UNSEEN
POWER

UNSEEN
POWER

HOW MUTUAL FUNDS
THREATEN THE POLITICAL
AND ECONOMIC
WEALTH OF NATIONS

ADAM HARMES

Published in 2001 by Stoddart Publishing Co. Limited
895 Don Mills Road, 400-2 Park Centre, Toronto, Canada M3C 1W3
180 Varick Street, 9th Floor, New York, New York 10014

Distributed in Canada by:
General Distribution Services Ltd.
325 Humber College Blvd., Toronto, Ontario M9W 7C3
Tel. (416) 213-1919   Fax (416) 213-1917
Email cservice@genpub.com

Distributed in the United States by:
General Distribution Services Inc.
PMB 128, 4500 Witmer Industrial Estates, Niagara Falls, New York 14305-1386
Toll-free Tel. 1-800-805-1083   Toll-free Fax 1-800-481-6207
Email gdsinc@genpub.com

05   04   03   02   01   1   2   3   4   5

Canadian Cataloguing in Publication Data

Harmes, Adam
Unseen power: how mutual funds threaten the political
and economic wealth of nations

Includes bibliographical references and index.
ISBN 0-7737-3283-7

1. Mutual funds - Economic aspects.   2. Pension trusts - Economic aspects.
I. Title.

HG4530.H37 2001   339.4'3   C00-932843-2

U.S. Cataloging-in-Publication Data available from the Library of Congress

Jacket design: Bill Douglas @ The Bang
Text design: Tannice Goddard

THE CANADA COUNCIL | LE CONSEIL DES ARTS
FOR THE ARTS | DU CANADA
SINCE 1957 | DEPUIS 1957

*We acknowledge for their financial support of our
publishing program the Canada Council, the Ontario Arts
Council, and the Government of Canada through the
Book Publishing Industry Development Program (BPIDP).*

Printed and bound in Canada

To my family

CONTENTS

ACKNOWLEDGEMENTS

The ideas in this book were developed as part of my recently completed Ph.D. thesis. As a result, my greatest debt is to my friends and colleagues in the Department of Political Science and the Centre for International and Security Studies at York University. Special thanks go to Stephen Gill and Isabella Bakker who have had an enormous impact on my development as a scholar. Without their encouragement, support and friendship, my Ph.D. — and this book — would never have been completed. In addition to Stephen and Isa, I owe a large debt of gratitude to Eric Helleiner. Eric's enthusiasm has always been infectious among his students and he is the reason that I became interested in the politics of international financial markets in the first place.

Others in the academic community who have influenced and supported me greatly, either directly or indirectly, include: Louis Pauly, Leo

Panitch, Greg Albo, Tim Sinclair, Randy Persaud, Ronen Palan, Rob O'Brien, Randy Germain, Shane Gunster, Angie Swartz, Marlene Quesenberry, David Dewitt, Heather Chestnutt, Steve Mataija, Joan Broussard, John O'Neill, Chris Robinson and the late Susan Strange.

Linda McQuaig, a terrific writer, analyst and friend, convinced me that economics was far too important to be left to economists and that developments in the dismal science could be made both exciting and accessible to a non-academic audience. My agents, Bruce Westwood and Hilary Stanley, have guided me through the world of publishing and I am forever grateful for their decision to take a chance on a rookie academic. At Stoddart, the wisdom and patience of managing editor Don Bastian, who is one of the nicest people I have ever met, made my foray into the world of popular publishing an entirely pleasant experience. Editors Steven Beattie, Elizabeth d'Anjou and Sue Sumeraj found every flaw in the manuscript and generously tolerated the ones I wanted to leave in. Elizabeth in particular went above and beyond by expertly dealing with the numerous computer problems we experienced and by meeting me for a late night editing session in a food court in downtown Toronto.

I also want to thank my family and friends for their unwavering support and their tolerance of my very busy schedule. My army buddies and drinking buddies kept me humble at all times by constantly asking when I was going to get a real job. Grant Pye, Jeff Gooley, John King, Matt Anderson, Mike Walker, Andrew Paterson, Ian Cameron, Bruce McEachern, Tony Welsh and the officers, NCOs and troops of the Queen's Own Rifles of Canada provided me with the support and ribbing I needed to get the job done. My greatest personal debt goes to my family. My mother's and father's love and support have been my anchor in trying times. My brother Dave, in addition to being a great roommate and sounding board for ideas, is my best friend.

To everyone: thank you, thank you, thank you.

1

MR. SMITH GOES TO BAY STREET

It's called the "balanced portfolio throw."

Players are given a handful of beanbags to throw at targets with labels such as "Stocks," "Bonds," "Mutual Funds" and "Savings Account." The object of the game is to hit as many different targets as possible in order to "diversify" your "portfolio" of beanbags. What makes the balanced portfolio throw so interesting is that it's a game for children — one of the many investment-oriented games on offer at this year's annual "FUNd Fair" in downtown Toronto. For children who were tired from tossing beanbags and jumping up and down in an inflated bouncing castle dubbed "The Trading Floor," a sugar fix was available in the form of cookies shaped like dollar signs. A few feet away, posing for photos, stood the costumed mascot of GT Global Mutual Funds, the company that started this annual investment carnival. Resembling a

Disney character, GT Global's Henry the Hedgehog (as in "hedge your investments") is a tall, goofy-looking fellow whose sole mission in life is to convince youngsters of the need to invest early and diversify often.

To reinforce this message among the 800-plus kids who attended the fair, GT Global (which has since been bought out by AIM Mutual Funds) offers two mutual fund starter kits designed to teach children the basics of investing. The kit aimed at the under-nine set includes a mock mutual fund certificate, a stuffed Henry the Hedgehog toy and a slickly produced storybook entitled *Henry's Mysterious Present: A Story About Mutual Funds*. In this Mother-Goose-goes-to-Bay-Street tale, the story begins with young Henry the Hedgehog being disappointed that the birthday present given to him by his Nana was some shares in a mutual fund and not the toy fire truck he'd hoped for. But as this financial fairy tale progresses, through a dozen colourfully illustrated pages, Henry and his friends are taught the benefits of deferred gratification and the magic of compound interest. They learn what a mutual fund is and what a portfolio manager does. And by the end of the book, all of the children come to the shouted realization: "We want mutual funds too!" Of course, no story about mutual funds would be complete without the inevitable fine print: "Nana said she was happy that they all wanted to start investing, and reminded them that *no one can promise* that a mutual fund will make money."

Even fairy tales, it seems, need to be screened by the folks in legal.

The significance of Henry the Hedgehog stems from the sociological observation that children are to society what canaries are to coal mines: a type of barometer that provides early warning of broader social changes. When teenagers started getting jobs at Microsoft and schools felt compelled to teach "computer literacy," we knew that the new information revolution was upon us. So today, when preteens are being enticed into the stock market and schools are starting to promote "financial literacy education," it is becoming apparent that a new social trend has emerged. As *Newsweek* has observed: "We have become a nation of stock junkies — splurging on mutual funds, scouring market tables and studying personal finance columns. Warren Buffett is a media idol. This is, most obviously, a sociological event."[1] To understand and situate this sociological event, it's useful to recognize that the contemporary process of globalization is both a trend and a deliberate political project.

The trend aspect of globalization is the information revolution and, like any revolution, its significance stems from the fact that it involves the masses. When computers were first invented, they were a technological coup that promised to usher in a new wave of increased productivity. But computers didn't really become a revolution until they entered the retail market. With the mass marketing of computer technology in the form of the personal computer, a product that had once been the preserve of scientists and engineers became a cultural phenomenon. As the 1990s progressed, average people began to interact with information technology on a daily basis. Through video games, the Internet and CD-ROMs, computers became associated with fun as well as work — and in the process were transformed from a form of capital good into a form of consumer good. The popular media began to institutionalize coverage of developments in the industry, and corporate leaders such as Bill Gates became household names with guru status. The necessity of computer skills became embodied in the phrase "computer literacy," and with the attainment of these skills, words and phrases such as "megabyte" and "surfing the net" entered the popular lexicon. Not coincidentally, there even emerged a rekindled interest in science fiction.

For many of us, the information revolution *is* globalization. It's the seemingly natural and inevitable process by which technology is making our world a smaller and more interdependent place to live. But globalization is also a deliberate political project, one in which the balance of power between different economic actors has shifted dramatically. Most important, it is the way that the financial community has come to exert an unprecedented influence over people's everyday lives. While many pundits have focused on how globalization has increased the power of the large multinational corporations, it's the financial community that wields the greatest clout in the global economy. We live in a time where shareholders, not CEOs, determine the fate of corporations, where the destiny of countries often seems to lie in the hands of unseen bondholders and currency traders rather than with the democratically elected representatives of citizens. The source of the financial community's new power is multifaceted, and much of it has to do with the way that governments have seen fit to deregulate controls on the activities of the financial institutions.

At the same time, a large part of the growing power of Wall Street and Bay Street stems from what is, arguably, the second most important revolution of the globalization age. This is the revolution of mass investment, and it is this revolution and its broader economic, political and cultural implications that are the focus of this book.

THE REVOLUTION OF MASS INVESTMENT

As with the information revolution, the revolution of mass investment was brought about when a once exclusive product began to enter the retail market. Through the rise of mutual funds and pension funds, a growing number of passive savers have been transformed into active investors. By the late 1990s, over 50 percent of U.S. households had a stake in the stock market, up from only 25 percent in 1987 and only 3 percent in pre-crash 1929.[2] In Canada the situation is similar, with over half the population now having some stake in the stock market.

To understand the origins of this revolution, it's useful to make a distinction between the rise of mass investment on the one hand and the rise of mutual funds, pension funds and other "institutional investors" on the other.

The rise of mass investment is the product of many factors. In its initial stages, mass investment grew out of postwar affluence and was part of the broader post–Great Depression compromise between workers and their employers. During this period, the predominant form of mass investment was through the defined-benefit pension plan. As the name suggests, in a defined-benefit pension plan the employer agrees to pay workers a set pension where the specific benefits are defined in advance, based on, for example, a percentage of salary or a flat rate per year of service. To pay for the pensions, companies would create an investment fund out of contributions deducted from workers' wages.

For workers, the advantage of the defined-benefit pension plan was that the risk of saving enough money for retirement was taken over (or socialized) by the employer. In other words, the amount that a worker received in pension benefits was negotiated in advance, and the employer was responsible for paying the pension even if the fund's investment returns proved to be inadequate.

By socializing retirement risk, defined-benefit pension plans acted as a form of retirement-income insurance for workers and as a means of imposing forced savings. For governments, forced savings had the added benefit of deferring wages into the future, and this helped to keep a lid on rising inflation. At the same time, defined-benefit pension plans also reflected the desire of employers to maintain a large core workforce consistent with large-scale, assembly-line manufacturing. Defined-benefit pension plans, which generally operate on the principle of "imperfect vesting" (where pension rights accrue to the employee only after a number of years of service), were used as a mechanism for reducing labour turnover.

When retirement risk is socialized in this manner, pension benefits are more like an entitlement program than an investment return because the burden of investment risk is not borne by the individual employee. This, in turn, implies that control over investment decision making lies with the employer, meaning that individual employees are more akin to passive savers than active investors.

By the 1990s, mass savings through defined-benefit pension plans were increasingly being transformed into mass investment through various forms of defined-contribution plans. As a 1999 report by the Cato Institute observes, "The rise of the worker capitalist is inextricably linked with the rapid and recent substitution of defined contribution plans, which create individual investors, from defined benefit plans, which create individual entitlements."[3] In a defined-contribution plan, the pension received by the employee is no longer guaranteed by the employer. Instead, workers and/or their employers contribute to an investment fund that pays retirement benefits based entirely upon its market value at the time of retirement. In this type of plan, all risk (of inflation, low market returns, etc.) is borne by the individual employee.

With investment risk being shifted from the employer to the employee, the risk of saving for retirement is increasingly being privatized in a way that is forcing a greater number of people to become active investors. And it is this shift in risk and control over pension investments to employees that characterizes the new era of mass investment.

In the same way that the socialization of retirement risk was a product of the postwar compromise between workers and their employers, the privatization of retirement risk is part of the broader trend towards free-market restructuring and the desire among employers for a more flexible and self-reliant workforce. The rise of defined-contribution pension plans, which transfer the burden of investment risk and control to employees, are a sign that job security has become a thing of the past. Employers no longer need to ensure workers' loyalty by offering them pensions to stay with their firms. Defined-contribution pension plans allow laid-off workers to carry their pension savings with them, freeing the employer from the responsibility of providing fixed retirement benefits.

Also important to the rise of mass investment has been the perceived pressure on the pay-as-you-go social security programs provided by governments. As products of the postwar compromise, social security programs socialize retirement risk and redistribute income; they are generally indexed to inflation. Operated as a form of compulsory defined-benefit pension plan, social security programs rely on taxes as well as savings, transferring income directly from current workers to pensioners. The defined benefits are guaranteed by the government's power to tax.

In the last few years, social security programs have come under growing pressure from both demographic and fiscal trends. Pointing to these trends, a 1998 report by the Organisation for Economic Co-operation and Development (OECD — a Paris-based organization whose members roughly constitute the "developed world") argues that

[t]he aging of populations of the OECD area has produced a rising
need for retirement products by increasingly wealthy and sophisticated individual investors. At the same time, the baby boom cohort
is causing looming fiscal problems in countries relying predominantly
on pay-as-you-go financed state pension provision systems.[4]

In response to these pressures, governments have increasingly sought to promote individual retirement savings through the use of tax incentives for personal savings plans such as RRSPs and through public education initiatives to inform people of the need to save for their own retirement. Reinforcing these efforts, conservative think tanks, lobby groups for the mutual fund industry and even the World Bank have sought to promote the notion of a coming "crisis" in social security programs.[5]

While much debate seems to exist over the extent to which social security programs are actually in crisis, the end result of these public education initiatives is that a growing percentage of the population does believe that a crisis is coming and have sought to ready themselves by increasing their personal investments. According to a survey by the American Employee Benefits Research Institute and Matthew Greenwald and Associates, conducted in July of 1996, only 10 percent of current American workers expect social security to be their most important source of future retirement income. At the same time, 30 percent listed personal pension plan contributions as their most important source. Another 23 percent listed personal investments outside of employer pension plans and 22 percent listed employer contributions to a pension plan.[6] Perceptions of a coming crisis in social security have contributed to a growing acceptance, particularly among young people, of the downsizing of government and of company-provided retirement benefits, and of the notion that this downsizing is inevitable. Illustrating this increasingly pervasive attitude, one 24-year-old personal banking representative remarked, "We no longer have the luxury our parents did of being able to wait, spend forty years in the same company and expect it and the government to take care of us when we are old."[7]

Two other factors have contributed to the revolution of mass investment. One, of course, is the bull market of the past decade and the way that investment companies and the media have been hyping it extensively. As *Business Week* magazine has observed, "never before has Wall Street raised expectations quite so high — and never before has the media joined in quite so willingly as cheerleaders and stockpushers."[8] In fact, according to Competitive Media Reporting, a New York research firm, advertising by U.S. brokerage firms alone increased by 95 percent in 1999, to over $1.2 billion.* The second factor, which is related to the bull market, is the growing sophistication of the mutual fund and investment management industry, which has made investing accessible to a much broader segment of the population.

THE RISE OF INSTITUTIONAL INVESTORS

Institutional investors can be defined as "specialized financial institutions which manage savings collectively on behalf of small investors."[9] These include mutual funds, hedge funds, pension funds and insurance companies. Institutional investors share a number of common features that have helped to draw people into the financial markets. The first of these features is risk pooling. By allowing individuals to hold a more diversified portfolio than they could by purchasing stocks and bonds on their own, institutional investors spread the risk of investing over a large number of individuals. The second feature characterizing institutional investors is professional management based on a fiduciary relationship to the individual investor. A fiduciary relationship is to fund managers what the Hippocratic oath is to doctors. It's their legally mandated duty to invest with your interests, rather than their own, taking precedence. In the investment world, fiduciary duty requires a fund manager to minimize risk, maximize returns and preserve capital on behalf of the individual investor. When fund managers resist the notion of ethical investing, they do so because they think using any criteria other than financial performance would be in conflict with their fiduciary duty and their need to get you the highest possible return. Professional management also generally implies greater resources, in terms of both investment expertise and of the ability to collect and analyze relevant market information. A final characteristic common to all institutional investors is size, and the resulting benefits from economies of scale — such as the ability to pay lower brokerage fees due to a higher volume of transactions.

---

* Unless otherwise indicated, all monetary amounts in this book are quoted in U.S. dollars.

Institutional investors, particularly mutual funds, have benefitted enormously from the rise of mass investment. In North America, they are beginning to replace individual ownership of stocks and bonds, as well as bank deposits, as the key repository for the savings of households. In fact, by 1995, institutional investors in the main regions of the developed world controlled over $24.4 trillion, up from only $3.2 billion in 1981 — an increase of almost 8,000 percent.[10]

Mutual funds and pension funds invest this money in stocks, bonds and currencies around the world. And in the process, they have become *the* dominant players, *the* power in the world's financial markets. "The emergence of institutional investors as the dominant holders of financial assets . . . is one of the distinguishing features of the present financial landscape," said a recent report by the OECD.[11] It's amazing how all those tiny nest eggs can add up when you put them together and let a handful of people decide how to invest them.

MASS INVESTMENT: THE VIEW OF ECONOMIC CONSERVATIVES

The first to formally notice the mass investment revolution was American management guru Peter Drucker. In his 1976 book, *Unseen Revolution: How Pension Fund Socialism Came to America*, Drucker argued that the rise of mass investment in corporate stocks meant that America was on its way to becoming a de facto socialist state where workers, through their retirement savings, were coming to own the means of production. Drucker notes,

In terms of Socialist theory, the employees of America are the only true "owners" of the means of production. Through their pension funds they are the only true "capitalists" around, owning, controlling, and directing the country's "capital fund." The "means of production," that is, the American economy . . . is being run for the benefit of the country's employees.[12]

More recently, conservative observers have updated Drucker by characterizing the revolution of mass investment as an emerging form of investor democracy or worker capitalism. David Hale, the global chief economist for the Zurich Group, argues that

> [t]oday, retirement plans are expanding their ownership of the stock market but are not producing a form of pension fund socialism. The U[nited] S[tates] is, instead, embarking upon a new experiment in the democratization of bond and equity ownership through a mixture of mutual funds, defined contribution pension plans and direct ownership of securities.[13]

Similarly, a 1999 report entitled *The Rise of Worker Capitalism* from the conservative U.S. think tank the Cato Institute suggests that "capital ownership, once the signature of wealth, has become widely diffused."[14] Underpinning this conservative portrayal of the revolution of mass investment is the notion that, because we're all investors now, the economic policies that are good for the financial community are somehow beneficial to the rest of us as well. This view of mutual funds and pension funds as the bridge between Wall Street and Main Street has become so widespread and accepted that we now tend to think of these funds as the "good guys" of global finance.

This portrayal of mutual funds and pension funds as the representatives of average people contributes to a disjuncture between popular perceptions relating to the different players within the financial markets. On the one hand, there are the bondholders, stock speculators and twenty-two-year-old currency traders in red suspenders. Boo! In the world of high finance, these are the wealthy landlords, the get-rich-quick schemers and the spoiled brats who five years ago we would have loathed in high school. On the other hand, there are the mutual funds and the pension funds. Yay! These are us, the good guys, the average people saving diligently for a better future. The contrast between how the two groups are portrayed in the media couldn't be more striking.

Bondholders are the aristocracy. Mutual funds are the masses.

Stock speculators are the manipulators who live off the buying and selling of others. Pension funds are the value investors with a real stake in the companies they finance.

Currency traders are the short-term hot money. Mutual funds and pension funds are the patient retirement savings in for the long haul.

Because of these contrasting perceptions, most of us tend not to associate mutual funds and pension funds with "the financial markets" at all. Today, the very notion of "the financial markets" conjures up images of vast wealth and power, not of families and pensioners nurturing their tiny nest eggs. In our mind's eye, we can almost see the evil foreign bondholder telling our governments to slash social programs and pay down the debt, or visualize the hyperactive currency traders who shoot almost $2 trillion a day around the globe, often leaving a trail of economic devastation in their wake. We don't think of mutual funds and pension funds when we think about the power of the global financial markets. And because of our attitude towards these funds as the good guys of global finance, investigations into the growing power of the financial markets have often neglected the role played by mass investment and the rise of institutional investors.

THE ARGUMENT OF THIS BOOK

This book presents a simple argument that seeks to challenge the conservative view that the rise of mass investment has led to an intersection between the interests of Wall Street and those of Main Street. Instead, it argues, the rise of mutual funds and pension funds has served to vastly increase the power of Wall Street *over* Main Street in ways that are not always in the interests of the average person.

But before going into the specific details of what this book is about, let's be clear on what it's not about. Unlike virtually every other book with "mutual funds" in the title, this one won't teach you a thing about how to invest. While you may learn something about the new dynamics that are driving the present boom in North American stock markets and why you might want to be concerned about them, you won't get any hot tips about the latest emerging market or technology or about which fund company is most deserving of your trust.

Another thing this book won't do is attempt to make you feel guilty about where your RRSP is currently invested. Many critics on the left as well as the growing "ethical" mutual funds industry are quick to point out how your investments often benefit from the poor working conditions of others or from the sale of unethical products such as weapons and cigarettes. Books such as Naomi Klein's *No Logo* have already done an excellent job showing us the misery that often lies behind the products we purchase. This book doesn't attempt to extend this argument to the realm of investing, or to show you how the growth in your RRSP is *benefitting* from recent trends such as corporate downsizing or cutbacks to social programs. What it will attempt to show you, however, is how the rise of mutual funds and pension funds is actually *causing* these trends.

Finally, it's important to be clear that this book isn't a rant about the evils of the mutual fund industry or a portrayal of individual fund managers as greedy and self-serving fat cats. When I began shopping this book around for a publisher, one of the first questions I was asked was "Who is the villain?" While many of the events described in this book could certainly be written up as a dramatic struggle between the forces of good and evil, it wouldn't be an accurate account of what's actually going on. Too often these days, journalists and authors are pressured to reduce complex economic and political processes to simple stories of heroes and villains. There's little doubt that such stories make for compelling sound bites and wider audiences. And sometimes they are actually true; the wealthy landlords often do exploit the downtrodden villagers. But what a focus on individual villains gains in simplicity, it often loses in usefulness for addressing the real problems at hand. Few of us really believe that the problems besetting the new global economy are solely due to evil deeds perpetrated by a small cabal of no-goodniks; or, by extension, that if these individuals were replaced by the morally righteous, the world would quickly become a more just and democratic place to live.

If there's any villain in this book, it's what economists call a "fallacy of composition." A fallacy of composition is based on the notion that the effect of the whole can be different from the sum of its parts. Adam

Smith wrote about the whole being greater than the sum of its parts in *The Wealth of Nations*, his seminal defense of free markets. To make the case for unfettered markets, Smith sought to demonstrate how the economic decisions of greedy individuals would be automatically coordinated towards beneficial social outcomes by the "invisible hand" of market forces. He argued that the sum total of individuals acting in their own narrow self-interest would add up to the most efficient allocation of resources thanks to the laws of supply and demand. A fallacy of composition is the flip side of this coin. As a concept, it refers to situations where individual decisions, even those that are both rational and ethical from the individual's point of view, can add up to very negative social consequences.

Examples of fallacies of composition, where individuals act rationally but markets do not, are abundant in economic theory. Probably the most familiar example is that of a run on a bank. Suppose for a moment you just heard a rumour that your bank was in trouble. Now, because you found the rumour on the Internet you're not too sure about its reliability. But you're still worried. "What if my bank goes bust and I lose all my savings?" you think. The prudent thing for you to do is to go down to your local branch and withdraw your money, just in case.

As an individual, you're doing the rational thing, erring on the side of caution. The problem is that it's also rational for everyone else to do the same thing. All of a sudden, you have a bank run. Everyone is down at the bank demanding their money back while Jimmy Stewart is up on the counter as in the movie *It's a Wonderful Life*, pleading with you to keep your money where it is. Of course, banks loan out your savings to other people, so they don't have enough cash on hand to give everyone their money back. "It's in Bob's house, it's in old man Peterson's house," pleads Jimmy. If, caught up in the obvious sense of panic, you decide to ignore Jimmy and demand your money back anyway, Jimmy will be forced to meet the demand for cash by selling off the bank's assets at panic prices, causing the bank to go bust and causing all but a few depositors to lose their money. Even if the original rumour was completely false, the rational prudence of many individual depositors will have added up to a self-fulfilling prophecy; the bank goes bust anyway and no one comes out ahead.

Fallacies of composition such as bank runs are one of the main reasons economists accept the need for some government intervention in the economy. To prevent bank runs, governments have set up systems of deposit insurance to convince depositors not to panic. And, if they panic anyway, governments stand ready to loan the banks enough money to meet the demand for withdrawals without having to sell off their assets at a loss.

The fallacy of composition described in this book is a simple one. We, as individual investors, put pressures on fund managers to achieve strong performance in the very short term. To meet our demands, fund managers then put short-term pressures on our governments and corporations in ways that lead to financial crises, cutbacks to social programs and mass layoffs. Then, faced with the stagnating incomes produced by these trends, we up the pressure on fund managers for higher returns. It's perfectly rational for average people who are receiving less from their governments and employers to seek offsetting gains from their fund managers. But what's rational for individuals in their role as investors adds up to a vicious circle of short-term horizons that hurts those same individuals in their roles as employees and citizens.

Our story of the fallacy of composition surrounding the mutual fund industry begins in Chapter 2 with a look at how institutional investors are changing the way that capital is allocated in the global economy. In doing so, it seeks to challenge two widely held myths about the way financial markets and the investment management industry are supposed to work. Drawing upon the insights of Adam Smith's invisible hand, conservative economic theory believes that financial markets are both rational and efficient; that prices will always reflect their true value; and that individuals, using those prices as an indicator of supply and demand, will allocate their resources in the most efficient manner possible. At the heart of this theory is the assumption that markets are made up of individuals. Millions of them. Some will buy, some will sell and the decisions of all will be somehow coordinated by the invisible hand of market forces.

The specific logic goes something like this: With so many investors in the markets, the prices of stocks, bonds and currencies will always reflect their true value because, even if some investors sell in a panic or buy in a frenzy, there will always be others to see the mistake and to move markets back in the opposite direction: that is, back to the point where prices once again reflect their underlying fundamental value. In fact, this view holds that the growth of mutual funds and pension funds increases the power of the "invisible hand." By bringing the savings of millions of average people into the financial markets, these funds are supposed to enhance market efficiency. They are supposed to do so by diluting the wealth of the powerful few with the investments of the ordinary many.

But mutual funds and pension funds are not about millions of individuals. They are about delegated control and about the whole being greater than the sum of its parts. In fact, as more and more of us have delegated control over our savings to the professional fund managers, there has been a massive concentration of power in the financial markets. So much so that, by April of 1999, Canadian mutual funds alone controlled over $350 billion (CDN), with two-thirds of this amount being concentrated in the top ten companies. In the United States, mutual fund assets now approach the $6 trillion mark. And while most of us would have trouble even imagining a trillion dollars ($1,000,000,000,000), the fund managers employed by Fidelity Investments — "where over 15 million investors put their trust" — will soon be responsible for precisely this amount.

Now, if you ask players in the industry about this concentration of power, they will, grudgingly, admit that it's true. But before you can get another word out, they'll quickly inform you that this is a good thing. You see, it all has to do with the fact that mutual funds and pension funds represent the retirement savings of average people. And because they're retirement savings, mutual funds and pension funds have long-term investment horizons. This is supposed to make them the "smart money," serving the investors who can afford to wait out irrational volatility: buy-and-hold rather than buy-and-panic investors.

While this logic sounds reasonable enough in theory, it doesn't

actually work out that way in practice. Mutual funds and pension funds
may have long-term investment horizons, but the men and women
who manage them often do not, because of the way that competition
within the industry puts fund managers under intense pressure to attract
and retain customers by making sure that their funds perform strongly
in the very short term.

Within the funds themselves, these pressures have become institutionalized in a way that can force fund managers to behave in a
short-term and trend-chasing manner. Many of them face performance
evaluations on a quarterly or even monthly basis, and some are even
employed under thirty- to sixty-day contracts. This arrangement has a
tendency to dramatically shorten one's investment outlook. Also important is the fact that most fund managers are evaluated and paid in
relation to the performance of their peers, a system that encourages
trend-chasing behaviour.

The upshot of all this (which will be explained in much greater detail
in Chapter 2) is that the growth of mutual funds and pension funds
has created a situation where capital is now moving around in a highly
concentrated and herd-like manner on the basis of extremely short-term
horizons. Short-term horizons mean that the financial markets are much
more prone to ignore economic fundamentals. And when they do, the
concentration of decision making and the herd-like behaviour of fund
managers mean that investors will all be moving in the same direction.
Add these together and it becomes much more likely that markets will
overreact to economic news and that prices will "overshoot" — that is,
they will fail to reflect the true value of the assets they are attached to
in the way that conservative economic theory predicts they should. In
economic terms, these trends have led to a decline in efficiency and to
a greater potential for market volatility and financial crises. In political
terms, they've led to a dramatic shift in the balance of power between
investors on the one hand and governments, corporations and workers
on the other.

After laying out this argument, the rest of the book goes on to outline the implications of the concentrated power of mutual and pension
funds, together with the trend-chasing behaviour and short-term focus

of fund managers, across a number of areas of the world economy. In doing so, it shows how mutual and pension funds have become the great unseen power behind a wide range of contemporary economic trends. From financial crises abroad to cutbacks to social programs, mass layoffs and growing inequality at home, we will see how the rise of mass investment and institutional investors represents far more than growth in the power of a single industry. It has, rather, led to a sea change in the organization of the financial markets more generally and a massive shift in the balance of power between Wall Street and Main Street — in favour of the former. This balance of power is important because the way we organize our financial system affects how we organize our economy at the international, national and company levels. When the organization of finance changes, so does everything else.

Globalization as a trend is about the information revolution. But globalization as a deliberate political project is about the growing power of the financial community and the way that the revolution of mass investment has turbocharged its efforts.

2

LONG-TERM MONEY, SHORT-TERM BEHAVIOUR

It had all the makings of a bona fide scandal.

Stock manipulation, accusations of a cover-up and the public's trust in the whole investment management industry were thrown into question. And it happened at the Royal Bank of Canada to boot — one of the largest and most respected banks in the country. Details of the scandal, which broke in the summer of 2000, became to the business sections of the *Globe* and the *Post* what the Canadian Alliance leadership race was to their main sections — a marginally interesting story that was being milked for all it was worth.

The actual crime, which was perpetrated by a couple of fund managers at RT Capital, the pension management arm of the Royal Bank, involved a stock manipulation gambit known as "high-closing." High closing is when fund managers attempt to "juice up" their performance numbers by purchasing enough shares in a company, at an overly generous price, to artificially boost the price of the stock. The idea is to buy the stock just before the market's closing bell so that the inflated price becomes the stock's closing price. This has the effect of temporarily bumping up the price of the stock, and with it the value of a fund manager's portfolio.

For a day or two, Canadian investors might have comforted themselves with the notion that the RT Capital scandal was an isolated event — a case of a few bad apples rather than a rotten barrel. Unfortunately, such hopes were dashed when a report in the *Globe and Mail* showed that the practice of high closing appeared to be widespread among both pension and mutual fund managers.[1] These accusations led many commentators to worry that the scandal could undermine the public's trust in the whole investment management industry. Particularly worrisome was the possibility that people would no longer trust the performance numbers they use when deciding which funds to invest in. "As far as trust in performance numbers goes, I think this sort of thing is potentially fatal. This is a big deal. People see this stuff and it confirms their worst fears that the mutual fund industry isn't working for them. This is very, very dangerous," said Duff Young, a mutual funds columnist and president of FundMonitor.com Corporation.[2]

"Very, very dangerous" or not, the scandal was a blessing in disguise for the media. Summer is usually a pretty boring time to be a business reporter. Not much happens because most of Bay Street vacates the city for the tree-lined shores of Muskoka cottage country. But last summer, thanks to RT Capital, the business press was producing exclusive after exclusive, and some of the more ambitious reporters were no doubt debating whether the scandal was big enough (of Bre-X proportions perhaps?) to stretch into a book-length exposé. (Who knows — given Canadians' short memory for scandals, and the ability of writers and publishers to crank out a book when haste is required, there may already be such a book on the market.)

While the media's coverage of the details and personalities involved in the scandal was excellent, the reporters and pundits did seem to miss what was, and wasn't, important about the illegal manipulation of stocks by fund managers at RT Capital. In fact, the scandal was both more important and less important than many in the business and regulatory community seemed to recognize at the time.

First, let's consider why the RT Capital scandal is less important than it was made out to be in the press. Doesn't it matter that some fund managers and traders broke the law? Doesn't it matter that they attempted to "juice up" their performance numbers by manipulating stock prices? And doesn't it matter that this type of stock manipulation appears to be a widespread practice in the industry?

Yes, it matters. But not that much.

As my normally non-business-savvy mother insightfully asked: "Isn't this similar to what the TV networks do during sweeps week?" Putting aside the fact that it's not currently illegal for TV shows to artificially boost their ratings during an evaluation period, the scandal at RT Capital amounts to pretty much the same thing. To make their numbers appear slightly better during their own evaluation period, the fund managers at RT Capital did the financial equivalent of the TV networks bringing out the big name celebrities and supermodels to make a show seem slightly more popular than it actually is.

In television circles, news that a network is artificially boosting ratings during sweeps week to attract advertisers is a non-event because everyone's doing it. The comparable practice is only an event on Bay Street because, there, it is illegal. But in the grand scheme of things, if everyone's manipulating performance numbers in more or less the same way, they tend to cancel each other out, because fund managers — like TV shows — are rated against each other.

So, if everyone's doing it, high closing probably has little real effect on one fund manager's performance numbers relative to others. This doesn't make it right, and the Ontario Securities Commission is correct in trying to stamp out the practice; petty crimes can lead to bigger ones. But it does mean that the scandal itself isn't really that important. After all, it doesn't put savings at risk and, given the fact that "juiced-up" stock prices tend to correct the following day, it has little impact on the individual companies whose stock prices are manipulated.

Yet the RT Capital scandal *is* important. Not because some fund managers broke the law, but because of the reason they felt the need to do it in the first place. On this question there was remarkable consensus among the experts. It was all about the intense pressures on fund managers to attract and retain customers by making sure that their funds perform strongly in relation to their competitors'. To give you a taste of this consensus, here's what the experts had to say:

- "Industry observers say the temptation is enormous for money managers to boost the value of their portfolios because they are under intense pressure to generate top performances and win clients. The temptation to manipulate stock prices is greatest at year-end because annual bonuses are tied to performance," reported the *Globe and Mail*.
- "People are under tremendous pressure to perform, and if you put people under pressure to perform it's natural that you're going to have individuals in that predicament," observed Tom Caldwell, chairman of Toronto-based Caldwell Securities Ltd.
- *Financial Post* columnist David Olive added his two cents on the issue by noting that this is "an era when money managers face unprecedented pressures to outperform their peers."
- Dominik Dlouhy, president of Dlouhy Investments, told the *Globe and Mail*, "I think lots of mutual funds do 'high closing.' They are driven to it by this insane idea that you measure performance every day. Everybody is into short-term horizons. The pressure is intense. The bigger concern is that the public keeps on looking at the horse that is leading by a nose in the daily performance stakes. This short-term attitude has changed investing into short-term gambling, and this breeds excesses like high closing."[3]

Mr. Dlouhy's comments are particularly insightful because they point to the real significance of the RT Capital affair: that stock manipulation is just a symptom of an underlying disease, one that is infecting our financial markets and is producing other symptoms far worse than the scandal at RT Capital. The underlying disease is the pressure on fund managers to perform strongly in the very short term. This is not how the financial markets and the investment management industry are supposed to work. Mutual funds and pension funds are made up of retirement savings. And because they're retirement savings, mutual funds and pension funds are supposed to have long-term investment horizons. This is supposed to make them the "smart money" within financial markets, the patient capital that makes markets more efficient through the buying and holding of securities over the long term.

If fund managers had long-term investment horizons, like they're supposed to, there'd be little incentive to manipulate stocks through the practice of high closing. Purchasing a large block of shares at an inflated price at the end of a trading day serves to artificially boost the stock's price; but only temporarily. If the same purchase is carried out in the middle of the day, the market would quickly correct itself and the price of the stock would return to its true value. But when it's done just minutes before the closing bell, the juiced-up stock doesn't have enough time to correct itself and the price of the stock remains artificially high until the market reopens the next day. And because the market corrects itself so quickly, high closing has no effect on a mutual or pension fund's real performance.

But real performance isn't what matters to fund managers. What matters to them, and what creates the incentive for high closing, is the need to perform strongly during their evaluation periods. Mutual and pension fund *money* may have long-term investment horizons, but the *people* who manage these funds often don't, because they're evaluated and paid based on their ability to perform strongly in the very short term. Most fund managers are evaluated on both a quarterly and yearly basis. So juicing up performance numbers through high closing works because, even though the boost is only temporary, and even though it will correct the following day, it does last long enough to boost a fund manager's numbers at the end of an evaluation period. This is important because strong performance numbers, even those that beat out the competition by only a little, can make all the difference in terms of attracting new customers. And this is what fund managers are paid to do. Performance numbers and the ability to attract new investors form the yardstick by which mutual and pension fund managers are paid.

When short-term performance pressures lead to illegal dodges like high closing, it's definitely a cause for concern. But the greater worry is the way that short-term horizons may be, as Mr. Dlouhy notes, changing investing into a form of short-term gambling. By shortening the investment horizons of the financial markets, the performance pressures on fund managers may be contributing to other, much larger, problems. To understand why these short-term pressures are so significant, and why they're making our financial markets much less efficient, we need to first understand how the financial markets are supposed to work.

HOW THE FINANCIAL MARKETS ARE SUPPOSED TO WORK

In the same way that governments have been reducing tariffs to promote free trade, so too have they been eliminating capital and exchange controls to promote the globalization of the world's financial markets. But unlike the process of trade liberalization, with all its attendant policy debates and political protests, we generally hear much less about the process of financial liberalization. And this is despite the fact that the globalization of financial markets has far outpaced what is going on in the realm of trade. The flow of money across borders today is exponentially larger and faster than the flow of goods and services could ever hope to be. To understand why we've decided to free up our financial markets, and why this is supposed to be a good thing, it's necessary to make a brief foray into the dismal science of economic theory.

In conservative economic theory, the case in favour of liberalized (that is, less regulated) financial markets is founded upon the belief that free markets are the most efficient allocators of resources. Financial markets are said to be efficient when the prices of stocks, bonds, currencies and other assets reflect their "true" value. When this occurs, economic actors such as governments, firms and households can use these prices as an indicator of supply and demand, allowing them to allocate their resources efficiently. In the big picture of economic theory, it's the law of supply and demand, expressed through prices, that constitutes the "invisible hand" of market forces. For example, if the value of a

currency or stock is falling, governments and corporations will take this
as a signal that they're doing something wrong and will alter their policy. When economists note that a particular government or firm is
changing their policy because of "market forces," this is what they're
talking about.

For a free-market economy to allocate resources in the most efficient
manner possible, prices in the financial markets *must* reflect their true
value. If they don't, prices send false signals to governments, firms and
households — signals that can cause them to make poor economic decisions. In his recent book on the U.S. stock market, *Irrational Exuberance*,
Yale University economist Robert Shiller provides a good description of
what can happen when prices don't reflect their true value:

> How we value the stock market now and in the future influences
> major economic and social policy decisions that affect not only
> investors but also society at large, even the world. If we exaggerate
> the present and future value of the stock market, then as a society
> we may invest too much in business start-ups and expansions, and
> too little in infrastructure, education, and other forms of human
> capital. If we think that the market is worth more than it really is,
> we may become complacent in funding our pension plans, in main-
> taining our savings rate, in legislating an improved Social Security
> system, and in providing other forms of social insurance.[4]

While Shiller's comments refer to stock prices, the same logic holds true
for other asset prices such as bonds and currencies. The bottom line
is that in a free-market economy prices must reflect their true value in
order to send efficient signals to economic actors and ensure that
resources are appropriately allocated.

But how do we know that financial markets will operate efficiently?
How do we know that investors will value the prices of stocks, bonds
and currencies in a way that reflects their true value? For conservative
economists, the answers to these questions are found in the theory of
efficient markets. This theory argues that financial markets should
always operate efficiently because they're comprised of millions of

rational and diverse individual investors. Rational investors are those who look at economic fundamentals when deciding how much a stock, bond or currency should be worth. Fundamentals for government bonds and currencies are things like the inflation rate, the unemployment rate and the size of the country's debt and deficit, as well as the government's plans for the future. Fundamentals for stock prices include all of the above, which can affect the stock market as a whole (for example, by pushing interest rates higher or lower) as well as factors specific to individual firms, such as earnings, market share, debt load and, again, the management's plans for the future. When you see those commercials with fund managers going out to "kick the tires" at a particular company, they're investigating the company's fundamentals.

So the first reason the financial markets are supposed to operate efficiently is because investors use economic fundamentals — as opposed to Ouija boards — to determine the price of a particular asset. And this means that prices should reflect the "true" value of assets, and should only change if the underlying fundamentals change. For example, if the federal government decides to implement more inflationary policies, this would constitute a change in the country's fundamentals, causing investors to sell the currency, leading to a fall in its value. As the currency fell, it would send an automatic signal to the government that it needs to alter its policies. And if it did alter its policies, investors would look at the new fundamentals and would then buy the currency, causing its value to go back up.

At this point in the theory, one problem that needs to be addressed is the fact that all investors may not interpret the fundamentals in the "correct" way. Determining the correct price for a stock, bond or currency is difficult because it's part science and part art. It involves the science of researching what the fundamentals *are* and the art of determining what they actually *mean*.

Determining what fundamentals mean is difficult because it also involves guesses about what could affect those fundamentals in the future. Two investors looking at the same set of economic fundamentals may come up with very different ideas about what the price of a particular asset should be. This is why the financial pundits you see on television are constantly disagreeing about whether Internet stocks are overvalued or priced correctly, or about what impact a merger will have on a particular company's stock price. The pundits aren't disagreeing because they are basing their views on different sets of information. Rather, they have different opinions about what those fundamentals mean and how they will affect prices in the future.

Now, if this is what actually happens, if investors constantly disagree about what the value of a particular asset should be, how are the financial markets supposed to come up with the "true" price, the price that reflects the fundamentals accurately and will send efficient signals to economic actors? This is where the second part of the theory of efficient markets comes in: the part about financial markets being made up of millions of diverse individuals.

When a market is composed of millions of diverse individuals, there will be a very large number of guesses about what a particular asset is worth. Some of the guesses will be high and some will be low because a diversity of investors means that they won't all evaluate fundamentals in the same way. But the magic of the market is that it works on the law of averages. The guesses that are a little high will cancel out the guesses that are a little low and the average will find the true value of the asset. So the financial markets should be efficient even if the guesses of investors are not 100 percent correct. As long they aren't all wrong in the same direction, the high and low guesses will offset each other. This is why it's important that the financial markets are made up of a large number of diverse investors. It increases the odds that investors won't all make similar guesses in a way that causes the price of an asset to be over- or undervalued.

This argument about poor guesses offsetting each other should also hold true if some investors completely ignore economic fundamentals and assign an asset an irrational price. Again, the law of averages should ensure that irrational investors will simply have the effect of cancelling each other out.

What happens, you might ask, if the guesses of a large number of irrational or incorrect investors *do* all go in the same direction? Doesn't this mean that the guesses will fail to cancel each other out? And, if this happens, won't prices become over- or undervalued in relation to the true value of the asset? For proponents of the theory of efficient markets, the answer to these questions is yes — but that it doesn't matter. It doesn't matter because, even if a large number of investors do the same thing and buy in a frenzy or sell in a panic, there will always be other, more rational, investors to spot the mistake and to move prices back in the opposite direction, back towards their true value.

In the lingo of financial theory, investors who spot mistakes and invest to offset them are called "arbitragers." Also known as "stabilizing speculators" or "contrarian investors," arbitragers represent the smart money within the financial markets, the money that focuses on economic fundamentals. Their activities work to bring prices back towards the assets' true values. For example, if a large number of investors have been too pessimistic about a particular stock, causing it to become undervalued, arbitragers should spot the mistake and start buying the stock. When the stock price eventually goes up, the arbitrager makes a profit from having bought low and sold high. More to the point, when arbitragers buy an undervalued stock they increase demand for the stock and thus help to push its price back up to its true value.

Any investor who focuses on fundamentals can act as an arbitrager because there is little risk involved. If an asset's price is clearly not justified by the fundamentals, an arbitrager is virtually guaranteed to make a profit by taking a contrarian position.

There is, however, one key exception to this rule. Arbitrage can be risky if the potential exists for the asset to be even more mispriced in the future. Let's say that investors were overly pessimistic about a particular currency and started selling it in a panic, causing the value of the currency to fall well below its fundamental value. At this point, the smart money should step in and take an offsetting position by holding onto, or buying, the currency. But what if other investors are *so* pessimistic about the currency that they continue to sell, and the value of the currency continues to fall? While the arbitrager will make a profit when the currency eventually corrects itself, it may take a while for this to happen. In the short term at least, the arbitrager will lose money.

For investors with short-term horizons, this is a problem. They can't afford to take an offsetting position if it means that they'll lose money temporarily. If you're an investor who's only a few months away from retirement, then short-term pain for long-term gain is not going to work for you as a strategy. If you buy an undervalued currency that's still falling, it may not correct in time for you to sell it at a profit. So if the financial markets are dominated by investors with short-term horizons, arbitrage may not in fact ensure that markets operate efficiently and that prices will reflect their true value. Luckily, though, the theory of efficient markets argues that this won't happen. Once again, the markets are saved by the fact that they are composed of millions of diverse individual investors.

In the same way a large number of investors provides the diversity necessary to prevent all guesses about asset prices from being wrong in the same direction, it also ensures that not all investors will have the same investment time horizons. Older investors with shorter horizons will be offset by younger investors with longer horizons. Average investors who are afraid of taking short-term risks will be offset by wealthier investors who can take the heat. Diversity in the financial markets means that there should always be enough long-term investors willing to act as arbitragers. And this means that the financial markets should always operate efficiently.

The idea that financial markets should always operate efficiently is the cornerstone of conservative economists' arguments on why governments should stay out of the financial markets' way. In their view, free financial markets will always value the prices of assets correctly, and this will provide the most efficient signals for economic actors, meaning that governments, firms and households will be able to allocate their resources in the most efficient manner possible.

Well, that's the theory, anyway.

HOW THE INVESTMENT MANAGEMENT INDUSTRY IS SUPPOSED TO WORK

For the most part, conservative economists haven't paid much attention to the rise of mutual funds and pension funds. They haven't seen any need to distinguish between different types of investors because they view all investors, whether individuals or institutions, as behaving in the same way. They see them as independent actors who allocate their investments in a rational and diverse manner.

This doesn't mean that conservative economists have completely ignored the rise of mutual funds and pension funds. But it does mean that they don't think institutional investors make any real difference to the workings of the financial markets. In fact, to the extent that they think about mutual funds and pension funds at all, conservative economists argue that they should have the effect of making the financial markets even more efficient.

The first way that mutual funds and pension funds are supposed to increase the efficiency of financial markets is by making them more rational. Institutional fund managers are professional investors who undergo extensive financial training. And unlike most individual investors, they invest for a living. This means that professional fund managers have the training, time and resources necessary to analyze all the relevant economic fundamentals when deciding where to invest. Any trend that has the effect of making investors pay more attention to fundamentals is bound to make the financial markets more efficient.

The second way that institutional investors are supposed to make the financial markets more efficient is by increasing the total number of investors. More investors operating in the markets increases the diversity of guesses about asset prices and, in turn, increases the chances that those guesses will average out and find the true price. It also increases the chances that smart investors who pay attention to fundamentals will cancel out the dumb ones, again making it more likely that prices will reflect the true value of assets. Mutual funds and pension funds are supposed to increase the number of investors operating in the financial markets by bringing in the savings of millions of ordinary people.

The final way that mutual funds and pension funds are supposed to make the financial markets more efficient is by increasing the number of investors who are operating with long-term investment horizons. Mutual funds and pension funds pool the retirement savings of millions of ordinary people. And because they're retirement savings, mutual funds and pension funds should be invested with the long term in mind. Think about your first trip to a bank or mutual fund company, when they make you fill out a form to determine your "investor profile." One of the key bits of information they're looking for is your investment horizon. In other words, when do you plan to cash in your fund and spend your savings? The bulk of people saving for retirement have a fairly long time before they need to cash in their funds. This means that short-term dips in the market are no big deal. A person with long-term horizons should only care that the market is going to go up over the long term.

So if mutual funds and pension funds are made up of primarily retirement savings, with long-term investment horizons, they too shouldn't care very much about short-term dips in the market. And when it comes to market efficiency, long-term horizons are a good thing. Long-term horizons mean that mutual funds and pension funds should be the financial-market arbitragers, the guys who can afford to wait out setbacks and offset short-term volatility by taking contrarian positions rather than following the herd. If a stock price rises for irrational reasons, mutual and pension funds should be the ones to sell it. And if a currency plummets below its true value, they should be the ones to buy it and hold, rather than buy and panic waiting for the rebound. As Thomas Hockin, president of the Investment Funds Institute of Canada, has argued, mutual funds and pension funds "are based on long-term commitments . . . It is not 'hot money,' volatile and fickle."[5]

Taken as a whole, therefore, the rise of mutual funds and pension funds should be making our financial markets more efficient. Professional fund managers and the long-term horizons associated with retirement savings should make the markets more rational. And by helping to transform millions of passive savers into active investors, mutual funds and pension funds should also be making the investor base much more diverse.

Again, that's the theory.

REDUCING DIVERSITY:
THE CONCENTRATED POWER OF
MUTUAL FUNDS AND PENSION FUNDS

The problem with theories is that sometimes "what ought to be" and "what is" are not the same thing. This doesn't mean that a theory that isn't reflected perfectly in practice is no longer valid or useful. But it does mean that textbook theories need to be constantly checked against the existing reality. And when it comes to supporting the conservative view of how the financial markets and the investment management industry are supposed to work, reality hasn't always been that helpful.

Institutional investors *ought* to be making the financial markets more diverse and efficient by diluting the wealth of the powerful few with the investments of the ordinary many. Unfortunately, this is not what is actually happening. Rather, mutual funds and pension funds are serving to concentrate power within the financial markets in a way that is reducing the diversity of the investor base. As a 1995 report by the International Monetary Fund (IMF) observed, "the effective investor base is changing from a very large number of small investors to a very small number of large investors."[6] And this means that decisions relating to investing are becoming increasingly concentrated as more and more individuals delegate control over their savings to the professional fund managers.[7] In the United States, institutional investors in 1995 controlled almost 40 percent of household financial assets, up from only 20 percent in 1980. Here in Canada, the situation is similar; institutional investors in 1997 controlled over 46 percent of household financial assets, up from only 21 percent two decades earlier.

Across the industrialized world, the trend towards delegating control over investment decision making is evident in the growing size of institutional investors' assets under management. In these countries, the total assets of mutual funds, pension funds and insurance companies grew from $3.2 trillion in 1981 to over $24 trillion by 1995. And while pension funds and insurance companies used to be the most important of the institutional investors, the biggest growth in the last decade has been among the mutual fund companies. In the first half of the 1990s, the assets of developed-country mutual funds soared at a growth rate of over 16 percent per year to a 1995 total of over $5.5 trillion.

Also, as you might expect, the biggest growth has been in the United States, which accounted for about half of the approximately $26 trillion controlled by rich-county institutional investors in 1996. To put this number in perspective, consider the fact that, in that same year, American institutional investors held securities such as stocks and bonds worth almost double the total U.S. national income and almost three times the assets held by banks. The assets of American mutual funds soared from a meagre $370 billion in the mid-1980s to well over $3 trillion by 1996. Two years later this amount had jumped to over $5.5 trillion. And, while pension funds have not grown at quite as fast a rate as their mutual fund counterparts, their assets in the United States have nonetheless ballooned from a little over $1 trillion at the start of the 1980s to another $5.5 trillion by 1995.

Individual investors aren't the only ones who've been delegating control over their investments to the professional fund managers. More and more, pension funds, particularly corporate-sponsored defined-contribution funds, have been delegating the management of their portfolios to mutual funds and other external asset management companies. And this trend is serving to further concentrate power and reduce diversity within the financial markets.

Pension funds can delegate control over their investments in one of two ways. First, rather than hire in-house fund managers, many pension funds will hire the services of an external asset management company to run their portfolios. Asset management companies provide fund management services to institutional funds (such as pension plans, trust funds and endowments) as well as to wealthy individuals. Some asset management companies operate as independent firms; all they do is manage money for institutional funds and individual high rollers. Others are owned by other financial services companies like the banks. For example, RT Capital is an asset management company owned by the Royal Bank. Finally, some asset management companies are run by mutual fund companies. Actually, it's the other way around. Many mutual fund companies are really just asset management companies that operate both wholesale and retail divisions. Their wholesale business is managing institutional funds, like pension plans. Their retail business is the selling of shares in individual mutual funds, which they set up and market to the broader public.

In addition to hiring external asset management companies and the wholesale divisions of mutual fund companies, pension funds have also delegated control by simply investing in the same retail mutual funds that are sold to the general public. So rather than doing the hard work of selecting individual stocks and bonds for their portfolios, many pension funds simply invest through a broad selection of mutual funds. The fastest-growing type of defined-contribution pension plan in the United States is the 401(k) plan, which is somewhat similar to Canada's tax-subsidized RRSPs. In 1997, assets held in 401(k) plans totalled $925 billion. In 1986, less than 8 percent of 401(k) assets were invested in retail mutual funds. But by 1994, mutual funds had captured over 30 percent of the 401(k) market.

The tendency for pension funds to invest in mutual funds rather than purchasing assets directly is even more pronounced when it comes to investing in "emerging markets." ("Emerging markets" is, of course, the new term for what we used to call the "developing" or "third" world.) A recent survey conducted by Kleinman International Consultants, the Frank Russel Company and the World Bank found that over 50 percent of all pension funds invest in emerging markets through mutual funds, and that less than 5 percent of them manage these investments in-house.

A final factor that has served to reduce the diversity of the investor base has been the trend towards concentration within the asset management industry itself. Specifically, despite the existence of a large number of these companies, the bulk of the business (and hence of the assets under management) is heavily concentrated in a small number of the largest firms. In the United States, the top twenty asset managers controlled 85 percent of 401(k) pension plan assets, with eleven of these twenty firms being mutual fund companies. The biggest of the big was Fidelity Investments, which, in 1997, managed $175 billion worth of 401(k) assets — about 19 percent of the total 401(k) market. Including its retail mutual funds as well, Fidelity controlled almost $1 trillion in 1999.

Examples of industry concentration can also be found here in Canada. By the end of 1999, Canadian mutual funds controlled almost $350 billion (CDN) in assets, with almost two-thirds of this amount being concentrated in the top ten companies. Mutual fund companies such as Investors Group and Trimark manage assets on the order of $30 billion (CDN) each. Large pension funds, such as the Ontario Teachers' Pension Plan Board and the Ontario Municipal Employees Retirement System, manage pools of assets that are even larger still.

The bottom line is that the rise of mutual and pension funds has led to a massive concentration of power within financial markets, a fact that does not sit well with the beliefs of conservatives and the assumptions of the theory of efficient markets. As a 1995 report by the IMF argues, rather than being composed of millions of diverse individuals, "the investor base in securities markets in industrialized countries, and increasingly in developing countries, is dominated by a relatively small number of large institutional investors."[8] Now, concentration on its own is not necessarily a bad thing. In some cases, it has brought a number of benefits to investors, such as greater product choice and fund management expertise. But, with an increasing number of individuals and pension funds handing control over their investments to a relatively small group of fund managers, it does mean that there is a smaller and less diverse group of individuals making decisions about asset prices.

Why does this matter? Remember that for financial markets to work efficiently through the law of averages, there needs to be a large and diverse number of opinions about the meaning of economic fundamentals. When markets produce many and varied views on the meaning of fundamentals, the chances go up that high and low guesses will cancel each other out and find the true price through the law of averages. But by concentrating investment decision making in the hands of a relatively small number of fund managers, the rise of mutual funds and pension funds is having the opposite effect — that is, it may be serving to reduce the number and diversity of opinions about fundamentals. And this tendency increases the chance that a large number of opinions could all go in the same direction, without enough opposing opinions to cancel them out. When this happens, prices can move away from their true value and become over- or undervalued.

Reinforcing the likelihood of this type of one-way buying and selling is the way that concentrated investment decision making makes for a closely knit and conformist investment community. When financial markets are composed of millions of diverse individuals, there will be a large variety of models (whether formal or informal) for analyzing economic fundamentals. This variety will produce a wide range of views about what those fundamentals mean. In today's financial markets, however, fund managers are much more likely to be carbon copies of one another. They are trained in the same way, they have similar views about what types of economic policies are "good" and "bad," and they are more likely to come up with similar models for evaluating fundamentals and similar opinions about what those fundamentals mean. Fund managers are thus more likely to react to changes in fundamentals in the same way, leading to the one-way buying and selling that can cause prices to move far away from their true value. As a 1993 report by the IMF argues, "when fund managers share homogeneous perceptions about both the evolution of financial variables and the impact of news, the potential exists for new information to produce massive purchases and/or sales and sharp movements in prices."[9]

A close-knit investment community (like many other communities) creates a kind of socialization process where individuals are assimilated into the logic of the whole. One detailed study, conducted by anthropologists William O'Barr and John Conley, set out to examine this process through a kind of "gorillas in the mist" strategy of observing fund managers in their natural habitat. The study found a willingness among fund managers "to accept inherited structures and strategies without question."[10] They also found a business culture that placed a high premium on conformity in everything from dress and language to management strategies. In part, this socialization process helps to explain why fund managers may adopt similar models for evaluating economic fundamentals (to say nothing of their penchant for pinstripes).

Therefore, by concentrating investment decision making, mutual funds and pension funds do seem to be reducing the number and diversity of views in the financial markets and, in turn, are increasing the potential for the kind of one-way buying and selling that can cause prices to move away from their true value. As a 1998 report by the OECD observes, "institutional investors may react to news in a similar manner, which — in the aggregate — may cause major portfolio shifts."[11]

SHORT-TERM HORIZONS AND HERD BEHAVIOUR IN MUTUAL FUNDS AND PENSION FUNDS

The conservative response to this claim about concentrated power and a reduced diversity of investment decisions is that it doesn't matter. It isn't that important that fewer people are making decisions if those people are much more likely to be fully rational and to allocate their capital based on economic fundamentals. As the dominant holders of financial assets, mutual funds and pension funds are supposed to make the financial markets more rational because they are managed by professional investors based on long-term investment horizons. This means that institutional investors should be more likely to focus on economic fundamentals and to act as arbitragers to bring any mispriced assets back to their true value.

Now, while this sounds reasonable enough in theory, it doesn't quite match the existing reality. As we saw in the case of the RT Capital scandal, mutual and pension fund managers are under intense pressures to perform strongly in the very short term. They are evaluated and paid based on their ability to retain old clients and attract new ones, and this means that they must produce strong performance numbers on a quarterly basis. So while the retirement savings that make up mutual funds and pension funds may have long-term investment horizons, the men and women who manage these funds often do not.

Where does this pressure to perform come from and why is it so intense? The short answer is that it comes from us, the average investors. As it turns out, we're a greedy and fickle bunch, a bunch that demands great returns fast or we take our business elsewhere. When we sit down to decide which mutual funds to invest in, most of us have a tendency to compare the most recent performance numbers with little concern for how the different funds have done over the long term. We check newspapers and Internet sites to find out how our mutual funds are performing on a daily basis. In fact, recent studies that look at how individual investors decide where to invest seem to confirm the notion that they over-emphasize recent performance. According to one study, 80 percent of all new money invested in U.S. mutual funds in 1996 went to the top third of funds, which received the coveted four- or five-star ratings from the popular fund-rating agency Morningstar.[12]

Another problem is that most of us seem to go for the sizzle rather than the steak. We decide which funds to invest in based on who was able to generate the highest return. The problem is that the highest return isn't always the best indicator of real performance. Real performance is how high a return a fund manager is able to get *after* you adjust for the amount of risk that he or she takes. If a fund manager makes a high-risk, all-or-nothing kind of bet on a single stock, and the risk pays off, the return is likely to be quite high. But if the bet doesn't pay off, you have lost all your money. In contrast, if a fund manager pursues a lower risk investment strategy the return will probably be lower, but your retirement savings will be safe. For most of us, the second strategy is the best one. Slow and steady wins the race. But despite this fact, many individual investors focus more on returns and less on risk when deciding where to invest. As *The Economist* remarked, "What interests [individual investors] is that George Soros made $1 billion betting against sterling, not whether he lay awake at night sweating over what he had risked to do so."[13] (We'll discuss the exploits of billionaire investor George Soros and his bet against the British pound sterling in Chapter 5.)

So, with so many of us focusing on raw returns without taking risks into account, fund managers are forced to do the same, concentrating on generating high returns in the very short term. In the case of mutual funds, part of the short-term pressure on fund managers comes from the need to attract new customers. But part of it comes from the need to retain old customers, because individual investors can redeem their shares at a moment's notice and take their business elsewhere. As a

1994 report by the IMF commented, "U.S. mutual funds need to meet performance standards over a very short time horizon, and open-ended funds face the risk of sizeable net redemptions if their quarterly performance lags behind the competition."[14]

The pressure to achieve strong short-term performance also applies to the external asset managers who compete to manage pension funds. Pension funds are supervised by trustees who represent the interests of the individual pension plan holders. These trustees choose an asset management company based on the same short-term performance numbers that individuals use to evaluate mutual funds. So, like mutual fund managers, external managers of pension funds must generate strong short-term results in order to keep old clients and attract new ones.

Within the mutual fund and asset management companies themselves, these short-term performance pressures have become institutionalized in the way that fund managers are evaluated and paid. Many of them are employed under three-year contracts, with performance evaluations as often as every quarter in the United Kingdom and Canada, and even monthly in the United States. This system has a tendency to dramatically shorten the investment outlook of many fund managers. And while pension fund managers tend to have somewhat longer investment horizons than those who manage mutual funds, a 1997 report by the World Bank cautions that "over 50 percent of pension fund investments are undertaken through the purchase of shares in mutual funds, so the distinction between mutual funds and pension funds is, in practice, more blurred."[15]

Short-term investment horizons make the financial markets much less efficient because they can create incentives for fund managers to ignore economic fundamentals and, instead, to observe and follow the behaviour of other investors. In other words, they run with the herd. Imagine a stock market that has become temporarily overvalued because of irrational investing. (This is a hypothetical example; any similarities to current stock-market conditions are purely intentional.) For a fund manager with long-term horizons who is aware that stock prices have risen above their true value, the rational thing to do would be to sell the stocks, anticipating that the market would eventually correct itself. By focusing on fundamentals and selling stocks, the fund manager would be acting as an arbitrager, helping to push stocks back down to their true value.

But as we saw earlier, the incentive to focus on fundamentals is reduced if the investor has short-term horizons. For a fund manager who is subject to short-term performance pressures, selling the overvalued stocks may not be the rational course of action because of the potential that the market could become even more overvalued before it eventually corrects. If you're a fund manager facing an upcoming performance review, you simply can't afford to wait for the market to correct itself over time if it means that your performance on paper will suffer because of unrealized gains. For example, in the run-up to the 1987 stock market crash in the United States, one study found that a large number of fund managers knew that the market was overvalued but felt pressure from short-term performance evaluations not to sell because they feared missing out on further price rises.[16] Therefore, as E. Philip Davis, a senior economist at the Bank of England, notes, in certain situations "funds may . . . adopt similar portfolios even if their own information suggests a different pattern could yield a better return."[17]

Short-term performance pressures can cause fund managers to ignore economic fundamentals whether asset prices are rising or falling. But this problem may be even greater when prices are falling because, as the OECD notes, "downside risk matters most to institutional investors who are averse to absolute risk."[18] Absolute risk for fund managers is the risk of allowing the value of their portfolios to drop below set minimum levels. For some pension funds, it refers to the need to maintain a minimum level of funding to ensure that pension obligations can be met. This means that a fund manager may be forced to sell in an irrationally falling market if not doing so would mean the value of his or her portfolio could fall below its minimum funding level.

Managers of mutual funds may also be forced to sell in a falling market to meet the demands of individuals who want to redeem their shares. Or they may sell because they face an upcoming performance review. Even if the market is falling irrationally and the fund manager knows that the market will correct itself eventually, short-term losses may affect the value of their portfolio during an evaluation. As a 1998 report by the IMF points out, "A mutual fund manager who allows losses to mount in anticipation of a subsequent reversal may find himself a former mutual fund manager before that reversal takes place, creating an understandable reluctance to let the position ride."[19]

Reinforcing these tendencies to ignore fundamentals and to follow the herd is the fact that most fund managers are paid on the basis of "relative performance." Relative performance means evaluation in relation to the performance of other fund managers. This is opposed to "absolute performance," which is a fund manager's ability to generate the highest possible return.

The system of evaluation by relative performance creates a huge incentive to do what everyone else is doing, regardless of what the fundamentals say. If a fund manager takes a risk by going against the crowd and it doesn't pay off, he or she is penalized with lower pay or a pink slip. If the risk does pay off, and a manager does outperform his or her peers, the rewards aren't much better than they would have been for doing the same thing as everyone else because the incentive structures of fund companies are often skewed against risk taking. This means that going against the herd involves large potential risks without the potential for large rewards. So it's not surprising that most fund managers will play it safe and follow the herd, even if they think the herd is wrong. And if the herd *is* actually wrong, it doesn't matter because the fund manager is paid based on how he or she performs relative to everyone else. As a 1997 report by the World Bank shows, "fund managers will follow the investment decisions of other fund managers to show clients that they know what they are doing. If they follow another fund manager's decisions and the investment turns out to be unprofitable, they are more likely to be thought of as unlucky than unskilled, since other fund managers will have made the same mistake."[20]

So when fund managers sit down to decide how they're going to divide up their portfolios, most of them start with what everyone else in the market is doing. As one senior fund manager — who asked to remain anonymous — said in an interview, "When you set your asset allocation, you have got to do it relative to what you last knew about where the industry was." Therefore, if a particular asset, region or country comes into (or goes out of) fashion, fund managers will often feel the need to follow the herd in order to limit their risk of performing below the level of the average fund. And when everyone is doing what everyone else is doing, the law of averages fails and it becomes much more likely that prices will move away from the true value of assets.

These tendencies towards herd behaviour can become even more acute when fund managers are investing outside the borders of their home countries. In these situations, the short-term and trend-chasing behaviours of institutional investors can be amplified by a lack of specific expertise, as well as by the costs and difficulties associated with collecting and analyzing information. Gathering information about foreign countries in general, and emerging markets in particular, can be expensive. Many fund managers and asset management companies are unwilling to devote the resources necessary to fulfill these tasks properly, given the fact that foreign investments usually count for a relatively small portion of their overall portfolios.

Another obstacle to good assessments of fundamentals in foreign markets stems from the predominance of fund managers with "balanced expertise" rather than "specialized expertise." A fund manager with balanced expertise is a generalist, knowledgeable in a broad sense about different types of assets and countries. A fund manager with specialized expertise may be an expert in a specific region of the world or a specific asset class such as bonds. Many institutional investors seem to favour balanced over specialized expertise because it's easier to compare generalists when evaluating on the basis of relative performance. But when fund managers lack specialized expertise about a specific region, especially one that comprises only a small part of their portfolio, they have little incentive to spend the time and resources necessary for a full consideration of economic fundamentals. As American economist Thomas Willett notes, "The combination of typically high information costs about developing countries and lower incentives to invest in information acquisition may make markets less forward looking with respect to monitoring developing countries and more reactive to major developments."[21]

This evidence of the short-term and herd-like aspects of institutional investors' behaviour challenges the conservative view that professional fund managers are more likely to focus on long-term economic fundamentals. And by extension, it undermines the claim that mutual funds and pension funds are making the financial markets more efficient by acting as arbitragers working to bring mispriced assets back towards their true values. Instead, the rise of mutual funds and pension funds, which are the dominant holders of financial assets, seems to have created a situation where capital is now moving around herd-like, in concentrated blocks, on the basis of investment decisions taken with extremely short-term results in mind. Short-term investment horizons mean that fund managers are much more prone to ignore economic fundamentals. And on the occasions when they do, concentrated decision making and herd behaviour mean that investors will all be moving in the same direction. Add these factors together and it becomes much more likely that the financial markets will overreact to economic news and that prices will overshoot — that is, they will move far away from the true value of the assets they represent. As E. Gerald Corrigan, a senior advisor at Goldman Sachs, observes, "One of the curses of these current financial markets is that they overshoot — repeatedly and substantially."[22]

THE ECONOMICS AND POLITICS OF PRICE OVERSHOOTING

How important is it if fund managers are prone to overreact and prices are more likely to overshoot far away from their true value? In economic terms, it matters a great deal. The whole case in favour of free financial markets is based on the idea that these markets should operate efficiently. If financial markets don't operate efficiently and prices don't reflect the true value of assets, they send false signals to those who make economic decisions at all levels — governments, firms and households. Misleading signals can cause these agents to make poor economic decisions. For example, if stock markets overshoot in a positive, upwards direction, corporations and households become richer on paper, and this sends signals that it's okay for them to save less, spend more and go into a greater amount of debt. This may be fine for a while, but it means that if the market eventually corrects, those firms and households will have set themselves up for a fall. And overshooting can work both ways. When the market eventually corrects, it may overshoot in a negative, downwards direction, causing excessive damage to the domestic economy. Firms with too much debt may go bankrupt and people with too little savings may lose their homes.

The same logic can apply to national currencies. If the value of a currency gets too high relative to its true value based on fundamentals, the government may feel overconfident and begin to borrow money in foreign currencies and pursue other policies that make sense only if the currency remains perpetually strong. Again, this may set them up for a fall if the value of the currency corrects. A falling currency, especially one that starts to overshoot in a negative direction, can cause the size of a government's foreign currency debt to balloon to crisis — currency crisis — proportions. Summarizing the problems of price overshooting, Joseph Stiglitz, a former chief economist of the World Bank and member of the President's Council of Economic Advisors, notes: "If asset prices do not reflect fundamentals well, and if these skewed asset prices have an important effect on resource allocation, then the confidence of economists in the efficiency of market allocations of investment resources is, to say the least, weakened."[23] In other words, price overshooting, and the problems it can cause, throws doubt on the value of freeing financial markets from government regulation.

The economic result of price overshooting, as we have just seen, is to send inefficient signals to governments, firms and households in a way that causes them to make poor economic decisions. The political result of price overshooting has been a dramatic shift in the balance of power between investors on the one hand and governments, corporations and workers on the other. Does this matter? In political terms, it matters a great deal, because economic policy in a capitalist democracy also has a true "price" — an equilibrium that depends on a balance of power between Wall Street and Main Street. Wall Street prevents governments and firms from pursuing policies that are economically unsustainable. Main Street prevents them from pursuing policies that are politically unsustainable. Capitalist democracies work best when there is a balance of power between these two groups. This doesn't mean utopia. But like they say, capitalism is the worst system ever invented, except for all the others so far.

Under normal circumstances, free financial markets impose discipline on governments and firms that may attempt to pursue economically unsustainable policies. If a government attempts to buy votes by stimulating the economy through overly inflationary policies and excessive spending, investors (who are hurt most by these policies) will bring the government back in line by selling the currency, causing its value to fall. If a corporation gets too ambitious and directs too much of its profits towards expansion rather than dividends, investors will sell their shares, causing the stock price to drop.

At the same time, in a free and democratic society, citizens and workers will provide discipline from the other direction; that is, they will discipline governments and firms that attempt to pursue policies that are politically unsustainable. If a government tries to drive inflation and social spending too low, causing unemployment to rise and wages to stagnate, citizens will vote them out of office. If a firm tries to lay off too many workers to deliver excessive profits to shareholders, workers will go on strike.

Any time that either Wall Street or Main Street gets too much power in a capitalist democracy, a crisis results. In the nineteenth century, investors had too much power and average people suffered. The policies that benefitted the financial community led to the politically unsustainable levels of unemployment and social hardship that emerged in the Great Depression. As we tacked left in the postwar years, Main Street achieved increasing influence over economic policy. But the policies that benefitted Main Street in the short term led to economically unsustainable levels of inflation, which emerged with the onset of stagflation in the late 1970s.

Price overshooting today has upset the political equilibrium once again. It has put too great a pressure on governments and firms to pursue the types of policies that benefit investors at the expense of

workers and citizens. Market overreaction and price overshooting transform the discipline of investors into a form of punishment. The
mandate of the Bank of Canada has always been to pursue an interest-
rate policy that balances the often conflicting goals of very low inflation
and very low unemployment, between the interests of Bay Street and
those of Main Street. A balance is necessary because too high inflation
is economically unsustainable and too high unemployment is politically
unsustainable. In normal times, aiming for such a balance rather than
the near-zero inflation that investors want will cause some investors to
move their money abroad and the value of the dollar to drop a little.
No big deal; a lower dollar boosts our exports anyway. But when the
financial markets are prone to overreact, a country is no longer being
disciplined by investors in proportion to the amount the policy actually
harms them. Instead, in such a climate, if a government implements the
policies that investors dislike, then rather than simply dropping a little,
the currency could plummet. Price overshooting is one of the reasons
our governments have been cutting social programs and pursuing a
near-zero inflation interest-rate policy. In the long term, these policies
could prove to be unsustainable as growing inequality begins to
produce political crises.

Speaking of crises, let's turn now to the role that price overshooting,
as well as the balance of power between Wall Street and Main Street,
has played in the currency crises of the 1990s.

3
MUTUAL FUNDS AND FINANCIAL CRISES

Michael Camdessus, the former head of the IMF, called it "the first financial crisis of the twenty-first century." Camdessus was referring to the 1994 Mexican peso crisis, and his remarks were an acknowledgement that something new was afoot: that the events in Mexico represented a new type of currency crisis, at least compared to those of the previous fifty years. On December 19, 1994, the Mexican government implemented what all agreed was a necessary devaluation of the peso. But necessary or not, the financial markets were pissed. It was like the old Rodney Dangerfield line about playing football in a rough neighbourhood. The financial markets didn't just sack the quarterback, they went after his family as well. The post-devaluation sell-off by investors was a bloodbath. In less than two weeks, the peso had dropped by over 50 percent and the Mexican stock market had lost almost half of its value in dollar terms. In response, the Mexican government was forced to jack up interest rates and to implement a painful package of austerity measures to restore investor confidence and comply with the conditions of the American-led bailout.

As is always the case with financial crises, what was extremely painful for millions of average people was merely something interesting to analyze for foreign economists. The peso crisis was interesting because it challenged the conventional wisdom about what causes financial crises and how much damage they're supposed to do. Mexico's economic fundamentals didn't indicate that a crisis was coming; when it came, the damage done was far out of proportion to that expected from a simple devaluation of the currency. While this may seem like an odd thing to say, economists — as we'll see below — can usually predict when a financial crisis is going to happen. But in the case of Mexico only a very few experts saw danger on the horizon, and they were largely ignored by government officials and investors. Also, when the crisis hit, economists had difficulty explaining why so much damage was done. The "punishment" inflicted upon Mexico came nowhere close to fitting the "crime." As *The Economist* remarked at the time, "on their own [Mexico's economic fundamentals] did not justify the scale of the capital outflow or of the depreciation of the peso; the markets simply lost their heads."[1]

While politicians and the media were quick to blame the Mexican government for causing the crisis, economists knew that things weren't quite that simple. The crisis didn't fit in with the standard models, which usually do point a finger of blame at the policy blunders made by governments. But this situation was different. Mexico didn't make the kind of mistakes that usually lead to a currency crisis; if it had, more economists and investors would have seen it coming. What made the peso crisis particularly troubling for economists was the fact that, despite what the head of the IMF said, it wasn't the first example of this new type of crisis. The first one had actually taken place a couple of years earlier, an entire continent away. Europe had seen a similarly unpredictable, if less damaging, crisis when a number of currencies fell to speculative attacks (that is, massive selling) in the autumn of 1992. And like the peso crisis, the speculative attacks in Europe didn't seem to be justified by the underlying economic fundamentals.

In the aftermath of the European and Mexican crises, economists began to develop new models to explain what had happened. It was an exciting time to be an academic as theories on what had caused this new type of currency crisis became a veritable growth industry in the economics profession, as well as the subject of vigorous debates in the pages of scholarly journals and at various conferences around the world. A few years after the peso crisis, the debate was still raging, but most economists had begun to reach a kind of consensus. They accepted the idea that a new type of crisis had emerged, but came to the broad conclusion that it had nonetheless been caused by policy blunders made by the governments involved. Helping to reinforce this explanation was the fact that it fit well with the prejudices of those at the IMF, on Wall Street and in the U.S. Treasury Department who didn't want to see blame assigned to the financial markets. If the financial markets were at fault, that would imply the need for government intervention, something that didn't sit well with their conservative leanings. But if blame for them could be assigned to governments, especially to governments that had failed to follow the conservative guide to economic policy, then the crises could actually be helpful in pushing those governments further down the free-market path.

And then came the 1997 East Asian currency crisis — the worst one yet. Every bit as unpredictable as the European and Mexican episodes had been, the Asian crisis hit country after country as the "Asian flu" spread across the region and as far afield as Latin America and even Russia. The Asian crisis challenged both the old models and the new consensus. Conservative pundits were quick to blame the crisis on governments in general and on Asia's "crony capitalism" in particular. This term implied that governments were to blame for the crisis because of the allegedly corrupt and outdated model that Asian development had been following, one that had failed to fully apply the wisdom of free markets and conservative economic policies. This was the explanation promoted by a number of economists as well as by the media and the international financial institutions. It was a great explanation. But, as we'll see in the next chapter, it turned out to be completely wrong.

Whatever else came out of the Asian crisis, it did seem to confirm that something fundamental had changed in the 1990s. Currency crises had become much less predictable and far more damaging compared with what was indicated by the underlying economic fundamentals. When the Asian crisis hit in 1997, I was at York University in Toronto working on my Ph.D. thesis, a snootier and more complicated version of this book. Focusing on the mutual fund industry, I had begun to gather evidence on the role played by institutional investors in both the European and Mexican crises. I was convinced that their role had been underestimated by the conventional wisdom. To me at least, it didn't seem to be a coincidence that a new type of currency crisis had emerged at precisely the same time that mutual funds and pension funds had come to dominate international capital flows. It also didn't seem to be a coincidence that what made these crises new was the fact that currency values were overshooting what was justified by the underlying fundamentals.

I had already completed my research on the short-term and herd behaviour of institutional investors and on the way that they had increased the potential for market overreaction and price overshooting. It seemed only logical that the rise of institutional investors had something significant to do with the simultaneous emergence of a new type of currency crisis that was characterized by price overshooting. It also seemed hard to believe, with all that we know about currency crises, that governments kept on making the same mistakes time after time. But then came the Asian crisis, which seemed to throw a monkey wrench into the model I was trying to develop. The trouble was that, while much of the capital outflows during the European and Mexican crises were controlled by institutional investors, in the Asian crisis they were controlled by banks. Undeterred, I began to delve deeper into the details of the Asian crisis — and I found that mutual funds, once again, did seem to play a significant role, one that made me more confident that my model might be correct.

In the next chapter, I'll show you the evidence I found. In this chapter, I'll outline my model and go through why I think the rise of mutual funds and pension funds best explains what is new about currency crises in the 1990s. Of course, it's important to remember that I developed this model when I was a graduate student, and that graduate students are, for the most part, the young people of the academic world. We have the advantage of not having too much invested in old models and theories and therefore are usually freer to challenge them. But at the same time, like all young people, we tend to be a bit arrogant and think that we know better than our elders. Most papers written by graduate students could be titled "Why Everyone Is Wrong Except for Me." So in the spirit of full disclosure, I'll leave you to judge my explanation on its own merits.

But first, let's start with what my elders have to say.

INTERNATIONAL ECONOMICS 101: THE "IMPOSSIBLE TRINITY"

Before we go into the various models that have been used to explain currency crises, it's necessary to outline some of the basics of international economics. The most important concept to get a handle on is something called the "impossible trinity," which is based on the Mundell-Fleming thesis (one of the two economists who came up with it is Nobel laureate Robert Mundell). The impossible trinity concept, which has come to be widely accepted, is that governments can pursue only two of the following three policy goals at any one time: capital mobility, fixed exchange rates and discretion over monetary policy.

The first of these, capital mobility, refers to the ability of investors to move their money into and out of a country as they see fit. Governments can prevent capital mobility through capital and exchange controls, or they can promote it by removing these controls. The globalization of financial markets has come about because governments have been steadily removing capital and exchange controls over the last few decades. The second policy goal, fixed exchange rates, involves keeping the value of the nation's currency stable in relation to other currencies in order to better facilitate international trade. Governments can lock in exchange-rate stability by fixing the value of their currency to another "anchor" currency, or they can abandon it by allowing the exchange rate to "float."

The final goal, discretion in monetary policy, relates to a government's power over interest rates, which it exercises through the national central bank. Discretion over monetary policy is useful because it allows governments to fight recessions and to maintain a sustainable balance between very low inflation and very low unemployment. If inflation starts to get too high, the central bank can pursue a "contractionary" monetary policy by raising interest rates. Higher interest rates cause firms and households to reduce their spending as more of their income goes to paying interest on debt and new credit becomes more expensive. Reduced spending lowers the demand for goods and services, meaning fewer jobs and wage increases, a situation that prevents prices (and thus inflation) from rising. If unemployment gets too high, the central bank will pursue the exact opposite strategy: an "expansionary" monetary policy of lowering interest rates. Lower interest rates mean that households and firms are able to spend more because they are now paying less interest on old debts. New credit also becomes cheaper. Increased spending raises the demand for goods and services, allowing companies to hire more workers, which reduces unemployment.

Capital mobility, fixed exchange rates and discretion in monetary policy are all desirable goals. Unfortunately, the logic of the impossible trinity dictates that a government can achieve only two of these at any one time. If a government decides that capital mobility is a priority, then it must choose between either a fixed exchange rate or discretion in monetary policy; it can't have both. When capital is mobile, any attempt to fight a recession or to stimulate job creation through lower interest rates will lead to exchange-rate instability as the value of the currency falls. Investors prefer very low inflation. So when governments decide to reduce unemployment by allowing a little bit more inflation, investors take their money abroad; this causes the value of the currency to fall. If the government decides instead that it would prefer a stable, fixed exchange rate, then it must give up the option of stimulating the economy through lower interest rates. The only way that a government can have both discretion over monetary policy *and* a fixed exchange rate is to prevent investors from taking their money abroad through capital and exchange controls.

The history of the international monetary system boils down to governments deciding which two of these three goals they will pursue. In the decades leading up to the Great Depression, barring a brief interval during the First World War, governments opted for capital mobility and fixed exchange rates at the expense of discretionary monetary policy. After the Second World War, the emphasis was on giving up capital mobility to allow governments to pursue both fixed exchange rates and discretionary monetary policy. Today, capital and exchange controls have fallen completely out of fashion. Most countries have once again promoted capital mobility, forcing them to choose between a fixed exchange rate and discretion over monetary policy.

Among economists and policy-makers, there's been a bit of a debate over whether it's best for countries to pursue fixed exchange rates or to retain discretion over monetary policy. I say a "bit" of a debate because most economists support the latter option; they recognize that governments do need the power to fight recessions and to respond to economic shocks. If Canada had had a fixed exchange rate when the effects of the Asian crisis hit in the summer of 1998, the Bank of Canada would have been forced to sharply raise interest rates to defend the value of the dollar. This would have prevented the dollar from falling, but it might have induced a recession. Most economists and policy-makers agree that our un-fixed, or "floating," exchange rate was useful because it allowed us to absorb the shock of the Asian crisis with a falling dollar rather than with a painful slowdown in economic growth.

Some economists and policy-makers do support fixed exchange rates. But they tend to be very conservative types who would prefer that countries only pursue very low inflation rather than try to maintain a sustainable balance between it and very low unemployment. These conservatives have promoted the fixed exchange-rate option in a few industrialized countries like Canada. It's no coincidence that the only advocates of a fixed exchange rate for Canada are found at the *National Post* and at ultra-conservative think tanks such as the C.D. Howe

Institute. The promotion of fixed exchange rates is regarded as somewhat more respectable in developing countries because of their history of episodes of hyper-inflation. In these countries, a fixed exchange rate has been seen as a useful mechanism for reducing inflation quickly and building confidence with foreign investors.

CURRENCY CRISES: THE CONSERVATIVE VIEW

I mentioned earlier that investors prefer very low inflation even if the price is high unemployment. Inflation is bad for investors because it erodes the value of their investments over time. No one likes rising prices, but for most of us the little bit extra we have to pay for goods and services is more than offset by the jobs and higher overall wages that come from lower unemployment. At the same time, high inflation benefits no one. This is why most central banks aim for a balance between very low inflation and very low unemployment. Nevertheless, many investors still prefer very low inflation and, to promote it, they have often advocated the policy goals of capital mobility and fixed exchange rates, which, when pursued together, force governments to give up their ability to reduce unemployment through a discretionary monetary policy. Many conservatives who support this approach argue that capital mobility is desirable because free financial markets are the most efficient allocators of resources. They also argue that, in the long term at least, discretionary monetary policy has no impact on unemployment and should therefore be abandoned anyway. This is a slightly more complicated argument, which we'll go through in Chapter 6. For now, suffice it to say that investors and some conservatives have often advocated the policy mix of capital mobility and fixed exchange rates at the expense of discretion in monetary policy.

The next important point to note is that the European, Mexican and Asian currency crises all occurred in countries that had adopted this policy mix — one that John Williamson at the Institute for International Economics dubbed the "Washington consensus" because of the support it has received from the U.S. government as well as from the IMF, which is based in Washington, DC. But does this mean that the Washington consensus policy mix of capital mobility and fixed exchange rates causes speculative attacks and currency crises? According to its conservative proponents, the answer is a resounding "No!" Most conservatives hold that speculative attacks against fixed exchange rates are always the result of policy blunders made by individual governments. They are never the fault of investors or of the decision to adopt free financial markets and fixed exchange rates.

At a more philosophical level, this argument reflects the way that conservatives think about the nature of free markets. In conservative theory, economic failure is always the fault of an individual actor, be it a person, firm, or state. This view rests on their belief that, because investors are rational and financial markets are efficient, prices will always reflect the underlying economic fundamentals of the corresponding assets. This means that investors are simply the messengers of economic failure, never its cause. From this perspective, the fall in currency and asset prices that occurs during a speculative attack is simply the act of an efficient market adjusting to poor economic fundamentals caused by unsound government policies. The beauty of this explanation is that it assumes away capital mobility and the behaviour of investors as a potential cause of currency crises. Also assumed away, based on the conservative belief in the virtues of fixed exchange rates and very low inflation, is a government's decision to adopt a fixed exchange rate in the first place.

To reinforce their argument that currency crises are caused by policy blunders made by individual governments, conservatives have drawn on two generations of models explaining what causes a speculative attack against a fixed exchange rate.

SPECULATIVE ATTACKS: THE FIRST GENERATION

The classic model of what causes a speculative attack against a fixed exchange rate was developed by MIT economist Paul Krugman and was then later refined by Robert Flood and Peter Garber.[2] According to this classic model, currency crises are caused by governments that fail to pursue policies consistent with making a fixed exchange rate work. More precisely, speculative attacks against fixed exchange rates are caused by governments that attempt to pursue an expansionary monetary policy to lower unemployment, or that go into debt to increase spending on social programs.

But why does this lead to a crisis?

When a government adopts policies that investors dislike, such as the expansionary monetary policies or increased social spending that can lead to higher inflation, investors take their money abroad, and this causes the value of the currency to fall. For a government with a fixed exchange rate, the only way to defend the value of the currency (other than abandoning the expansionary policies) is to use the foreign currency reserves held by the national central bank to buy up the currency, propping up its value. In other words, when investors sell the currency causing its value to fall, the central bank will buy the currency to push its value back up. The problem is that this strategy will only work for so long because central banks have a limited supply of foreign currency reserves. As long as the government maintains its expansionary policies, investors will continue to move their money abroad, and the downward pressure on the currency will continue. When the government runs out of foreign currency reserves, and investors are still selling it and moving their money out of the country, the government is forced to let the value of the currency fall. In financial parlance, this is known as a "devaluation."

Speculative attacks occur because investors can see what's going on. When they realize a government is starting to run out of the foreign currency reserves it needs to defend the currency, they see an opportunity for profit and launch a speculative attack. This means that investors start to pull their money out of the country all at once, selling the currency as well as other assets such as stocks and bonds. With investors leaving all at once, the government runs out of reserves quickly and is soon forced to devalue the currency.

Even though a speculative attack occurs abruptly, it is fully justified by the fundamentals, because sooner or later the government would have run out of foreign currency reserves and would have been forced

to devalue the currency anyway. All a speculative attack does is antici-
pate and bring forward an otherwise inevitable devaluation. This is why
economists are usually able to predict speculative attacks and currency
crises. All they need to do is look for certain "leading indicators,"
which provide evidence that a government with capital mobility and
a fixed exchange rate is also trying to pursue expansionary policies.
Specific indicators are things like an increase in the money supply,
growing deficits and debt, and a drop in the central bank's stock of foreign currency reserves.

In many ways, the classic model of a speculative attack against a
fixed exchange rate can be understood as the inevitable outcome of policies that attempt to violate the iron law of the impossible trinity,
or Mundell-Fleming thesis. If a country with capital mobility and a fixed
exchange rate attempts to pursue a discretionary monetary policy at the
same time, something has to give because you can't achieve all three goals
simultaneously. As a 1998 report by the IMF notes, "Since Mundell and
Fleming, it has been well understood that a small country with a fixed
exchange rate and freely mobile capital cannot pursue an independent
monetary policy . . . [and that] . . . an overly expansionary monetary policy will be vulnerable to a speculative attack."[3] So, in the classic model,
the focus is on the *inconsistency* between capital mobility, a fixed exchange
rate and the attempt to pursue an expansionary monetary policy. The
model doesn't argue that the expansionary monetary policy is a bad policy. Rather, it just shows, using the logic of the impossible trinity, why
this policy will eventually force a government to abandon its fixed
exchange rate. Conservatives tend to ignore this part of the model. They
love capital mobility and fixed exchanges rates, so they tend to put all the
blame on individual governments and their attempts to reduce unemployment through an expansionary monetary policy.

SPECULATIVE ATTACKS:
THE SECOND GENERATION

In the 1980s, Krugman's classic model became the conventional wisdom on currency crises. It seemed to explain all episodes where fixed

exchange rates fell to speculative attacks. Then came the 1990s and the emergence of the new type of currency crisis discussed earlier. The European crisis of 1992, the Mexican peso crisis of 1994 and the Asian crisis of 1997 all challenged Krugman's model because the speculative attacks that occurred did not seem to be justified by the underlying economic fundamentals. The countries involved didn't appear to be pursuing the kind of expansionary policies that usually lead to a speculative attack against a fixed exchange rate. And when the speculative attacks did occur, they seemed to do a lot more damage than most economists expected. Barry Eichengreen, a senior economist at the University of California, Berkeley, notes, "What is new about recent crises, compared to those of the preceding fifty years, is their violence and the damage they do."[4]

So a new generation of models explaining currency crises began to appear.[5] To explain why these crises didn't seem to be justified by the underlying fundamentals, these second-generation models included the idea of a "self-fulfilling" speculative attack. Remember that in Krugman's classic model, a speculative attack against a fixed exchange rate occurs only if a government is trying to break the rules of the impossible trinity by pursuing an expansionary monetary policy. In this situation, a speculative attack merely brings forward an otherwise inevitable devaluation of the currency, one that is fully justified by the fundamentals.

A self-fulfilling speculative attack, on the other hand, doesn't simply bring forward a devaluation of the currency; it causes one. To understand how a speculative attack can become self-fulfilling, imagine a situation where a government has no intention of pursuing expansionary policies and, all other things being equal, is willing to defend its fixed exchange rate forever by raising interest rates if the currency starts to drop.

The problem is that investors know that governments are political animals, accountable to voters. They know that the higher interest rates that are often necessary to defend a currency can carry a heavy political cost because they slow down the economy and cause unemployment to rise. If investors trust the government and believe that it

has the "political will" to defend its fixed exchange rate, then everything is fine. In this situation, as long as investors don't launch a
speculative attack, the fixed exchange rate is sustainable because the
government has no intention of undermining it with an expansionary
policy. But if for some reason investors start to doubt the government's
resolve, they may see an opportunity for profit and launch a speculative
attack. If investors think the government is no longer willing or able to
defend the currency with higher interest rates, because of the political
costs involved, they may launch an attack that will force the government to devalue the currency. In such a case, the speculative attack is
self-fulfilling because it leads to a devaluation and currency crisis that
would not otherwise have occurred.

But what, you might ask, would make investors think that the
government is no longer willing or able to raise interest rates to defend
the currency and cause them to launch a self-fulfilling speculative
attack? Well, that's the million-dollar question in the quest to explain
the new type of currency crisis that emerged in the 1990s. And in
attempting to answer this question, economists have divided themselves
into two broad camps. Those in the first camp believe in what we
might call the "financial panic" explanation. They argue that self-
fulfilling speculative attacks are triggered by the fickle and herd-like
behaviour of investors. This group argues that the new type of currency
crisis is caused by inefficient financial markets rather than by government policy blunders: investors start to doubt the government's resolve
to defend its fixed exchange rate and launch an attack for irrational
reasons, reasons that have little to do with a country's economic fundamentals. A related possibility, promulgated by the "conspiracy theory"
faction of the financial panic camp, is that a speculative attack can be
deliberately launched by a small cabal of large investors who want to
profit from forcing a government to devalue its currency. Either way,
the emphasis of the financial panic explanation is on the role of inefficiencies in the financial markets rather than on policy blunders made
by individual governments; the idea is that if financial markets only
focused on the fundamentals, crises of this sort wouldn't have happened.

As you can probably guess, the financial panic explanation doesn't sit well with the friends and well-wishers of Wall Street and Bay Street. The notion that financial markets are to blame for the new type of currency crisis is at odds with the idea that financial markets are efficient and implies the need for government intervention. So in response to this explanation, a second camp emerged, which we can call the "government blunder" theory. The government blunder explanation updates Krugman's classic model by arguing that investors will only launch a self-fulfilling speculative attack when an economy enters what they call a "zone of vulnerability." A zone of vulnerability has to do with the underlying strength of the domestic economy and refers to the emergence of conditions that make it harder for the government to raise interest rates to defend the fixed exchange rate.

For example, if a government is already unpopular with voters, or if unemployment starts to get too high, it becomes politically difficult for politicians to endure the slowdown in growth and job losses that would result from higher interest rates. Sharp interest rate hikes can also be difficult for a government that is running large deficits and debts, especially if the private sector is also carrying a high level of debt. Debt makes raising interest rates more costly because it leads to higher interest payments for both the government and firms. This can cause government debts to rise even faster, make firms with high debt loads go bankrupt and, if the banking system is a little weak, can hurt the banks too as bankrupt firms default on their loans. From the perspective of the government blunder explanation, when an economy enters a zone of vulnerability, it becomes profitable and rational for investors to launch a self-fulfilling speculative attack. It's rational because investors know that the government will be politically unable to defend the currency with higher interest rates, meaning that a speculative attack has a high chance of succeeding.

The government blunder explanation blames politicians for failing to prevent the emergence of a zone of vulnerability. Conservatives argue that governments can prevent a zone of vulnerability by reducing the "labour-market rigidities" that they believe lead to higher unemployment as well as to higher debt because of increased spending on social assistance programs. Labour-market rigidities are government policies, such as minimum wages and generous unemployment insurance and welfare programs, that prevent workers from accepting lower wages and going back to work. So by focusing on the way that government policy fails to prevent the emergence of a zone of vulnerability, the government blunder explanation once again lays the blame for currency crises on the actions of individual governments. And, in doing so, it absolves the financial markets of any responsibility.

The financial panic and government blunder camps also disagree about why the new type of currency crisis does so much more damage than is justified by the economic fundamentals. According to proponents of the financial panic explanation, the excessive damage results from the herd behaviour of investors, which causes them to overreact to a devaluation and to punish a country more severely than is justified. Proponents of the government blunder explanation accept that excessive damage is caused by herd behaviour, but — as always — they blame governments for causing it. They argue that herd behaviour is caused by the failure of a government to be fully open and transparent about what its country's economic fundamentals actually are, such as how much debt the public and private sectors are actually carrying. A lack of transparency is said to give rise to "information asymmetries," which is a fancy way of saying that some investors, due to inside information or better analysis, may have more information about fundamentals than others. These asymmetries are supposed to lead to herd behaviour because it becomes rational for investors with less information to follow other investors who are seen to have more.

After much debate between the two camps, a sort of uneasy consensus has emerged that leans towards the government blunder explanation. The consensus argues that government blunders create a zone of vulnerability that increases the potential for a self-fulfilling speculative attack, but that the exact timing and strength of an attack may be partially due to panic by investors. The bottom line is that the consensus holds governments to blame and absolves the financial markets from responsibility for currency crises. As Eichengreen comments, "What emerges from . . . competing models and interpretations is a single, synthetic understanding of why crises occur. Crises do not occur randomly. Rather, they afflict countries whose governments set themselves up for a fall."[6]

SOME GAPS IN THE CONSERVATIVE VIEW OF CURRENCY CRISES

The conservative explanation for currency crises, both old and new, is that they are caused by government blunders. Either they try to break the rules of the impossible trinity by pursuing expansionary policies or they fail to take measures to prevent the emergence of a zone of vulnerability (characterized by high unemployment and debt). In both cases, governments are to blame. The behaviour of investors is not to blame, nor is the decision to adopt the Washington consensus policy mix of capital mobility and a fixed exchange rate in the first place.

When the government blunder explanation is applied to individual currency crises, ones where leading indicators do show evidence of either expansionary policies or of an emerging zone of vulnerability, the conservative focus on government policy mistakes has much to recommend it. The problem starts when you apply it to all currency crises in the last fifty years as a group. Conservatives fail to explain why so many governments are so darned stupid. You see, it seems that almost every time a government has opted for the Washington consensus policy mix of capital mobility and a fixed exchange rate, it has ended up in a currency crisis.[7] Almost without exception, governments seem to have made the type of blunders that lead to a speculative attack. Now, I may be a bit naive (remember, graduate student), but I have trouble with the idea that almost all governments, of widely differing political leanings, across a large number of countries, can really be this stupid. I mean, when one fixed exchange rate falls to a speculative attack, it's perfectly reasonable to assume that the government is at fault. When it happens to two or three countries, I'm still prepared to believe that government blunders are the main cause. But when virtually every modern fixed exchange rate ends in a crisis, you have to start thinking there might be something more structural at work.

That's problem number one. The second problem with the conservative focus on government blunders is that it doesn't seem to fully explain why the damage done by currency crises in the 1990s is so much greater than is reasonably justified by the underlying economic fundamentals. If information asymmetries really are the main cause, what changed in the 1990s to make them worse than before? And why were the more transparent European economies also affected by market overreaction?

DEMOCRACY AND THE POLITICS OF CURRENCY CRISES

Why have so many fixed exchange rates ended in crisis? And why are governments so prone to pursue policies that undermine the workings of their fixed exchange rates? The short answer to both of these questions is democracy. Governments don't implement policies that undermine their fixed exchange rates because they're stupid. They implement them because they are accountable to voters, and voters don't like the hardships that are produced by the Washington consensus policy mix of capital mobility and a fixed exchange rate. If you think back to the logic of the impossible trinity, you'll remember that a government that decides to pursue capital mobility and a fixed exchange rate is forced to give up the option of fighting recessions and reducing unemployment through a discretionary monetary policy. But voters *want* governments to do both of these things because, in addition to causing hardships for those who lose their jobs, recessions and higher unemployment slow down the economy and lead to stagnating wages.

The next problem with the Washington consensus policy mix of capital mobility and a fixed exchange rate is that countries don't exist in a vacuum. They exist in a world where something always happens, and the something that matters to a fixed exchange rate is what economists call a "negative shock." A negative shock is any event that causes investors to take their money out of the country, putting downward pressure on the currency. Negative shocks always happen because, in a globalized economy where capital is mobile, countries are increasingly affected by economic events outside their borders. When the U.S. Federal Reserve raises interest rates to fight inflation, investors pull money out of Canada, causing the value of our dollar to fall. When a crisis abroad makes investors nervous, they may flee Canada for the greater safety of U.S. markets, again causing our dollar to fall. The important point is that negative shocks will always happen. When they do, countries will always experience a downward pressure on their currency.

For a country with a floating exchange rate, like Canada, negative shocks are no big deal. We can just let our currency fall, wait for the effects of the shock to pass, and wait for our currency to rise back up. This is more or less what we did when the dollar came under downward pressure in the summer of 1998 following the Asian crisis. But for countries with a fixed exchange rate, negative shocks can cause more of a problem.[8] When a shock puts downward pressure on the currency, the government is forced to defend the fixed exchange rate by raising interest rates. This keeps the value of the currency stable, but higher interest rates slow down the economy and often lead to a rise in unemployment. Higher unemployment then starts to create the zone of vulnerability that makes countries vulnerable to a speculative attack, because it makes it more politically difficult for the government to raise interest rates in the future. Higher unemployment can also hurt the government's fiscal position and lead to higher debt. People who are unemployed don't pay taxes, so the government's revenues fall. People who are unemployed collect Employment Insurance and welfare, causing the government's spending to go up. And to make matters worse, higher interest rates mean that the government will be paying higher interest payments on the debt that it already has. All this further contributes to a zone of vulnerability because higher deficits and debts make it more difficult for the government to raise interest rates when the next shock comes along.

At the same time, voters don't like high unemployment, so they often start to put pressure on the government to do something about it. And governments, who are subject to the discipline of the political marketplace, are pressured to reduce unemployment by pursuing an expansionary monetary policy. The problem, of course, is that an expansionary policy is inconsistent with having capital mobility and a fixed exchange rate, so it eventually leads to a speculative attack. In a nutshell, this is why governments are so prone to pursue policies that make little economic sense, and why almost every fixed exchange rate has ended in a crisis. The Washington consensus policy mix of capital mobility and a fixed exchange rate will eventually produce hardships for voters when governments are forced to raise interest rates in the face of a negative shock. As interest rates rise the economy slows down and unemployment goes up. In a democracy, too-high unemployment is politically unsustainable, so governments aim to reduce unemployment through expansionary policies.

Some conservatives have sought to blame currency crises on the negative shocks that force governments to raise interest rates in the first place. The problem with this view, as mentioned above, is that negative shocks will always happen. As MIT economist Rudiger Dornbusch and his colleagues once argued, "An exchange-rate strategy that is only viable with good news is a bad strategy."[9] If the Washington consensus policy mix of capital mobility and fixed exchange rates is only politically sustainable as long as no negative shock occurs, the strategy is clearly an unworkable one.

At this point, conservatives would remind us of their argument that governments can avoid the high unemployment and rising debt that contribute to a zone of vulnerability by removing labour-market rigidities and cutting spending. The problem with the conservative solution, however, is that it once again ignores politics, confusing symptoms with the underlying malady. To understand why this is the case, it's useful to refer to the work of the late political economist Karl Polanyi. Polanyi is not well known among the broader public, but he's a superstar in political economy circles.

To explain the problem with the conservative focus on labour-market rigidities, Polanyi developed the notion of "fictitious commodities."[10] For a free market to work efficiently, business needs to have guaranteed access to the inputs of production — the things that are used to make products. This means that natural resources, labour and capital have to be made "for sale" through the creation of markets where everything has a price based on the laws of supply and demand. The problem, according to Polanyi, is that natural resources, labour and capital are fictitious commodities. They are inputs of production, not products produced for sale. For Polanyi, this means that prices and the laws of supply and demand can't be applied to them in quite the same way.

To understand why this is the case, let's look at a quick example. When you went to the bookstore to buy this book, it's quite likely that you found it in the "reduced to clear" bin. A reduced-to-clear bin and its storewide counterpart, the clearance sale, are used by stores to get rid of products for which there is little demand. The sign "reduced to clear" on a product means that the store is reducing the price of that product to clear the damn thing off its shelves. When there is little demand for a product, the only way the store can sell it is to lower the price, sometimes drastically. This is how the normal supply and demand price mechanism works. This little example may seem simple, but it actually explains one of the fundamental tenets of conservative economic theory.

While most economists agree that the price mechanism and the laws of supply and demand apply to all products that are produced for sale, conservatives believe that these laws can also be applied to the inputs of production in exactly the same way. Take the case of labour. Conservatives argue that the same laws that apply to the reduced-to-clear bin can be applied to workers. If unemployment is high, workers are unable to sell their labour. This, in turn, means that there must be little demand for labour relative to the supply. How can unemployment be reduced? According to conservatives, the answer is that workers must reduce to clear; that is, they must reduce their "price" by accepting lower wages and fewer benefits. When this happens, employers, like shoppers at the dollar store, will see a bargain and begin to hire them.

According to this theory, if a government wants to reduce unemployment, all it has to do is remove the labour-market rigidities that prevent workers from reducing their wage demands. This means getting rid of minimum wages and cutting spending on social programs like unemployment benefits and welfare. Conservatives argue that these programs prevent workers from accepting the lower wages that are needed to reduce unemployment, because no rational person would work for a wage that's less than what Employment Insurance pays for doing nothing.

If you're sitting in a university library reading this theory in an economics textbook, it makes perfect sense. If a product isn't selling, you lower the price. If unemployment is too high, you reduce to clear. So what's the problem? According to Polanyi, the problem is that labour isn't a real commodity like a book. Labour is actually people, and people have a nasty habit of not sitting quietly by while their wages and benefits are reduced. When you put a book in the reduced-to-clear bin and drastically lower its price, the book doesn't complain. The book doesn't worry that it has a family to feed or despair over what other books will think if they see it in the clearance bin. With people, there's no such luck. People *do* tend to complain when their wages and benefits are cut. They go on strike, they demand that the government intervene in the economy and, if things get really bad, they hurl rocks at the provincial legislature. In a democracy, if enough voters are complaining, the government is forced to do something about falling wages or it gets voted out of office. This is the discipline of the political marketplace.

What Polanyi's notion of fictitious commodities tells us is that high unemployment is just a symptom of an underlying problem. This problem is the way that capital mobility and fixed exchange rates can force governments to defend the currency by raising interest rates and slowing down the economy. When a government cuts social spending to reduce debt and remove labour-market rigidities, all it ends up doing is replacing the problem of high unemployment with the problem of falling wages, something that voters will be equally displeased about. When this happens, the government will still be put under pressure from voters to pursue expansionary policies, which means that the fixed exchange rate will still be politically unsustainable. Thinking back to the impossible trinity, it would appear that in a democracy governments must retain discretion over monetary policy to fight recessions and to prevent unemployment from getting too high or wages from getting too low. If this is the case, if giving up discretion over monetary policy is too politically difficult in a democracy, then countries that adopt the Washington consensus policy mix of capital mobility and a fixed exchange rate will be prone to crisis because this mix is politically unsustainable. To get a handle on how important democratic pressures are to the sustainability of a fixed exchange rate, we can now examine the role played by democracy in that mother of all financial crises, the Great Depression.

DEMOCRACY AND THE ORIGINS OF THE GREAT DEPRESSION

The first important point to note about the Great Depression is its similarity to modern currency crises, in that it took place in the context of capital mobility and a system of fixed exchange rates. In many ways, capitalism at the turn of the last century was similar to today's era of economic globalization, with its emphasis on free markets, capital mobility and stable currencies. Prior to the Second World War, investors could move their money across borders, and governments locked in stable currencies by adopting a gold standard system of fixed exchange rates, pegging currency values to the price of gold. The whole system was fairly stable until the First World War. After the war, something changed and the free-market economy eventually collapsed, in 1929, with the onset of the Great Depression.

To explain the collapse of the free-market system, conservatives of the day blamed government intervention in the economy for undermining the natural workings of the "invisible hand" of market forces. Karl Polanyi, the political economist mentioned earlier, agreed with the conservative explanation as far as it went, but argued that government intervention in the economy was the inevitable outcome of "weaknesses and perils" inherent in the free — or, as he termed it, "self-regulating" — market itself.[11] In his 1944 book, *The Great Transformation*, Polanyi

developed a concept called the "double movement" to explain why
the free-market system produced hardships that eventually led to its
downfall. The first half of the double movement was the decision
by governments to pursue capital mobility and fixed exchange rates.
The second half was the way that this policy combination produced
hardships for average people, causing them to demand government
intervention to protect jobs and stimulate wages. This government intervention then served to undermine the workings of the free market
and eventually led to its collapse. In other words, Polanyi argued, the
free-market economy of the early twentieth century collapsed because
it was politically unsustainable.

As a further demonstration of the importance of democratic pressures
to the collapse of the free-market system, University of California
economist Barry Eichengreen contrasts the problems that beset the post–
First World War gold standard with its relative stability in the decades
before the war. In doing so, he argues that the only reason the pre-war
combination of capital mobility and the gold standard system of fixed
exchange rates was stable was the absence of democracy. In the decades
leading up to the First World War, mass democracy and trade unions
were in their infancy. Citizens and workers were limited in their ability to influence government policy. Meanwhile, what we now know
about economics — the impossible trinity, the influence of monetary
policy on inflation and unemployment — was much more limited.
Capital mobility and the gold standard system of fixed exchange rates
was simply seen as the natural order of things; it was a system to which
few could imagine an alternative. As Polanyi observed, "belief in the
gold standard was the faith of the age . . . and was the one and only
tenet common to men of all nations and all classes."[12]

With average people having little political influence and even less
knowledge of economics, governments were not under the same
pressures as they are today to use macroeconomic policy to reduce
unemployment or to stimulate wages. This insulation from democratic
pressures created a unique set of conditions that increased the stability
of the gold standard. As Eichengreen argues, "the insulation enjoyed by
the monetary authorities allowed them to commit to the maintenance

of [the gold standard]. The effect was self-reinforcing: the market's confidence in the authorities' commitment caused traders to purchase a currency when its exchange rate weakened, minimizing the need for intervention and the discomfort caused by steps to stabilize the rate."[13] In other words, because democracy was limited, investors were confident that governments would have the political will necessary to defend the gold standard with higher interest rates. If interest rates rose and produced hardships for citizens, investors didn't have to worry that the government would give in to political pressures and pursue an expansionary policy. They had complete confidence in the willingness and ability of a government to defend its fixed exchange rate.

In fact, limitations on democracy actually altered the nature of capital flows. Normally, when a currency comes under downward pressure, investors are prone to sell even more of the currency because they worry that the government won't have the political will to defend it with higher interest rates. But given the limitations on democracy, investors would buy, rather than sell, a falling currency because they had complete trust that the government would raise interest rates. The beauty of this situation was that, when investors bought the currency, its value would start to go back up on its own. This effect made the gold standard system of fixed exchange rates more stable because governments didn't have to hike interest rates as high to defend the currency, so such a defense actually produced fewer hardships for average people.

After the First World War, all of this changed because of the rise of democracy.

Before the war, fewer hardships didn't mean no hardships. Specifically, despite its relative stability, the gold standard system of fixed exchange rates often did lead to difficulties for average people on occasions when governments were forced to implement contractionary policies. While unemployment wasn't a huge problem thanks to an absence of social programs and other "labour-market rigidities," defending the gold standard often did lead to falling wages. And, as Polanyi notes, "In human terms such a postulate implied for the worker extreme instability of earnings, utter absence of professional standards, abject readiness to be shoved and pushed about indiscriminately, complete dependence on the whims of the market."[14] In response, average people began to demand reforms. And in the years following the First World War, these demands grew as citizens sought payback for the blood they'd spilled in the trenches of Europe.

During the First World War, the gold standard, along with most other forms of international cooperation, was suspended. After the war, as countries attempted to reinstate it, they confronted a very different set of circumstances. First and foremost were the demands of citizens for higher wages, better working conditions and social programs for veterans. Second was the problem that prices had risen considerably since before the war, meaning that any return to the gold standard at its previous rate would require higher interest rates to lower inflation and wages. For obvious reasons, the demands of citizens and those of returning to the gold standard were in fundamental opposition to each other.

Nevertheless, by 1925, countries had begun to reinstate the gold standard. But all was not the same as before. Democracy had served to alter the nature of capital flows. Investors no longer fully trusted governments to defend the gold standard, so when a currency came under downward pressure they would sell it, thus increasing the amount by which governments would have to raise interest rates. So, in economic terms, the rise of democracy made the gold standard much more politically costly for governments to defend.

And then came the crash of the U.S. stock market in October of 1929. Governments responded to this negative shock by sharply raising interest rates to defend their fixed exchange rates. Newly won benefits for workers acted as labour-market rigidities and unemployment began to soar. Economist John Maynard Keynes advocated going off the gold standard and stimulating the economy by using discretionary monetary policy and government spending to create jobs. But governments were so committed to defending the gold standard, mostly out of a lack of understanding of what else they could do, that they continued to raise interest rates, driving millions out of work. Eventually, the political costs became too great to bear and governments abandoned the gold standard. But it wasn't until the Second World War, which was in economic terms a massive government spending program, that the economy was stimulated enough to fully end the depression conditions.

According to Polanyi and Eichengreen, the Great Depression originated in the hardships that were produced by the conservative policy combination of capital mobility and the gold standard system of fixed exchange rates. And following Polanyi's notion of the "double movement," these hardships led to political demands for reform and to the rise of democracy. Democracy, and the government intervention that it brought about, undermined investor confidence and the stability of the gold standard. When the U.S. stock market crashed and produced a severe negative shock, investors panicked and put currencies under downward pressure. While governments today would have responded by abandoning their fixed exchange rates, policy-makers at the time naively chose to defend their currencies with higher interest rates, a policy that led to the massive unemployment that became the Great Depression. Eichengreen summarizes the argument thus: "Polanyi saw the spread of universal suffrage and democratic associationalism as a reaction against the tyranny of the market forces that the gold standard had helped to set loose. The consequent politicization of the policy environment, he recognized, had destroyed the viability of the gold standard itself."[15] In other words, the gold standard eventually collapsed because it was politically unsustainable.

What does Polanyi's explanation of the collapse of the gold standard tell us about modern currency crises? Most importantly, it tells us why governments seem to be so prone to pursue policies that undermine the workings of a fixed exchange rate, and why virtually every modern combination of capital mobility and a fixed exchange rate has ended in crisis. Where conservatives argue that currency crises are caused by government blunders, such as expansionary policies or the creation of a zone of vulnerability, Polanyi would argue that these "blunders" are often inevitable because of the hardships produced by the Washington consensus policy mix. He would argue that this policy mix is prone to crisis because the need to defend a currency with higher interest rates in the face of a negative shock inevitably leads to a politically unsustainable situation — either rising unemployment and debt or falling wages.

In today's era of economic globalization, many economists have argued that capital mobility has become a given; that, because of developments in information technology, it is no longer possible for governments to prevent investors from taking their money abroad. Whether true or not, the same logic would also seem to apply to democracy and to the need for governments to retain discretion over monetary policy in order to fight recessions and to reduce unemployment. And if both capital mobility and democracy are givens in the modern world, then the decision to adopt a fixed exchange rate is the only government blunder that leads to currency crises.

This contradiction between democracy and a fixed exchange rate explains why currency crises continue to afflict countries whose governments adopt fixed exchange rates. It does not, however, explain why currency crises in the 1990s have become so much less predictable and more damaging in terms of what is justified by the underlying economic fundamentals. To solve this mystery, we need to examine the role played by mutual funds and pension funds.

MUTUAL FUNDS AND CURRENCY CRISES IN THE 1990S

In the last chapter, we saw how concentrated power, herd behaviour and a focus on short-term horizons in the growing world of mutual funds and pension funds has increased the potential for market overreaction and for prices to overshoot the true value of assets. In the rest of this chapter, we'll see how market overreaction and price overshooting explain why currency crises in the 1990s have become so much less predictable and more damaging. Let's start with the first issue, unpredictability.

Investors love the Washington consensus policy mix of capital mobility and fixed exchange rates because it prevents governments from pursuing the expansionary policies that they dislike. When this love is combined with the herd behaviour of institutional investors, the result seems to be that fund managers get a little too excited when a government adopts a fixed exchange rate. They love it, and they show their love by pouring so much money into the country that asset prices — such as stocks, bonds and the value of the currency — can overshoot what the assets are actually worth. And when prices overshoot and assets become overvalued, it can lead to the formation of what economists call a "speculative bubble."

A speculative bubble can start when a change in economic fundamentals, such as a government adopting a fixed exchange rate, causes investors to take a more favourable view of a country's assets and to invest accordingly. As money flows in and asset prices rise, the favourable view is reinforced among investors, leading to further capital inflows and, eventually, to an overvaluation of asset prices. In this situation, it can be rational for investors not to sell, even if they know that the market has become overvalued. This is because they also know that it could become even more overvalued in the future. And if you recall from the last chapter, this attitude is especially prevalent among fund managers because of the pressures on them to perform as well as their peers in the very short term.

But why does it matter if a speculative bubble emerges? Well, to conservatives, it actually shouldn't matter all that much, because they don't believe that overvalued asset prices will have any long-term effect on the real economy. Imagine a country whose stock market has become overvalued in the manner of a speculative bubble. When this happens, most economists believe that investors and corporate managers are aware that stock prices are overvalued. So even though the bubble may last for some time, they assume that corporate managers will act rationally and will not base any real business decisions on the fact that their stock price has risen so high. This means that when the market eventually corrects, even sharply, it should have little impact on corporations or on the real economy.

In many cases, this is how speculative bubbles do work. Prices rise and then eventually correct, with nothing having changed except the temporary value of assets on paper. The problem is that the conventional wisdom has generally ignored situations where inflated asset prices can artificially alter the fundamentals themselves. If you think back to the theory of efficient markets outlined in the last chapter, you'll remember that the conservative argument in favour of free financial markets rests on the assumption that they are the most efficient allocators of resources. When financial markets operate efficiently, the prices of assets reflect their true value, and economic actors can use these prices as an indicator of supply and demand, allocating their resources accordingly. But if prices are prone to overshoot the true value of assets, they send false signals to economic actors, causing them to make poor economic decisions. And when economic actors make decisions based on overvalued prices, it becomes much more likely that the real economy will be affected. In fact, a bubble in asset prices can lead to a bubble in the underlying fundamentals themselves.

One of the most prominent people to recognize how a bubble in asset prices can lead to a bubble in the fundamentals themselves is billionaire investor George Soros. Soros is probably the world's most famous and colourful speculator. He was reported to have made over a billion dollars speculating against the British pound during the 1992 European currency crisis. Prime Minister Mahathir of Malaysia blamed Soros personally for causing the Asian crisis of 1997. Soros even wrote a book, *The Crisis of Global Capitalism*, in which he argues that the free-market policies of the Washington consensus have gone too far and are becoming politically unsustainable.

In his book, Soros also describes how price overshooting and speculative bubbles can lead to the emergence of a bubble in the fundamentals themselves:

> The important point is that the future, when it occurs, will have been influenced by the guesswork that preceded it. The guessing finds expression in the stock prices and stock prices have ways of affecting the fundamentals. Similar arguments apply to currencies, credit and commodities . . . When stock prices find a way to affect the fundamentals, a self-reinforcing process may be set in motion that may carry both the fundamentals and stock prices quite far from what would be the conventional equilibrium [or true price of the asset]. This would justify the trend-following behaviour that

can carry financial markets into what I call far-from-equilibrium territory. Eventually the divergence between image and reality, expectations and outcomes, is bound to become unsustainable and the process is reversed.[16]

In other words, when asset prices find a way to influence the underlying economic fundamentals, a bubble can emerge in the fundamentals themselves. When this happens, the bubble in fundamentals appears to justify the bubble in asset prices, making the existence of a bubble much harder to identify. At the same time, when a bubble in asset prices leads to changes in real economic decision-making, then, when the bubble eventually bursts, it is much more likely that the real economy will be affected.

But how can overvalued asset prices affect real economic decisions in a way that leads to a bubble in the underlying fundamentals themselves? American economist Hyman Minsky argues that, because a speculative bubble often begins with a real change in fundamentals, it is possible that economic actors may not be aware that stock prices are overvalued.[17] They may believe that the small change in fundamentals does, in fact, justify the large rise in stock prices, and so may begin to make real economic decisions based on these overvalued prices. When stock prices overshoot the stocks' true value, households and corporations become wealthier on paper. This "wealth effect" can cause them to save less and spend more. For example, if the stock market is overvalued, the value of your RRSP will go up and you may decide that you don't need to save as much this year. Instead, you may decide that you can now afford to buy that new house, car or big-screen TV that you've always wanted. Similarly, rising stock prices make it easier for corporations to borrow money because stocks can be used as collateral for loans. If the stock is worth more, the corporation can borrow more.

When households and corporations spend more, they create a greater demand for goods and services, stimulating the economy. This means that corporations sell more and their earnings go up. An increase in earnings is one of the key fundamentals that we use to determine the true value of a stock's price. So when overvalued asset prices lead to less saving, more spending and a growth in corporate earnings, a bubble begins to appear in the actual economic fundamentals that underlie the asset prices. Even though the increased corporate earnings are somewhat artificial and unsustainable, because they are based on falling savings and rising debt, they *appear* to justify the original bubble in stock prices, making it much more difficult to see that a bubble has, in fact, emerged. So investors may be caught off guard when the stock market eventually corrects itself. Even worse, because households and corporations make real economic decisions based on the overvalued stock prices, it means that when the market eventually corrects, it is much more likely that the real economy will be negatively affected.

We now have the building blocks of a model to explain the currency crises of the 1990s and the role played by mutual funds and pension funds in causing them. This model combines the three factors we have discussed so far: Polanyi's insights on the politics of fixed exchange rates; the way that the concentrated power of mutual funds and pension funds, together with the herd behaviour and focus on short-term horizons of their managers, has increased the potential for market over-reaction and price overshooting; and the way that price overshooting can lead to a bubble both in asset prices and in the economic fundamentals that underlie them. Let's put these three factors together to see why currency crises in the 1990s have become much less predictable and far more damaging than is justified by the economic fundamentals.

Currency crises in the 1990s start with a country's decision to adopt the Washington consensus policy mix of capital mobility and a fixed exchange rate. Fund managers, who are all trained and socialized in the same way, tend to view this policy mix as "good" and to evaluate the changes in a country's economic fundamentals in the same way. This means that fund managers often react to policies of capital mobility and a fixed exchange rate with excessive optimism, leading to large capital inflows and to an increase in the value of the country's assets. Meanwhile, because fund managers are paid on the basis of "relative performance," they need to do what everyone else is doing in order to avoid underperforming the average. So, when a country comes into fashion by adopting capital mobility and a fixed exchange rate, fund managers tend to follow the herd, pouring more and more investment into that country's assets. The concentrated power and herd-like movement of all these mutual funds and pension funds can cause asset prices to become overvalued in the manner of a speculative bubble.

Now, because this rise in asset prices began with a real change in fundamentals (the adoption of capital mobility and fixed exchange rates), economic actors may believe that the rise in asset prices is fully justified and begin to make real economic decisions based on the overvalued prices. The overvalued asset prices can create a wealth effect as firms and households that have become wealthier on paper react by saving less and borrowing more to spend more. Increased spending creates a greater demand for goods and services, which stimulates the economy and fuels growth. Strong growth, in turn, helps to reinforce the view that asset prices are valued correctly; the price bubble becomes justified by a bubble in the underlying economic fundamentals.

Rising asset prices can also make rising debt appear to be sustainable. Determining what level of debt is sustainable for a firm means looking at how much it owes in relation to the value of its assets. This is often expressed as a "debt-equity ratio": a firm's total amount of debt divided by the value of its equity. (Equity includes both the physical assets a company owns and the value of its stock.) If stock prices rise, a firm can justify an increase in debt since, even though the total amount of debt increases, the debt-equity ratio doesn't increase. The same thing happens to the prices of other assets, like real estate. When an economy is growing fast, real estate prices tend to go up, so the value of a firm's physical assets, such as factories, also rises, providing further justification for increasing debt. Not only corporations but also households tend to increase their debt during such an economic bubble using the same logic.

The bubble in economic fundamentals can also lead to a sort of bubble in political fundamentals. This effect is important. Remember Polanyi's argument about the politics of currency crises? The Washington consensus policy mix of capital mobility and a fixed exchange rate lead inevitably to hardships for voters because, when negative shocks put downward pressure on the currency, the government is forced to defend the fixed exchange rate by raising interest rates. Higher interest rates slow down the economy and can lead to either rising unemployment or falling wages — either way, the result is pressure from voters to do something about it.

But all this changes when a bubble in the country's economic fundamentals begins to emerge. The bubble serves to temporarily offset or reduce the hardships normally associated with defending a fixed exchange rate. Large capital inflows from fund managers can cause a currency to become overvalued, which means that the government doesn't have to raise interest rates as high to defend the currency. Meanwhile, the bubble in economic fundamentals caused by increased spending helps to fuel growth and reduce unemployment, making voters happy and preventing them from putting pressure on the government to pursue expansionary policies. If voters are happy because of rising growth, investors become even more confident in the government's ability to defend the fixed exchange rate because they start to believe that it's politically sustainable.

This is why currency crises in the 1990s have become much less predictable than their earlier counterparts. Everything looks fine because the bubble in economic and political fundamentals appears to justify the original bubble in asset prices, making the fixed exchange rate seem politically sustainable.

The problem is that everything is not, in fact, fine. Short-term inflows of investment, falling savings and rising debt mean that the bubble in fundamentals is both artificial and unsustainable over the longer term. It also means that when a correction eventually occurs, the real economy will be significantly affected. This can happen for a number of reasons, all of which stem from the way that the bubble in asset prices sends false signals to economic actors.

First, as already mentioned, overvalued asset prices can cause households and firms to save too little and borrow too much. This is fine until the market corrects. But when it does, fewer savings and higher debts can lead to bankruptcies.

Second, a bubble in political fundamentals can lead to overconfidence in the government's ability to defend its fixed exchange rate. This overconfidence can also send false signals to economic actors. For example, firms and governments that believe that a country's fixed exchange rate is sustainable may begin to borrow money in foreign currencies. This makes sense as long as the fixed exchange rate holds. But if it doesn't, these governments and firms have set themselves up for a fall. A falling currency, especially one that starts to overshoot in a downwards direction, can cause the size of foreign currency debt to grow rapidly. To understand why this happens, let's assume that a government decides to fix the value of the domestic currency to the U.S. dollar at a one-to-one exchange rate. If a firm — or the government itself — borrows a million dollars in American currency, it will need one million units of its own currency to pay the loan back. But if the fixed exchange rate collapses and the value of the domestic currency falls by 50 percent in relation to the U.S. dollar, the government or firm will now need two million units of its own currency to pay back the loan; in effect, the size of the debt has doubled. When an exchange rate plummets in a country with significant foreign debt, the rise in debt levels can lead to a high rate of bankruptcies.

Overconfidence in a fixed exchange rate can also affect the economic decisions made by investors. When fund managers invest in a foreign country, they are buying assets, such as stocks and bonds, that are priced in the currency of that country. The risk is that if the country's fixed exchange rate doesn't hold and its currency falls, the fund will lose money because the value of the investment will fall in relation to the manager's home currency. To mitigate this risk, fund managers often use derivatives to hedge against the risk of a fixed exchange rate collapsing. A derivative is a specialized financial product that, in essence, allows a fund manager to place an offsetting side bet on the value of the currency; one that ensures that the fund manager will not be affected by movements in the exchange rate. If the value of the currency falls and the fund manager loses money on the original investment, he or she will make money on this side bet and offset the loss. The same holds true in reverse; if for some reason the value of the currency rises, increasing the value of the original investment, the fund will lose money on the side bet. The fund manager breaks even either way; the fund is not affected by changes in the value of the currency.

Unfortunately, like any type of insurance, derivatives cost money. When fund managers are overconfident in a government's ability to defend its fixed exchange rate, they may not bother to hedge their currency risk.

Now, when fund managers have foreign investments that are not hedged against currency risk, it makes them much more prone to panic if they start to think that the fixed exchange rate could collapse. And this is where the vicious circle of a self-fulfilling speculative attack can do its most severe damage. If a currency starts to fall and investors start to worry that the government won't be able to defend the fixed exchange rate, a lack of currency hedges mean that fund managers will start to panic and pull the vast sums of pension and mutual fund money out of that country, causing its currency to drop even more. As its currency drops, the country's foreign debt, in both the public and the private sector, starts to rise, adding to the sense of panic among fund managers. They worry that these rising debts will make the option of raising interest rates too expensive, because it would mean firms and the government would have to pay much more interest on their debts. This worry causes fund managers to pull even more money out of the country, causing the currency to fall even further, causing foreign currency debts to rise faster, causing fund managers to panic even more — and so on and so on.

Thus, the bubble in asset prices and economic fundamentals sends false signals to economic actors, which causes them to make poor economic decisions. When the bubble eventually bursts, the damage to the real economy can be quite severe.

But what causes the bubble to burst? Well, this is where the politics of currency crises comes in. It all starts with a negative shock that is large enough to force governments to raise interest rates in defense of the currency. Remember, these shocks are inevitable. Sooner or later an important country will raise interest rates because of conditions in its domestic economy. When this happens, some investors will take their money out of that country and its currency will come under downward pressure, forcing the government to raise interest rates. Higher interest rates will slow down the economy, causing unemployment to rise or wages to fall. The higher interest rates will also lead to a rise in the government's debt for several reasons: interest payments will rise, tax revenue will fall as unemployment goes up and wages go down, and the cost of social programs will rise as the unemployment and welfare rolls swell. Together, these factors can lead to political pressures from voters, putting the country into the zone of vulnerability described in second-generation models of currency crises.

The specific timing of a speculative attack depends on how soon investors realize what's going on. They may react to a rise in unemployment or debt, a slowdown in growth or a "political" event such as a protest or strike. Whatever the trigger, once a self-fulfilling speculative attack begins it will lead to the vicious circle of a falling currency, rising debts and the panic by investors described above.

Worse yet, such a crisis can spread from country to country. Crises can spread for both fundamental and financial reasons. The fundamental reasons boil down to trade links. If a country goes into crisis, it may affect another country that relies on it as a market for exports, because falling growth will mean fewer purchases. Investors may then begin to sell off the assets of the affected country and, if that country was in a similar zone of vulnerability, this sell-off can initiate another self-fulfilling speculative attack. A crisis can also spread for financial reasons: institutional investors that lose money in one market may be forced to cover their losses by selling off assets in another market. This can particularly apply to emerging-market mutual funds that invest in a specific region of the world. Fund managers may be faced with redemptions by individual investors, forcing them to sell off assets across the whole region. Again, if other countries are in a similar zone of vulnerability, the sell-off can initiate a series of self-fulfilling attacks, causing the crisis to spread still further.

And that, as they say, is that. This is my version of what caused the new type of currency crisis that emerged in the 1990s. These crises have been less predictable and more damaging than indicated by the fundamentals because the herd-like way that mutual funds and pension funds are managed caused asset prices to overshoot, leading to a bubble in the underlying economic fundamentals. This bubble in the fundamentals appears to justify the bubble in asset prices, making the onset of a crisis much more difficult to predict. When a correction eventually occurs, the poor economic decisions that were based on the bubble in asset prices ensure that when the fixed exchange rate collapses, it does a great deal of damage to the real economy.

With the model thus outlined, let's see how well it corresponds to what actually happened.

4

THREE CRASHES AND A BOOM

When analyzing historical events it is useful to keep in mind that history always repeats itself — but never in exactly the same way. The first part of this adage is the concern of this chapter; the second part is the minefield we need to avoid. Trying to figure out what causes a recurring kind of historical event — such as war, revolution or, in this case, the new type of currency crisis that emerged in the 1990s — means focusing on the common denominators. This is what theoretical models attempt to do: figure out why history keeps repeating itself without getting too bogged down in why it never repeats itself in exactly the same way. So if we're going to understand the reasons behind this new type of currency crisis, we need to focus on what was the same about all of the crises of this type rather than on what was different. While it's important for us to recognize that the European, Mexican and Asian crises took place under different specific circumstances, it's even more important for us to recognize that some very similar forces were at work in each one.

Few economists would disagree with this need to focus on common factors. But what I hope to convince you of is that the common factors that matter most are those outlined in the model I presented in the last chapter; that is, the politics of fixed exchange rates, the herd behaviour of mutual fund and pension fund managers, and the way that a speculative bubble in asset prices can lead to the emergence of a bubble in the underlying economic fundamentals. So with these factors in mind, let's see what actually happened.

EURO-TRASHED: THE POLITICS OF THE EUROPEAN CRISIS

The story of the 1992 European crisis begins in 1979, when a number of countries in Europe adopted a system of fixed, but adjustable, exchange rates known as the Exchange Rate Mechanism (ERM). The ERM was part of a broader European project aimed at increasing the level of economic, political and, eventually, monetary integration among the countries of the region. Economic integration means trade. Through the creation of the Common Market, the countries of Europe sought to integrate their markets by promoting freer trade. But unlike more limited agreements such as the North American Free Trade Agreement (NAFTA), the European project included mobility for labour as well as business. Immigration controls were relaxed to allow Europeans to live and work in any of the participating countries.

To promote trade, the Europeans wanted stable exchange rates, so in 1979 they adopted the ERM system of fixed, but adjustable, exchange rates. In doing so, the countries involved agreed to keep the values of their currencies fixed within a set target band in relation to the value of the German mark. When exchange rates are fixed but adjustable, it means that governments will more or less do whatever is necessary to defend the value of their currency, but retain the option of adjusting it in situations where maintaining it becomes too politically difficult. And between 1979 and 1987, this is exactly what governments did.

In the years following 1987, the Europeans deepened their commitment to economic and monetary integration by promoting greater capital mobility and agreeing to defend their fixed exchange rates at all costs. These commitments were formalized in 1991 with the signing of the Maastricht Treaty. The ultimate goal was Economic and Monetary Union (EMU), including the adoption of a common currency. To qualify for participation in EMU, countries had to meet several conditions, or "convergence criteria," which were laid out in the Maastricht Treaty. These criteria committed governments to lowering inflation, defending their fixed exchange rates (and giving up the option of adjusting them) and cutting back on their spending to reduce deficits.

In terms of the logic of the "impossible trinity," the Maastricht Treaty combination of capital mobility and fixed exchange rates meant that governments were forced to give up the option of reducing unemployment through a discretionary monetary policy. Predictably, this led to falling wages, as it was often necessary for governments to defend their fixed exchange rates by raising interest rates. And it was at this point that the discipline of the political marketplace put pressure on governments to do something to protect the incomes of workers.

Having given up the option of stimulating their economies through discretionary monetary policy, European governments turned to regulation and social spending to deal with the problem of falling wages. They promoted greater job security for workers through regulations, and made their social programs, such as unemployment insurance and welfare, increasingly generous. As Kathleen McNamara, a political economist at Princeton, argues, "When exchange rate stability increased in the 1980s, so did budget deficits throughout Europe, as unemployment benefits and public spending programs were used to promote political and broader economic stability."[1] However, while this did help somewhat to calm the restless masses, it also created labour-market rigidities and a rise in unemployment. The other problem was that, in some of the weaker economies like Italy, policies of this type were financed through increased government borrowing and an even larger rise in deficits and debts.

At the start of the 1990s, the hardships produced by the combination of capital mobility and fixed exchange rates increased substantially with the onset of a global recession and the unexpected economic costs of German reunification. After the fall of the Berlin Wall, Germany set about its project of reunification. To smooth the reunification process, the West German government began spending large sums of money in East Germany, reconstructing its economy and exchanging its currency for West German marks on a one-to-one basis. By 1991, all this extra spending began to create inflationary pressures and the German central bank, the Bundesbank, responded by raising interest rates. Higher interest rates in Germany acted as a negative shock for the rest of Europe, which caused investors to take their money abroad (to Germany, to benefit from the higher interest rates). This put downward pressure on other European currencies, which forced governments to raise interest rates to defend their exchange rates. This produced even greater hardships as the economies of Europe slowed, unemployment rose and deficits and debts grew.

With high unemployment and growing debts, many European countries started to enter the zone of vulnerability that economists believe increases the chance of a speculative attack. But investors didn't launch a speculative attack. They believed that governments and the citizens who voted for them were still committed to the Maastricht Treaty process and, thus, to maintaining their fixed exchange rates.

They were wrong.

In 1992, a number of European countries held referendums on the Maastricht Treaty. Denmark's vote, held in June, revealed that voters were tired of the hardships that had been produced by the policy combination of capital mobility and a fixed exchange rate. The result of the referendum was a resounding "No" vote, which shook the confidence of investors. To make matters worse, early polling pointed to a similar rebuke from voters in the upcoming referendum in France. This was the point when investors realized that the demands of the political marketplace might make governments unwilling to continue to defend their currencies and meet the other criteria laid down in the Maastricht

Treaty. This realization that fixed exchange rates might not be politically sustainable eventually led to a series of self-fulfilling speculative attacks and currency devaluations. As George Soros commented, "The exact moment of the reversal can be identified as the defeat in the Danish referendum . . . it generated the breakdown of the exchange-rate mechanism."[2]

As country after country came under speculative attack from investors, governments were forced to devalue their currencies and, in the case of the Italian lira and the British pound sterling, to abandon their fixed exchange rates altogether. Countries that were able to maintain their fixed exchange rates over the long term did so only through temporary currency devaluations and/or restrictions on capital mobility. In the aftermath of the crisis, the British economy boomed as the government, having given up its fixed exchange rate, was able to lower interest rates to stimulate the economy and reduce unemployment. In countries that maintained their fixed exchange rates, unemployment soared to a mid-decade average of around 12 percent. Only when these countries switched from fixed exchange rates to a common currency a few years later did the problem of unemployment begin to be addressed.

So what *caused* the European crisis? Was it the negative shock produced by German reunification? Partially. But remember, some sort of negative shock will always happen. If it wasn't German reunification, it would have been something else. Blaming the collapse of a fixed exchange rate on a negative shock is like building your house out of straw and then blaming the wind for knocking it over.

What about the failure of European governments to prevent the emergence of a "zone of vulnerability"? Couldn't the governments of Europe have simply removed labour-market rigidities and cut spending as many conservatives suggested? They could, but the zone of vulnerability probably would have come about anyway, meaning that the pressures on governments not to raise interest rates in defense of their currencies would have remained. As we saw in the last chapter, if a government removes labour-market rigidities by cutting spending on social assistance programs, all they end up doing is replacing rising unemployment with falling wages, something that voters are just as reluctant to tolerate for very long.

The European currency crisis was not the result of unlucky circumstances or government blunders. Rather, it was caused by the fact that the policy mix of capital mobility and fixed exchange rates is politically unsustainable because it forces governments to give up the option of fighting recessions and reducing unemployment through discretionary monetary policy. This policy mix is incompatible with democracy and with the need for governments to be able to respond to the demands of voters.

But if this is what caused the crisis, why was it so unpredictable for investors? Well, this is where the role played by mutual funds and pension funds becomes important.

CONVERGENCE PLAYS: THE ROLE OF MUTUAL FUNDS AND PENSION FUNDS IN THE EUROPEAN CRISIS

When the governments of Europe decided to commit to the Maastricht Treaty criteria of capital mobility, fixed exchange rates and lower deficits, fund managers got excited. They looked at the yields on government bonds issued by the weaker economies and realized that, if the commitment to the Maastricht Treaty deficit reduction criteria and fixed exchange rates held, it would improve the fundamentals of these weaker economies, causing the yields on their bonds to rise and converge with the yields on bonds in the stronger economies such as Germany. This realization led to an investment strategy known as "convergence plays" and fund managers began to pour money into the weaker economies, buying their bonds in record amounts.

As money poured in, it produced a sort of bubble in the underlying political fundamentals. Large capital inflows made it easier for countries to defend their fixed exchange rates, and this helped to limit the hardships that normally emerge when governments are forced to raise interest rates in defense of their currencies. At the same time, with fund

managers so willing to buy government bonds, it became easier for
countries to borrow money to finance the increased social spending
they needed to offset the hardships being produced by the Washington
consensus policy mix. The bottom line is that large capital inflows
created an artificial situation where governments were under less pressure from voters to pursue the expansionary monetary policies that
would undermine their fixed exchange rates. And this lack of pressure
from voters made fund managers more confident that governments
were willing and politically able to defend their fixed exchange rates.
They knew that rising deficits were a problem, but they believed that
they were only transitional because governments were so committed to
the criteria of the Maastricht Treaty, including deficit reduction, that
they would eventually cut their spending.

What investors didn't recognize was that the lack of political pressures on governments was somewhat artificial and unsustainable because
it depended so heavily on continuing short-term capital inflows and on
rising levels of debt. Fund managers believed that the lack of political
pressure on governments meant that they would eventually cut their
deficits. In fact, however, this lack of political pressure only existed
because of rising deficits and the way that they were used to fund social
spending to offset the hardships of falling wages and rising unemployment. Nevertheless, the optimism of fund managers was reinforced by
this bubble in the political fundamentals, which made them confident
that Europe's fixed exchange rates would hold. And as occurs in all
bubbles, greater confidence led to even more capital inflows. British
pension funds, for example, increased their investments in foreign bonds
from 0 percent of their portfolios in 1986 to over 4 percent by 1991.
In the United States, the optimism of fund managers actually led to the
creation of a specialized type of mutual fund designed to profit from
the anticipated convergence of weaker-economy bond yields. As a 1993
report by the Group of Ten countries stated, "'convergence trades'
spawned a whole new segment of the mutual fund industry, the short-
term global income fund."[3]

Concentrated decision making by fund managers, together with
their herd behaviour and the emergence of a bubble in the underlying

political fundamentals, led to excessive capital inflows to the extent that the volume of "convergence plays" grew to over $300 billion by 1992. As Bank of England economist E. Philip Davis argues, "The overall pattern of convergence plays could be seen as a form of overreaction of financial markets to the prospects of EMU, encouraged by forms of herding."[4] And just as excessive inflows led to a bubble in the under-lying political fundamentals, so too did they set the stage for a sharper correction, one that prevented a more orderly realignment of exchange rates. As George Soros notes, "Everyone rushed out to buy high-yielding bonds in the weaker currencies. This made the ERM more rigid than it had been before, and set it up for a radical break rather than a gradual adjustment."[5]

What this meant in practical terms was that the bubble in political fundamentals caused by excessive capital inflows led fund managers to place too much trust in the ability of governments to defend their fixed exchange rates. As a result, they began to make poor economic decisions such as not bothering to hedge against the risk that the fixed exchange rates might collapse. When fund managers have complete trust in a government, it can make them much more prone to panic if anything happens to call that trust into question. It also means that when the excessive volume of inflows turns into outflows, the sheer size of the reversal will make it impossible for governments to defend their currencies with higher interest rates.

So, when the Danish and French referendums on the Maastricht Treaty returned a "No" vote and a very weak "Yes" vote respectively, it was a large shock for fund managers. As MIT economist Paul Krugman notes, these votes revealed, to most observers' great surprise, that the enthusiasm of Europe's policy elite for EMU was not shared by the broader public.[6] At this point, fund managers' confidence in the political sustainability of the fixed exchange rates evaporated. And when fund managers started to panic and pull out their money en masse, excessive inflows quickly turned into massive outflows, which were too large to defend against even with sharp interest-rate hikes.

Mutual funds and pension funds played a key role in the 1992 Euro-pean crisis. If fund managers hadn't overreacted, governments would have realized sooner that their fixed exchange rates were politically unsustainable and might have been able to adjust their currencies before capital inflows grew to unmanageable levels. Without the pressures of massive inflows over a short period of time, and the corresponding potential for massive outflows, the governments of Europe might have been able to adjust their exchange rates in a more orderly fashion.

So the European crisis was the result of political hardships created by the policy mix of capital mobility and fixed exchange rates, and by the way that herd behaviour by fund managers served to mask these hardships until it was too late. But conservatives at the time didn't see it this way. They placed all the blame on the governments of Europe and none of it on the behaviour of the financial markets. The result was that investors and policy-makers saw the European crisis as an unfortunate, but isolated, event. And this meant that when the next crisis came along only two years later in Mexico, they were equally surprised.

OLD TEQUILA, NEW BOTTLE: THE BUILDING OF THE PESO BUBBLE

Both politically and economically, the 1990s seemed to usher in a new era. The fall of the Berlin Wall and the collapse of communism in the Soviet Union fuelled Western triumphalism about the victory of capitalism. In North America, this triumphalism was extended from capitalism in general to a case in favour of the free-market policies of the Washington consensus. When a number of developing countries began to replace past policies of government intervention with a free-market approach imported from the United States, it seemed to further confirm that a new era had emerged. Investors in particular became increasingly optimistic as changes around the world seemed to support the types of policies that would best serve their interests. So enamoured were they with policy shifts in the developing countries, that they came up with a new designation for them, "emerging markets," to reflect this new-found dedication to the virtues of free markets and sound money.

Leading the emerging-market charge was the Institutional Revolutionary Party (PRI) government of Mexico, whose new leader,

President Carlos Salinas de Gotari, held a degree from Harvard's Kennedy School of Government, and whose key advisors were a coterie of MIT-trained economists. In the late 1980s, Mexico was still recovering from the effects of the 1982 debt crisis. But all this began to change in 1990 when Salinas managed to negotiate a debt reduction package with the American Treasury Secretary Nicholas Brady. While the so-called Brady Plan had only a modest impact on real debt reduction and Mexico's growth prospects, it did seem to mark a turning point in the eyes of foreign investors. The debt reduction package was seen as part of a much larger reform process based on the Washington consensus policy mix of free markets, capital mobility and a fixed exchange rate.

In the same year, Salinas undertook a number of measures to promote his free-market vision and to build confidence with foreign investors. He deregulated the economy, privatized many state-owned enterprises (particularly in the banking sector) and cut government spending to reduce Mexico's deficits and debt. To convince investors that he was serious, Salinas promoted capital mobility by allowing foreigners to purchase government bonds and certain types of corporate stocks. He supported fixing Mexico's exchange rate to the U.S. dollar and, to top it all off, he proposed that Canada, the United States and Mexico begin negotiating a free trade agreement.

For North American fund managers, this was a dream come true. At home, a fall in U.S. interest rates, combined with a rapid growth in the assets held by mutual funds and pension funds, caused many of them to look abroad for new opportunities. And with Mexico well down the path to a free-market nirvana, fund managers reacted to Salinas's policies with excessive optimism — so much so that annual portfolio flows into Mexico rose from next to nothing in 1989 to over $30 billion by 1993. And as capital flowed in, Mexico's economic fundamentals seemed to improve dramatically. Between 1990 and 1992, the value of the peso rose, stock prices increased and inflation fell. Capital inflows led to a large drop in interest rates, which helped to quickly put the government's financial house in order. A deficit of around 2.8 percent was transformed into a surplus of 1.6 percent in two short years.

The short-term capital inflows pushed up the peso to a point where it became overvalued. And while an overvalued peso would eventually make Mexican goods more expensive on world markets and lead to a fall in exports, it did help to improve Mexico's purchasing power and its ability to buy foreign goods. The capital inflows and the rising value of the peso combined to fuel a boom in consumer spending. As a study by Jeffrey Sachs, Aaron Tornell and Andres Velasco demonstrates, "The increase in private consumption was largely financed by the massive capital inflows that took place. The link was the banking system, which converted much of this additional flow of resources into real estate and consumption loans."[7]

The boom in consumption generated support for Salinas's free-market reforms. As political scientist Timothy Kessler argues, "The main reason for Salinas's apparently deliberate strategy of overvaluing the peso was that virtually all of the economic interests that exercised influence over the PRI's political future were united, either implicitly or explicitly, in support of the status quo. For bankers and large industrialists, the middle class, and workers, Mexico's [fixed exchange rate] provided important economic benefits."[8] For Mexico's recently privatized banks, the large capital inflows produced enormous profits as they were transformed into domestic loans. In the business sector, the fixed exchange rate helped to reduce the cost of credit by allowing Mexican firms to borrow money in dollars; this contributed to rapid growth. For the middle class and unionized workers, the fixed exchange rate brought benefits in terms of greater purchasing power and an ability to purchase imported products. "For this reason," continues Kessler, "political opposition to maintaining the exchange rate was extremely limited."[9]

Because they did improve Mexico's economic and political fundamentals, large capital inflows made the fixed exchange rate appear to be politically sustainable. This appearance of sustainability led to further inflows, and to the absence of political pressures for expansionary policies. As Krugman observed, "because the financial markets offered an immediate, generous advance on the presumed payoff from free trade and sound money, it was easy to make a case for doing the right thing and brush aside all the usual political objections."[10]

Confidence in Mexico's reform process was so high that it led to a massive growth in the number of specialized emerging-market mutual funds. In fact, between 1988 and 1994, the category of emerging-market equity funds grew from 91 funds with $6.1 billion in assets to 820 funds with over $120 billion in assets. The number of equity funds specializing specifically in Latin America rose from 4 in 1988, with a total of $520 million in assets, to 105 in 1994, with over $14 billion in assets. In the specific case of Mexico, capital inflows from U.S. equity funds alone rose from $18 million in 1990 to over $5 billion by 1993. The end result of these massive capital inflows was the emergence of a speculative bubble in Mexican asset prices as well as in the economic and political fundamentals.

This created a kind of virtuous circle, as the bubble in fundamentals seemed to justify the bubble in asset prices, as well as investor confidence in the ability of the government to maintain its fixed exchange rate. As Krugman puts it, "the unprecedented depth and breadth of policy reform was largely due to the perception that such reforms brought macroeconomic and financial recovery — a perception driven by the way that financial markets rewarded the reforms . . . So once again something of a circular logic was at work."[11]

But, in fact, all was not well in Mexico. As was the case in the run-up to the European crisis, overvalued asset prices began to have a real effect on economic decision making. As mutual funds stampeded into the Mexican stock market, share prices rose. Meanwhile, Mexico's banks were busy converting short-term capital inflows into real estate loans, and this led to a rise in real estate prices. Rising asset prices made households and corporations feel richer, and the resulting wealth effect led to a decline in the national savings rate. In the business sector, the combination of rising asset prices and confidence in the sustainability of the fixed exchange rate caused many firms to borrow heavily in dollars to take advantage of lower interest rates in the United States. Mexican companies borrowed so much abroad that, by 1991, over half of their total debt was in U.S. dollars.

At this stage, Mexico was setting itself up for a fall. The situation was unsustainable, because the boom was heavily dependent on short-term capital inflows, an overvalued peso, a deteriorating trade balance, rising foreign debt and a decline in national savings. In other words, Mexico was having a short-term party on a credit card that would eventually have to be paid off.

POLITICS AND POWER:
THE BEGINNING OF THE END

Over the next few years, Mexico's experiment with the Washington consensus policy mix of free markets, capital mobility and fixed exchange rates began to produce a number of hardships for both businesses and average people. First and foremost was the way that the overvalued peso made Mexican goods more expensive on world markets, leading to a growing trade deficit. Between 1990 and 1994, Mexico's trade deficit (or, to use the broader and more precise measure, its current-account deficit) rose from 3 percent of gross domestic product (GDP) to almost 8 percent. At the same time, GDP growth was dropping steadily (from 4.5 percent in 1990 to a mere 0.6 percent by 1993) and unemployment was rising. Compounding these problems was a rise in inequality. As Krugman reported, "the benefits of growth, which in any case was barely positive in per capita terms, were also very unevenly distributed . . . there is not much question that as Latin American stock markets were booming, unemployment was rising and the poor were getting poorer."[12] This situation was beginning to fuel political discontent.

Mexico's recently privatized banking sector also began to experience difficulties. Faced with a huge amount of capital inflows that had to be converted into domestic loans, Mexico's banks had loaned out money to firms with somewhat less than perfect credit ratings. And as economic growth declined and these firms started to get into trouble, many of them began to default on their loans. The banking system became increasingly fragile. Between 1991 and 1994, the bad loans on the books of Mexico's banks rose from 3 to 7 percent. As Sachs, Tornell and Velasco argue in their study, the "transformation of short-run foreign capital into peso loans was responsible in part for the fragility of the banking system."[13] In other words, excessive capital inflows by foreign mutual funds had led to an overshooting of asset prices, which caused banks to make poor economic decisions.

In many ways, with unemployment and private-sector debt rising, and the trade balance and growth declining, Mexico seemed to be entering the zone of vulnerability described in second-generation models of speculative attacks. A few economists, such as MIT's Rudiger Dornbusch, were calling for a devaluation. To deal with the growing imbalances in the Mexican economy, Dornbusch wanted Mexico to adjust its fixed exchange rate drastically downwards. But the politics of the Washington consensus intervened to make a devaluation politically difficult. In 1993, President Clinton was cutting every deal imaginable to get the NAFTA, which Mexico wanted badly, through the U.S. Congress. Had the peso been devalued, there would have been a flood of Mexican goods into the United States, which could have undermined the Clinton administration's argument that the NAFTA would not cost American jobs.

At the end of the day, the Mexicans didn't devalue and the NAFTA made it through the American Congress. While this gave a further boost to the confidence of fund managers, it did seem as though growing imbalances in the Mexican economy were leading to the emergence of a zone of vulnerability, one that would make it harder for the government to defend its fixed exchange rate with higher interest rates. But, as occurred in the run-up to the European crisis, investors retained their confidence until evidence emerged that these economic hardships were beginning to produce political pressures from voters. The first bit of evidence appeared on January 1, 1994, the same day that the recently negotiated NAFTA came into effect. It started in Mexico's southern state of Chiapas with a violent uprising by the Zapatistas, a small group of armed peasants who were opposed to President Salinas's reform program in general and to the NAFTA in particular.

While a quick mobilization of the military, combined with a public relations campaign to downplay the threat posed by the Zapatistas, did help to pacify jittery foreign investors, fund managers began to worry that Mexico's bad old days of political instability might be returning.

A little over two and a half months later, these worries were greatly amplified when President Salinas's chosen successor, PRI presidential candidate Luis Donaldo Colosio, was assassinated. For mutual fund managers, Colosio's assassination raised serious questions about Mexico's political stability. And the continuing Chiapas conflict was eroding faith in the government's claim that the Zapatistas had no popular support.

Combined with a rise in U.S. interest rates, these internal political shocks put downward pressure on the peso as new inflows from foreign mutual funds began to dry up. Within a few days of the Colosio assassination, the peso had fallen to the lower end of its fixed-exchange-rate target band in what amounted to a drop of about 10 percent. And this downward pressure on the peso forced interest rates to rise by 7 percentage points. More importantly, it made fund managers nervous that Mexico would no longer be willing to defend its fixed exchange rate, making it vulnerable to a speculative attack. So, as in the European crisis, fund managers only began to get nervous when something changed to indicate that the political fundamentals were not what everyone had thought they were. The Chiapas uprising and Colosio assassination were to Mexico's fixed exchange rate what the Danish "No" vote was to the European ERM: a political shock that made investors worry about the political sustainability of the fixed exchange rate. As Sachs, Tornell and Velasco conclude, "it seems clear that March 1994 represented a turning point for Mexico's macro-economic performance. After political shocks led to the cut-off in foreign lending, the time was ripe for a policy change."[14]

If the Salinas government was going to change its policies, there seemed to be two potential options: either give up the fixed exchange rate and devalue the currency, or defend the peso through a further rise in interest rates. Both options had their downsides, and it appeared as though Mexico's experiment with the free-market Washington consensus had put it between a rock and a hard place. Raising interest rates to defend the peso would exacerbate Mexico's rising unemployment, growing private-sector foreign debt, increasingly fragile banking system and deteriorating political fundamentals. Devaluing the currency, while making the most economic sense in terms of dealing with Mexico's problems, would panic foreign fund managers and threaten President Salinas's dream of a comfortable retirement as the head of the World Trade Organization. Faced with these conflicting pressures, the government searched for a solution that would allow them to have it both ways. It was at this point that the hard place got a little bit harder.

Within a few hours of the Colosio assassination on March 23, officials at the Mexican central bank received a call from Robert Citrone.[15] Still under thirty, Citrone had recently become the emerging markets' point man for the world's largest mutual fund company. He was paid well, travelled extensively and exerted an influence over countries startling for his young age. As the head of Fidelity Investments' "New Markets Income Fund," a speculative bond fund set up in May of 1993, Citrone was someone who finance ministers took seriously.

When Citrone called up the Mexican central bank, it wasn't to offer his condolences for the Colosio assassination. It was to get a guarantee from the Mexicans that they would take the necessary measures to maintain the peso's value. And two weeks later, under the auspices of a consortium known as the "Weston Forum," Citrone and a handful of other fund managers met with Mexican officials to demand that the fixed exchange rate be defended. The June 14, 1994, *Wall Street Journal* reported as follows:

Mexico was asked to curb the speed of the peso's daily devaluation . . . [and] to insure investors against currency-exchange losses on $5 billion of peso-denominated securities if the peso dropped below the prescribed range. The investors also asked that Mexican banks be allowed to increase their foreign-currency liabilities to 25 percent of total assets from 20 percent. This could boost the banks' peso buying, but then leave them at greater risk if the peso fell . . . The investor group also suggested the government issue long-term *tesobonos*, government bonds with built-in devaluation insurance; increase its swap lines with foreign central banks; and, perhaps most important, back all these measures with central-bank peso purchases to push the currency up.[16]

These demands were reinforced the day before the Weston Forum fund managers met with Mexican officials when some of the funds refused to purchase a block of newly released short-term treasury certificates. Interest rates soared and the stock market dropped.

While we may never know how much influence the Weston Forum actually had, the government seemed to give in to its demands. Also from the *Wall Street Journal*:

> So far, the fund managers have reason to be pleased with Mexico's response. Soon after the Weston Forum meeting, Mexican officials launched a peso rescue operation. They issued longer-term *tesobonos* as the investor group asked, and cut back on the auctions of Mexican treasury bills, or *cetes*, to reduce short-term rates. Then, senior Mexican finance officials flew to Washington to announce a trilateral currency support program among the U.S., Canada and Mexico. After these meetings, Mr. Aspe, the finance minister, visited with Fidelity's fund managers.[17]

So, to achieve its conflicting goals of defending the peso and not raising interest rates, the Mexican government decided to relieve investors of their exchange-rate risk by converting peso-denominated bonds, known as *cetes*, into dollar-denominated *tesobonos*. This is the equivalent of a government borrowing in a foreign currency. When the Mexican government sold bonds that were denominated in pesos, it could pay them off in their own currency. If the value of the peso fell, investors would be the ones to lose out. This is what exchange-rate risk is all about. But when the government gave into the demands of the Weston Forum fund managers and converted its peso bonds into dollar bonds, it set itself up for a fall. If the fixed exchange rate ever collapsed, and the value of the peso fell against the U.S. dollar, the size of Mexico's foreign currency debt would balloon overnight.

At the end of 1993, only about 6 percent of Mexico's debt was in dollars. By November of 1994, this amount had risen to well over 50 percent as Mexico allowed foreign mutual funds to convert their peso bonds into dollar bonds.

By relieving fund managers of their exchange-rate risk, the Salinas government was able to avoid having to devalue the peso and give up its fixed exchange rate. The downside was that the government had, at the behest of foreign mutual fund managers, set itself up for a potential fall. If the fixed exchange rate did collapse, all that dollar debt would put Mexico into a severe world of hurt.

DECEMBER 1994: THE TEQUILA CRISIS

Short-term capital inflows from mutual funds are a bit like tequila. They both feel great when they're going in. If you have too much of either, you start to do stupid things that you'll end up regretting. At some point, too much of either changes euphoria into illness. And, whether it's capital flows or tequila, when it starts rapidly going out the way it came in, it's always a very unpleasant experience.

In the years leading up to the peso crisis, the Mexican government had consumed quite a lot of capital inflows. It felt great for a while, but then the government started to do stupid things, like converting its peso debt into dollar debt after the March 1994 Colosio assassination. This made it feel better temporarily and encouraged it to consume even more capital inflows. Over the summer, Mexico appeared to have stabilized. To deal with an upcoming election, the government pursued an expansionary monetary policy to stimulate the economy and to reduce some of the growing economic hardships. This policy soothed voters and contributed to the September re-election of the PRI, now led by Ernesto Zedillo. And even though the expansionary policy had to be offset by running down Mexico's foreign currency reserves to prop up the peso, fund managers began to feel that political stability was returning and that the fixed exchange rate would be politically sustainable.

Again, all seemed to be well — until a series of negative shocks crashed the party. In November of 1994, the U.S. Federal Reserve raised interest rates and, in Mexico, a political scandal erupted when the Attorney General accused the government of blocking the investigation of his brother's murder, which had occurred in September. This combination of an external economic shock with an internal political one revealed just how fragile the Mexican economy had become. Nervous investors began to sell Mexican assets and the government was forced to defend the fixed exchange rate by spending almost 25 percent of its remaining foreign currency reserves to prop up the peso. Two weeks later, a resurgence of instability in Chiapas fuelled rumours that the government would no longer be able to defend the peso and this increased the downward pressure on the currency, forcing Mexico to spend even more of its foreign currency reserves. Unable to withstand the pressure of both political instability and dwindling reserves, the government, on December 20, announced a 15 percent devaluation of the peso. And that's when all hell broke loose and the foreign mutual funds started heading for the exits.

Fund managers panicked. Many of them had had so much confidence in the sustainability of Mexico's fixed exchange rate that they hadn't bothered to hedge against the risk of a devaluation. David Hale, the chief economist of the Zurich Group, commented that the confidence of fund managers had been so complete that many of them had "assigned their domestic equity analysts to follow Mexican companies as if they were part of a new North American economic zone without any exchange-rate risk. As a result, they were totally unprepared for the political shocks of 1994 and experienced both anger and humiliation when the peso collapsed."[18] In fact, when the Mexican government announced the 15 percent devaluation of the peso, fund managers with short-term horizons were under immediate pressure to sell. As *Business Week* reported, "what began as an understandable sell-off picked up speed because scores of portfolio managers at mutual funds and pension funds had no choice. They had to worry about near-term performance and about meeting investment criteria. And mutual fund managers had to worry about the prospects of massive redemptions."[19] Fidelity Investments, for example, according to various media reports, reduced its investments in Mexican bonds from $7 billion in early 1994 to less than $1 billion by mid-1995.

Faced with massive capital outflows, the Mexican government was forced to completely abandon its fixed exchange rate and let the value of the peso float freely. But as the peso continued to drop, the earlier decisions of the government, which had seemed so rational when money was flowing in, came back to haunt it in full force. Mexico's foreign currency debt, both public and private, started to balloon, making many fund managers worry that the country would not be able to meet its obligations.

This is when the herd really began to move, leading to a vicious circle of capital outflows, rising debt and further capital outflows. Worries about Mexico's debt, combined with the by-now familiar short-term focus and herd behaviour of mutual fund managers, who raced to pull their money out, caused the value of the peso to fall even further — and caused fund managers to worry even more about Mexico's rising dollar debt. Within a few weeks of the initial devaluation, the Mexican economy was sliding rapidly downhill. The value of the peso fell, the stock market plummeted and public and private sector debt exploded. Thousands of firms went bankrupt, unemployment soared, growth fell and industrial production dropped by 15 percent.

And then the crisis began to spread.

When panicky individual investors saw the value of their emerging-market mutual funds dropping rapidly, they began to withdraw their savings. Funds that specialized in Latin American bonds, for example, experienced redemptions in the area of $550 million in the final quarter of 1994 and the first quarter of 1995. To meet this demand for cash, "[m]any funds were obliged to sell assets in other unrelated markets, thus spreading contagion elsewhere," noted Bank of England economist E. Philip Davis.[20] So other countries in the region began to experience downward pressure on their currencies and falling asset prices. In the end, it took a full-scale bailout by the United States and the IMF to restore investor confidence and end the crisis.

In the aftermath of the disaster, economists sat down to evaluate where Mexico had gone wrong. As Krugman notes, the conventional wisdom among conservatives was that the crisis "was not about the way the world at large works: it was a case of Mexico being Mexico."[21] They ignored the larger question posed by former World Bank economist Guillermo Calvo: "Why was so large a punishment imposed for so small a crime?" My own answer, of course, is that the herd behaviour of mutual fund managers created a bubble in asset prices and a bubble in the underlying fundamentals themselves. And because the bubble sent inefficient signals to economic actors and caused them to make poor economic decisions, when it eventually burst, it had a severe impact on the real economy.

More specifically, fund managers reacted to Mexico's free-market reforms with excessive optimism and massive capital inflows, which caused asset prices and the peso to overshoot. This helped to improve Mexico's economic and political fundamentals by offsetting the hardships that would normally have resulted from defending a fixed exchange rate. This bubble in the underlying fundamentals reinforced the optimism of investors as well as their confidence that the fixed exchange rate would be politically sustainable, and so sent inefficient signals to the government, firms and foreign investors, causing them to make poor economic decisions: Mexican firms borrowed too heavily in dollars and fund managers didn't bother to hedge their exchange-rate risk. And, worst of all, the government gave in to pressures from foreign fund managers, setting itself up for a massive fall by converting peso debt into dollar debt. As Moises Naim, editor of the prestigious journal *Foreign Policy*, argues, "developing countries often chastise the IMF and the World Bank for the conditions these institutions impose on their loans, such as policy reforms or budget cuts. But now that mutual fund managers exert an unprecedented influence on the behaviour of governments, the conditionalities of the IMF and the World Bank look enlightened and flexible — even benevolent — by comparison."[22]

At the end of the day, these factors were ignored by conservatives. They blamed the crisis on government blunders rather than on market inefficiencies, the existence of a bubble in the underlying fundamentals and the way that the concentrated power of fund managers helped to shape the disastrous decisions made by the Mexican government. Krugman concludes, "We should have looked more closely at the arguments of some commentators that there really were no serious mistakes at all, except for the brief series of fumbles that got Mexico on the wrong side of market perceptions, and set in motion a process of self-justifying panic. And we should therefore also have realized that what happened to Mexico could happen elsewhere."[23]

Indeed.

CAPITALISM MEETS CAPITALISM: THE BUILDING OF THAILAND'S BUBBLE

Views on what caused the 1997 Asian financial crisis come in one of two forms. The first view, which corresponds to the "financial panic" explanation outlined in the last chapter, is that the Asian crisis was caused by excessive lending and then panic by foreign banks. The second — and most widely promoted — view argues that the crisis was caused by government blunders. This is generally referred to as the "crony-capitalism" explanation, as I mentioned in Chapter 3. The crony-capitalism explanation also focuses on excessive lending and capital outflows by foreign banks, but blames governments for causing them. Proponents of this view argue that the Asian model of development was based on a type of cronyism where government officials gave implicit guarantees to firms that they would be bailed out if they got into trouble. Implicit guarantees such as these can give rise to a condition that economists call "moral hazard." Basically, moral hazard occurs when a government-created safety net distorts markets by encouraging excessively risky behaviour. In the case of the Asian crisis, the risky behaviour in question was excessive borrowing by domestic corporations and excessive lending by foreign banks.

While the financial panic and crony-capitalism explanations each cite different causes for the 1997 crisis, their common ground is a focus on the role played by flows of banking capital. They focus on banking flows rather than mutual fund flows because, while the flows from foreign mutual funds were large in absolute terms, they were only about one-quarter the size of bank-driven flows. However, I argue that, despite their relatively small size, the inflows from foreign mutual funds played a significant role in causing the crisis because it was these flows, rather than any implicit guarantees from governments, that were the real cause of excessive borrowing by domestic firms and the excessive lending by foreign banks. Specifically, the herd behaviour of foreign mutual fund managers contributed to a boom-and-bust cycle in Asian asset markets that *preceded* the currency crisis. And it was this boom and bust in the asset markets that led directly to the massive inflows, and then the panicked outflows, from foreign banks.

In any case, the story of the Asian crisis begins in the early 1990s when a number of countries in the region sought to attract foreign investment by reorienting their economies along freer market lines. For the sake of keeping the story simple, I'm going to focus primarily on Thailand because that is where the crisis began. Thailand was the domino whose fall started the chain reaction felt throughout the region and around the world. To attract foreign investment, the Thai government abandoned exchange controls, allowed foreigners to purchase domestic stocks, deregulated domestic banks and finance companies and created the Bangkok International Banking Facility to facilitate borrowing from foreign banks. To make the country attractive to foreign fund managers, the government fixed the Thai currency — the baht — to the U.S. dollar.

As in Mexico, reforms in Thailand took place in the context of low interest rates in the industrialized countries, growth in the assets of North American mutual funds and the fad-like popularity of "emerging markets" in general. In these conditions, fund managers began to pour money into the Thai stock and property markets. As one observer at the Korean Institute of Finance noted at the time, "Given these sound economic fundamentals and the region's commitment to liberalization, bond market dealers, fund managers, and other institutional investors have seen enormous opportunities to make money and have been purchasing East Asian assets in large quantities."[24]

Fund managers were so exuberant that total portfolio flows into Thailand rose from about $650 million per year during the late 1980s to the staggering amount of $5.5 billion in 1993. About $3 billion of this amount went into stocks following reforms to the Stock Exchange of Thailand (the SET). In fact, by 1993, foreign investors had become the largest purchasers of shares on the SET, with American fund managers accounting for almost half of this amount. With foreign capital pouring in, a bubble began to emerge in the value of asset prices. The value (or capitalization) of the Thai stock market as a whole more than doubled in a single year, from $58 billion at the end of 1992 to over $130 billion by the end of 1993.

As asset prices began to overshoot their true value, they sent inefficient signals to domestic companies, encouraging them to engage in short-term speculation on rising stock and real estate prices. Walden Bello, a co-director of a Thailand-based research institute, observed that "the promise of easy profits via speculation subverted the real economy as manufacturers in Thailand and the Philippines, instead of plowing their profits into upgrading their technology or skills of their workforce, gambled much of them in real estate and the stock market."[25] Also, to get more bang for their buck, many Thai companies began to borrow heavily from foreign banks, either directly or through the intermediaries of domestic banks and finance companies. All this borrowing led to a large rise in Thailand's foreign debt: from $21 billion in 1988 to $89 billion in 1996, with private-sector debt accounting for over $66 billion of this amount.

For obvious reasons, this version of events contradicts the story told by proponents of the crony-capitalism explanation. They argue, rather, that the heavy borrowing resulted from implicit guarantees of bailouts by government officials, which led to excessive risk taking on the part of both borrowers and lenders. Now, there are some fairly technical reasons why we may want to doubt this version of events. But I think the easiest way to refute the argument is to look at the conversion undergone by one of its original advocates.

In a 1998 paper titled "What Happened to Asia?" Paul Krugman outlined the crony-capitalism explanation, with its focus on implicit guarantees and the problem of moral hazard.[26] To be fair, the bulk of Krugman's argument, as we'll see later, was absolutely bang on. But his focus on implicit guarantees was challenged by a number of economists, particularly Steven Radelet and Jeffrey Sachs of the Harvard Institute for International Development. Radelet and Sachs argued that excessive lending could not be explained by implicit guarantees because, if these guarantees had really existed, they would have "crowded out" other forms of investment.[27] Think about it this way: if you could give your money to a bank or firm that was covered by an implicit guarantee that made your investment virtually risk free, why on earth would you invest in any assets that weren't covered by such a guarantee? The answer is that you wouldn't. But investors *did* put their money into assets that weren't covered by any government guarantees. So, to put it quite simply, the crony-capitalism explanation is not supported by the facts.

One year after writing his original paper, Krugman abandoned his view on implicit guarantees and crony capitalism, noting,

> If one really takes [the moral hazard] argument seriously, it implies not only that there should be over-investment and excessive risk-taking by entrepreneurs with access to guaranteed finance, but also that the availability of implicit guarantees should tend to crowd out "legitimate" investment that bears the full burden of risk. Yet as Radelet and Sachs point out, in the run-up to the crisis all forms of investment in the emerging Asian economies were booming, including direct foreign purchases of equity and real estate, investments that clearly were not protected by any form of implicit guarantee.[28]

The crony-capitalism explanation, which is a variation on the government blunder theme, received wide attention in the aftermath of the Asian crisis. But its popularity had more to do with its fit with the prejudices of conservatives than with the actual evidence. So, given the inherent logic of Radelet and Sach's argument, and the fact that it seems to have convinced Krugman, it would seem that we need to look elsewhere for an explanation of the excessive borrowing by Asian domestic firms and the concomitant excessive lending by foreign banks.

The alternate explanation suggested here is that large capital inflows from foreign mutual funds led to a bubble in asset prices, which created the incentive for, and appeared to justify, the excessive borrowing by domestic firms. Evidence for this version of events starts with the fact that portfolio inflows from foreign investors peaked in 1993, one year *before* the peak of banking inflows. Further evidence is the fact that, between 1992 and 1993, when portfolio inflows to Thai stocks rose from $4 million to a peak of over $3 billion, and the capitalization of the SET more than doubled, the market-to-book value of Thai companies' assets rose from 141 percent to 249 percent. Market-to-book value is one of those complicated ratios that can indicate when assets are becoming overvalued. The higher the percentage, the more likely it is that overvaluation exists. Therefore, as Michael Pomerleano speculated in a paper for the World Bank, "a possible implication is that the 'exuberant' valuations in East Asia were associated with large portfolio equity inflows in an illiquid market. In such a situation, marginal inflows might have had a disproportionate impact on valuations."[29]

As the prices of Thai assets began to overshoot their true value, they sent false signals to economic actors. Domestic firms borrowed too much and foreign banks loaned too much. Following the peak of portfolio inflows into the stock and property market in 1993, rising prices encouraged Thai firms to speculate with borrowed money. Banking inflows more than doubled in 1994. It seems that Thai firms were willing to borrow so much because artificially rising asset prices greatly increased the incentives to engage in asset speculation. They were also willing to borrow in foreign currencies (mainly dollars) because the rapidly growing economy made Thailand's fixed exchange rate appear to be sustainable. Foreign banks were willing to lend so much because rising asset prices and high growth made borrowers' underlying fundamentals seem much sounder than they actually were. Because assets such as property and stocks can be used as collateral for loans, the bubble in asset prices appeared to justify the increase in debt.

As bank loans flowed into Thailand, they were channelled by firms and finance companies into real estate and the stock market in the hopes of realizing quick profits. This led to a bubble in the fundamentals themselves as banking inflows boosted asset prices which then justified more bank loans and so on. As Krugman argues, the "overpricing of assets was sustained in part by a sort of circular process, in which the proliferation of risky lending drove up the prices of risky assets, making the financial condition of the intermediaries seem sounder than it actually was."[30]

Also important here was the way that the Asian "model" of development relied on much higher levels of debt than what is the norm in North America. Here, firms will usually borrow no more than one dollar for every dollar they have in assets. Asian firms, in contrast, have traditionally borrowed about four dollars of debt for every one dollar in assets. This is considered to be quite normal and safe because of the way that the Asian economies organize their domestic financial systems. So when asset prices rose, and appeared to justify greater debt, it combined with the already high debt-to-equity (assets) ratio of Asian firms. So, the amount that firms thought they could safely borrow skyrocketed.

Consider a hypothetical example: If a firm had $1 million in assets, then it could safely borrow $4 million in loans. If the value of its assets artificially doubled to $2 million because of a bubble in stock and property prices, then it could now borrow $8 million and still maintain it's four-to-one ratio of debt to equity. To foreign lenders, all appeared to be well, because the debt-to-equity ratio hadn't changed. The problem was that if the bubble in asset prices ever burst, the debt-to-equity ratio of Thai firms would soar. Consider what would happen in this example if a correction in stock and property prices sent the value of our hypothetical firm's assets back down to $1 million. The firm would still have $8 million in debt, so its debt-to-equity ratio would explode to eight to one. This would make lenders very nervous. Worse still, if lenders began to panic and pulled their money out of many such firms, there would be a self-fulfilling speculative attack. The sudden outflow of capital would put downward pressure on the fixed exchange rate and, as occurred in Mexico, the value of Thailand's foreign currency debt would rise, leading to more panic, and so on.

But lenders seemed to ignore this danger. They believed that the rise in asset prices and rapid economic growth were justified by changes in the fundamentals rather than by the herd behaviour of foreign fund managers. And because rising asset prices and growth appeared to justify rising debt and made the fixed exchange rate appear to be sustainable, they thought that everything was fine. As Bello argues, the "fundamentals of borrowers [were] often ignored in favour of what many investors and lenders saw as the real collateral or guarantee that they would eventually get a high rate of return from their investments, which was the 8 to 10 percent growth rate of the country."[31]

With everyone ignoring the circular process that gave rise to a bubble in asset prices, debt and the underlying fundamentals themselves, Thailand had set itself up for a fall.

THE ONSET OF THE "ASIAN FLU": 1996, NOT 1997

While Thailand's fixed exchange rate played an important role in the crisis by contributing to the exuberance of foreign fund managers and convincing firms to borrow in dollars, the politics of fixed exchange rates that we observed in the European and Mexican crises did not play as significant a role in Asia. This is because the boom — and, as we'll see below, the bust — in Asian asset markets occurred well before Thailand's fixed exchange rate began to produce any real hardships for average people. It did, however, produce hardships for Thai corporations when a negative shock hit in 1996. Following a 1995 agreement between the United States and Japan to boost Japanese exports, the value of the U.S. dollar began to rise and the Thai baht, which was fixed to the dollar, began to rise with it. In Thailand, the rising value of the baht began to produce hardships for domestic firms because it made their goods more expensive on world markets. The result was a fall in the growth rate of Thai exports down from 24 percent in 1995 to zero growth in 1996. And as export growth declined, Thailand's trade (or current-account) deficit rose sharply in 1996, to over 8 percent of its GDP.

To proponents of the financial panic explanation, such as Radelet and Sachs, "these signs seemed merely to suggest growing imbalances and the need for a modest adjustment, but not an impending major crisis."[32] Investors remained basically optimistic because of the way that the bubble in asset prices and growth appeared to justify the bubble in debt, as well as making both the fixed exchange rate and the level of foreign debt appear to be sustainable. And this is why few economists or investors believed that a crisis was on the horizon. As Radelet and Sachs commented, "One of the most unusual aspects of the Asian crisis is the extent to which it was unpredicted by market participants and market analysts . . . [and, this is why] . . . capital inflows remained strong through 1996, and in most cases till mid-1997."[33]

This "out of the blue" aspect of the Asian crisis is why some economists felt that the Asian crisis was caused by a seemingly irrational panic among foreign banks in 1997. They argued that when certain firms and finance companies in Thailand went bankrupt, foreign lenders overreacted, calling in their loans and initiating a self-fulfilling speculative attack. The problem with this explanation is its focus on the activities of banks and the way that it downplays the activities of foreign fund managers. In fact, the actions taken by foreign fund managers in 1996 may have provided a signal that a crisis was coming. As Radelet and Sachs themselves note,

> Stock prices provided the only indication of growing concern
> among market participants in the months preceding the crisis. The
> Thai stock market fell continuously after January 1996, a full eight-
> een months before the crisis began. The main index fell 40 percent
> in 1996 alone, and dropped an additional 20 percent in the first
> six months of 1997 as concern grew over the health of property
> companies and financial institutions. The Seoul [stock market] also
> fell sharply during 1996 and early 1997. In the case of Thailand, the
> stock market decline was matched by a slight decline in foreign
> bank lending in the first half of 1997.[34]

It appears that when the baht began to rise with the U.S. dollar, leading to a large rise in Thailand's trade deficit, fund managers began to worry that the government might give up its fixed exchange rate in order to stimulate exports. Radelet and Sachs again: "[the] biggest warnings came in Thailand, where expectations of currency depreciation grew markedly in 1996 and early 1997."[35]

Fund managers, who had purchased assets priced in the Thai

currency, had the most to lose if the fixed exchange rate collapsed and if the baht was devalued. So in 1996 they began to pull out their investments. This outflow of capital led to a fall in stock prices and in the real estate market. Over the course of the year, falling asset prices began to hurt the solvency of Thai corporations, causing fund managers to pull out even more of their investments, which led to further declines in asset prices. As Krugman comments, the asset bubble's collapse "involved the same circular process [as its growth] in reverse: falling asset prices made the insolvency of intermediaries visible, forcing them to cease operations, leading to further asset deflation."[36] With asset prices that had been used to back large debts falling rapidly, the large loans made to Thai companies began to look rather precarious. Foreign bankers started to worry that these firms were now carrying too much debt in relation to the value of their assets.

In January of 1997 these fears were amplified when two prominent firms — Finance One and the Samprasong Land Company — announced that they were defaulting on their loans. These announcements fuelled expectations that the government would abandon its fixed exchange rate to stimulate the economy and prevent further problems. At this point, the Thai economy was caught in a classic zone of vulnerability. Then, as Walden Bello notes, "The scent of panic attracted speculators who sought to make profits . . . on the baht's eventual devaluation."[37] Speculators such as George Soros began to sell the Thai currency in large quantities. To defend the currency, the Bank of Thailand spent billions of its foreign currency reserves, until it was eventually forced to abandon the fixed exchange rate in July of 1997.

Much like in Mexico, news that the government was devaluing the currency created a full-blown panic and a vicious circle of capital outflows, rising foreign currency debt and further capital outflows. As Thailand spiralled into recession, the so-called "Asian Flu" began to spread across the region. Again, foreign fund managers appeared to have played a significant role in transmitting the crisis. The specific circumstances varied across countries, but the fundamental dynamic of large debts supported by a bubble in asset prices seems to have been present throughout the region. As Krugman reveals, "in all of the afflicted countries there was a boom–bust cycle in the asset markets that *preceded* the currency crisis: stock and land prices soared, then plunged."[38] In Malaysia, the stock market began to fall sharply in March of 1997 even though banking inflows into Thailand still remained strong. As a report by the IMF notes, "The initial pressure on the [Malaysian currency] appears to have emanated from institutional investors closing out long equity positions, reflecting their concern that the stock market was overvalued."[39]

As was the case in the European and Mexican crises, the herd–like behaviour of foreign mutual fund managers played a significant role in the Asian crisis of 1997. Once again, excessive optimism and capital inflows by institutional investors had led to a bubble in asset prices and thus to a bubble in the underlying fundamentals themselves. These bubbles sent inefficient signals to economic actors, which caused them to make poor economic decisions — particularly in accumulating large amounts of debt priced in foreign currencies. It was difficult to see the crisis coming because of the way that the bubble in asset prices and in the underlying fundamentals seemed to justify each other and make the fixed exchange rate appear to be sustainable. When a negative shock came along, as they always do, the currencies came under pressure and the poor decisions made by economic actors came back to haunt them. Falling currencies and asset prices led to rising debts. Rising debts led to a crisis of confidence among investors and creditors. And falling confidence led to further capital outflows, falling asset prices and downward pressure on currencies.

BOOM OR BUBBLE? APPLYING THE LESSONS OF CRISIS TO THE U.S. STOCK MARKET

In economic terms at least, it was a great time to be the President of the United States.

As he stood before Congress to deliver his annual State of the Union address, the economy was expanding at a record pace, the stock market was booming and the political horizon, both at home and abroad, seemed to point to a new era of peace and prosperity. The President was jubilant and his address conveyed his sense that all was right with the world:

> No Congress of the United States ever assembled, on surveying the state of the Union, has met with a more pleasing prospect than that which appears at the present time . . . The great wealth created by our enterprise and industry, and saved by our economy, has had the widest distribution among our own people . . . The requirements of existence have passed beyond the standard of necessity into the region of luxury. Enlarging production is consumed by an increasing demand at home and an expanding commerce abroad. The country can regard the present with satisfaction and anticipate the future with optimism.

Despite its eerie similarities to political speeches of our own times, this excerpt from the State of the Union Address was not delivered by Bill Clinton. In fact, it was spoken by Calvin Coolidge on December 4, 1928, less than a year before the U.S. stock market collapsed in 1929.

If that Great Crash and the more recent events in Europe, Mexico and Asia offer us any lesson about predicting financial crises, it's that a bust is almost always preceded by a boom. The "dirty thirties" followed the "roaring twenties." The crises in Mexico and Asia followed on the heels of the Mexican and Asian economic miracles. Booms don't always lead to busts, but bubbles usually do. So predicting a crisis is about try- ing to determine whether or not a healthy boom has transformed itself into an unhealthy bubble. In the late 1990s, the topic of greatest con- cern is the U.S. stock market and the way that its meteoric rise has been breaking record after record.

According to the optimists, this rise is justified by the fundamentals; a particular mix of technology and policy that has brought about a "new economy." The specific argument boils down to the way that the information revolution, and a variety of free-market reforms pursued by the government, have helped to give a massive boost to U.S. productivity (the amount of economic output per worker). Without question, a strong productivity rise has occurred over the 1990s, and this fact *has* justified a rise in stock prices. The question is whether the growth in productivity justifies *as much of* a rise in U.S. stock prices as we've seen over the last decade. In other words, has a healthy boom based on improvements in the fundamentals transformed itself into an unhealthy bubble based on the irrational exuberance and herd behaviour of investors? If this is the case, if a bubble does exist, it should reveal itself in some of the same financial dynamics that were at work in the currency crises of the 1990s, but with one key difference: the United States does not have a fixed exchange rate.

I mentioned in the last chapter that it seemed to be no coincidence that a new type of currency crisis had emerged at precisely the same time that mutual funds and pension funds had come to dominate international capital flows. In a similar fashion, is it really a coincidence that the longest-running stock market boom in history has also emerged at precisely the same time as the revolution of mass investment and the rise of mutual funds and pension funds? The riddle we need to solve is not unlike that of the chicken and the egg. Are people investing in the stock market in record numbers because of the new economy, or has the new economy emerged because people are investing in the stock market in record numbers?

As I'm writing this chapter, a news item on the radio is outlining the findings of some recent psychological research. Apparently, pessimistic people, those who adhere to the glass-is-half-empty school of thought, have a distinct tendency to be happier people. So in the interests of our collective joy, let's start by looking at the pessimistic view that the current U.S. boom may, in fact, be a bubble. In doing so, we need to go beyond the traditional definition of a bubble — where prices simply get away from fundamentals — and attempt to determine if a bubble in stock prices has created a bubble in the underlying fundamentals themselves, as happened in the run-up to each of the three major financial crises of the 1990s.

How well does this "double bubble" model apply to the U.S. stock market? As we saw in the last chapter, any bubble worth its salt usually begins with a small, but nevertheless real, change in the underlying economic fundamentals of a country. We can identify three such changes in the fundamentals of the U.S. economy over the course of the 1990s. The first is the development of information technologies and the Internet, and the way that they've given at least some form of boost to productivity. The second is the policy shift within the Clinton administration towards what has come to be known as "the financial markets strategy." This strategy was to give the financial markets the spending cuts and deficit reduction that they wanted in order to build investor confidence. The third development is the restructuring of U.S. corporations. Successive waves of corporate downsizing helped to further build investor confidence by making the labour market more "flexible" and helping to keep a lid on rising wage demands and inflation.

Combined with the massive growth in the assets of mutual funds and pension funds, these developments helped to improve investor confidence, and fund managers responded by pouring the nation's savings into the stock market. As they did so, stock prices rose rapidly. The Dow Jones eventually crossed the 10,000-point mark. The money pouring in from mutual and pension funds, coupled with rapidly rising stock prices, form one indicator that a bubble may have emerged in the U.S. stock market. Another indicator is the way that escalating stock prices have begun to have a real effect on the decisions of economic actors. As stock prices rose, households and corporations felt richer, and the resulting wealth effect sent signals that it was okay to save less, borrow more and spend more. Of course, all this extra spending created a greater demand for goods and services, which helped to stimulate economic growth and corporate earnings, thus appearing to justify rising asset prices. In other words, it's possible that a bubble in the stock market has created a bubble in the economic fundamentals of the United States, and that this second bubble is giving the appearance that the original bubble in stock prices is justified and sustainable. Sound familiar?

One unique feature of the present U.S. boom is the revolution in mass investment. Over 50 percent of U.S. households now have a stake in the stock market. This means that the wealth effect produced by rapidly rising stock prices has been felt across a much larger segment of the population than it would have been even a decade ago. Over the course of the 1990s, the savings rate among households (the percentage of after-tax income that households put aside) has been declining steadily; by the end of the 1990s, it went negative for the first time in the post–World War Two era. By the end of 1998, the deficit in private net saving, which includes both households and corporations, had reached almost 5 percent of GDP, the highest it has been since the 1930s. This means that households and firms have not only financed greater spending through a running down of their savings, but that they have been getting into a greater amount of debt as well. In fact, total private borrowing for both households and corporations exceeded $1 trillion for the first time in history by the end of 1998. For firms, the rise in asset prices has made the rise in debts appear justifiable. As a 1999 IMF report states, "Nonfinancial firms have been taking on more debt over the past few years . . . [yet] . . . ratios to equity have not risen significantly."[40]

How important is this decline in savings and rise in debt? Well, to get a handle on just how important it is, we can take a look at some numbers from 1997 and 1998. In 1997, U.S. households were saving an average of 2.1 percent of their after-tax income. By the end of the first quarter of 1998, the savings rate had fallen to 0.5 percent, a drop of 1.6 percentage points over the course of one year. U.S. after-tax income totalled about $6 trillion that year. Doing the math, a drop of 1.6 percentage points in the savings rate on $6 trillion of national income means that the fall in the savings rate pumped almost $100 billion of extra consumer spending into the economy, an amount large enough to have a real effect on growth and corporate earnings.[41] And it is this rise in growth and corporate earnings that appears to justify the rise in asset prices. The result is a virtuous circle — an economy that seems to have discovered the secret to perpetual motion. Alas, as any physicist will tell you, perpetual motion is impossible. In the case of the economy, the problem lies in the fact that households have been saving less and borrowing more in order to sustain their spending habits. Such a situation is unsustainable; for the stock market to continue rising, households will have to borrow and spend in ever-increasing amounts.

Now, there are a number of potential monkey wrenches that could be thrown into the works of the U.S. economy to trigger a stock-market correction. The most likely scenario is for something, such as higher interest rates or households hitting a debt wall, to cause American consumers to cut back on their borrowing and spending. As the IMF observes in a 1999 report, the current "deficit in private net savings . . . has no precedent in the United States in the postwar period . . . suggesting that a correction through a drop in demand is a potential risk to the U.S. and world economies."[42] In any case, if a stock-market correction does occur, it could have a significant impact on the real economy. Falling stock prices could lead to a reversal of the wealth effect, causing consumers to save more and spend less, which would lead to a decline in growth and corporate earnings and, in turn, to further stock price corrections. Noting this potential for a major correction, *National Post* financial columnist Tracey LeMay argues that "Low or non-existent savings leaves families horribly exposed to potential dangers. An economic slowdown could cause consumers to pull back more deeply than in past recessions."[43] In fact, seeking to model this type of worst-case scenario, a study by economists Wynne Godley and Bill Martin argued that if the U.S. savings rate rebounded back towards 4 percent, the vicious circle of falling spending, growth and stock prices could cause a fall in the U.S. dollar, a decline in the average annual growth rate to 0.4 percent and a rise in unemployment to over 11 percent.[44]

Admittedly, this is the absolute worst-case scenario. It's unlikely to happen. The difference between the current boom in the U.S. stock market and those that preceded the Mexican and Asian financial crises is the fact that the United States doesn't have a fixed exchange rate that would prevent the Federal Reserve from lowering interest rates to stimulate the economy. But this doesn't mean that a major correction is outside the realm of the possible. Many of the characteristics of the so-called new economy, such as the unprecedented fall in national savings and rise in debt, do suggest that the U.S. boom is actually another of the artificial bubbles that helped to cause the new type of financial crisis that emerged in the 1990s.

A final, and much less clear cut, similarity between the current U.S. stock market and the situations that led to the Mexican and Asian financial crises is the extent to which market participants have attempted to justify soaring asset prices in terms of the onset of a new economic era. After all, the old Wall Street truism can work both ways: When a finance minister feels the need to promise investors that he won't devalue the currency, you can bet that he will. Likewise, when investors feel the need to justify why a boom is not a bubble and why it can continue indefinitely, it becomes much more likely that it won't. For pessimists, then, there are certainly enough reasons to be concerned. If you're an optimist, you might take solace in the old joke that pessimistic economists have predicted twenty-five out of the last four market corrections. At the end of the day, I guess we'll just have to wait and see whether pessimists are, in fact, happier people.

5

HEDGE FUND FOLLIES

No book on the power exercised by large institutional investors, and no discussion of recent currency crises and other episodes of financial volatility, would be complete without a discussion of hedge funds. Hedge funds have received a lot of attention recently because what they do is inherently interesting, even to those who find the world of economics and high finance inherently boring. Almost any time you hear people ranting about evil speculators manipulating stock prices or causing financial crises, they're probably talking about hedge funds. Over the course of the last decade, hedge funds have become the fodder for numerous conspiracy theories; they have been accused by some politicians of manipulating currencies and stock markets, of causing the currency crises that we discussed in the last chapter and even of posing a threat to the stability of the world economy as a whole. And while it's unlikely that hedge funds are anywhere near as important or problematic as their critics contend, the fact remains that at least some of the conspiracy theories are actually true.

Why have hedge funds been singled out for so much scorn, especially when compared with other large institutional investment vehicles such as mutual funds and pension funds? As I see it, there are two main reasons. The first is that hedge funds invest primarily on behalf of very wealthy investors, a group that is unlikely to generate much sympathy even at the best of times. The second reason is that the problems hedge funds are alleged to have caused are seen as being the result of either conscious strategies or deliberate recklessness. Where the problems caused by mutual funds and pension funds are the unintentional result of a fallacy of composition, the problems caused by hedge funds conjure images of the old robber barons of American capitalism, using their vast resources and power to manipulate markets for their own economic benefit. In this chapter, I'm going to try to separate the hype from the reality and, in the process, hopefully provide some insights into one of the most interesting set of actors in the financial world. But before we take a look at their recent exploits, we need to get a handle on what hedge funds actually are, how they operate and why supporters of the industry don't think they're really a threat to anyone.

WHAT ARE HEDGE FUNDS?

The raison d'être of hedge funds is to avoid government regulation. And because they are basically unregulated, there isn't any legal or universally accepted definition of what a hedge fund is. Probably the easiest way to think about hedge funds is as a type of unregulated mutual fund, one that caters almost exclusively to wealthy individuals and institutions, and makes use of high-risk investment strategies. To avoid the government regulations that can prevent the use of these high-risk strategies, hedge funds are either set up "offshore" or are structured as private investment partnerships. In legal terms, this is the equivalent of you and a bunch of your friends pooling your money to get more bang for your investment buck. As long as you have fewer than one hundred partners and you don't advertise yourself as an investment fund to attract other investors, you can pretty much avoid most of the regulations that normally apply to institutional investors. But just in case you and your friends are thinking of setting up your own hedge fund, you should be aware that there is one catch. You have to be rich. To qualify for exemption from government regulations, all of the "partners" in your hedge fund must be "accredited" investors. This means that each of you has to have a net worth of at least $1 million or an annual income of over $200,000.

For those of us who try to study hedge funds, their unregulated nature is a problem. Since they don't have to file many reports with the government, there isn't much hard data on their activities. Most of the data comes from private hedge fund tracking companies and from research carried out by international financial institutions. Based on this data, most estimates place the size of the hedge fund industry at somewhere between 2,500 and 3,500 funds, which manage a total of somewhere between $200 billion and $300 billion in investment capital. Most hedge funds are quite small and, as a result, fairly benign and uninteresting. The ones that have attracted the most attention are known as "macro" hedge funds. While the term "macro" implies "big," in this context it actually refers to a type of investment strategy rather than to the size of the fund. A macro strategy is one where the fund manager attempts to profit from changes in macroeconomic variables, such as shifts in interest rates, currencies and entire stock markets, rather than movements in the prices of individual stocks or bonds. Nonetheless, most of the largest hedge funds, those managing over $5 billion, do employ a macro strategy.

As an industry, hedge funds have grown rapidly in the last decade as more and more wealthy investors have sought to generate higher returns through investment strategies that aren't subject to the constraints of government regulation. As one observer of the industry has commented, "The rapid growth of the hedge fund market coincides with a period of significant expansion of the upper tier of American wealth, the number of Americans with more than $1 million having tripled during the last decade alone."[1] This is important because, as we saw above, to invest in a hedge fund you have to be wealthy. Most funds have minimum investment requirements ranging anywhere from $250,000 to $10 million. This is why they are able to take greater risks than mutual funds, and why governments haven't seen a need to regulate them; they believe that wealthy investors are able to take care of themselves.

While the assets controlled by hedge funds are fairly significant in absolute terms, supporters of the industry argue that hedge funds are, for the most part, too small to matter in terms of raising issues for policy-makers. Steven A. Lonsdorf, president of the investment consulting firm Van Hedge Fund Advisors, argues that the assets controlled by hedge funds are "not a significant amount of capital when compared to the level of capital in the global financial markets."[2] Also important, according to the IMF, is the fact that the assets of hedge funds "pale in comparison with the capital of other institutional investors such as pension funds, mutual funds, insurance companies, and investment and commercial banks, which, in the mature markets alone, exceeds $20 trillion."[3]

If hedge funds are having any impact on markets at all, supporters of the industry tend to see their growth as a positive development. They argue that hedge funds have a number of qualities that better position them to act as the smart money, or arbitragers, within the financial markets (remember this term for the investors who are able to make markets more efficient by going against the herd?). One reason that hedge funds should be able to go against the herd is that their managers are paid on the basis of absolute performance. As we saw in Chapter 2, most mutual fund managers are paid on the basis of relative performance — that is, in relation to the performance of their peers. This system encourages herd behaviour. Hedge fund managers, in contrast, are paid according to their ability to generate the highest return possible. For example, hedge fund managers are typically paid a management fee of around 1 percent of the fund's total assets, plus about 20 percent of annual profits. Because their remuneration is unrelated to the performance of their peers, they aren't under the same pressures as mutual fund managers to do what everyone else is doing.

"Many [hedge fund managers] see themselves not as speculators at all but as arbitragers. That means they are looking for assets whose prices are temporarily out of line with their fundamental values, selling those they deem expensive or buying those they think cheap. By doing this, in principle, the hedge funds can help to make markets more efficient," notes *The Economist*.[4]

ADVENTURES IN LONG-TERM CAPITAL MANAGEMENT

Financial crises are normally very public affairs. It's rare for the world to be brought to the brink of an outright financial catastrophe with the broader public being mostly unaware. While such a situation may be well-suited to the pages of a fictional bestseller, it really isn't supposed to happen in the real world. But in 1998, it pretty much did.

In 1998, a hedge fund called Long-Term Capital Management (LTCM) brought the world economy to the brink of collapse. And while the financial system was saved by our protectors at the New York Federal Reserve, the incident dispelled forever the notion that hedge funds were too small to matter.

The first problem with the too-small-to-matter view of hedge funds relates to their use of "leverage." Leverage is the amount of money that a fund can borrow against its existing capital. Most institutional investors are restricted by government regulations in terms of how leveraged they can become. Hedge funds, on the other hand, can borrow huge amounts of money with little collateral — sometimes as much as a hundred times their actual assets. They borrow money from banks based on the strength of their fund managers' reputations. As long as they are making money, high leverage helps them to make enormous profits by giving them more bang for their buck.

LTCM was a hedge fund set up in 1994 by some of the brightest minds in the financial world; two of its staff were Nobel-prize laureates in economics. LTCM's investment strategy was to identify temporary differences in interest rates through the use of sophisticated mathematical models and profit from these differences by employing extensive leverage; profit margins were small, so the fund borrowed huge amounts of money from banks so that its total return on each transaction was high. In the first three years of its existence, this strategy proved to be immensely successful. LTCM generated returns of over 40 percent in both 1995 and 1996, and slightly lower ones in 1997. In 1998, the fund had borrowed even more money and taken on even larger positions, to the extent that it was estimated to have leveraged about $4.7 billion of its own capital into over $1 trillion in nominal investments. LTCM's problems began on August 17 when, as investor uncertainty grew in the wake of the Asian currency crisis, the Russian government announced an effective devaluation of the ruble and a "time out" on paying its debts. As panic began to spread among investors, stock and bond markets became increasingly volatile. The differences among interest rates began to widen abruptly. But LTCM had bet on a narrowing of interest rates. Its losses grew rapidly; on September 2 the fund reported losses of over 50 percent for the year through to August 31.

With the value of the fund's assets dropping rapidly, the banks that had loaned money to LTCM demanded that the fund either put more cash down as collateral or pay off its loans. LTCM attempted to raise the money it needed by liquidating its positions. But when a firm's positions are so large, selling off assets has the effect of driving their price sharply downwards. Unable to raise the cash it needed, LTCM faced imminent failure. It was at this point that the Federal Reserve Bank of New York stepped in and arranged a bailout by a group of prominent commercial and investment banks, many of whom had loaned money to LTCM in the first place and thus had much to lose if it collapsed. To help further calm down the markets, the U.S. central bank ("the Fed") responded with a series of small interest-rate cuts, which succeeded in warding off both the collapse of LTCM and any full-blown panic by investors.

Under normal circumstances, investors who make high-risk bets that don't pay off are left to fail by the government, which prefers to let market discipline take its course. But in the case of LTCM, the Fed was forced to intervene because the fund had become so extensively over-leveraged that its failure posed a threat to the financial system as a whole. As William McDonough, president of the Federal Reserve Bank of New York, commented,

> Had Long-Term Capital been suddenly put into default, its counterparties would have immediately "closed out" their positions . . . [and] . . . if many firms had rushed to close out hundreds of billions of dollars in transactions simultaneously, they would have been unable to liquidate collateral or establish offsetting positions at previously existing prices. Markets would have moved sharply and losses would have been exaggerated. Several billions of dollars of losses might have been experienced by some of Long-Term Capital's more than seventy-five counterparties.[5]

If LTCM had collapsed, it could have brought the whole financial system down with it. Selling off its assets at panic prices would have panicked other investors and caused asset prices to fall rapidly. The banks that had loaned money to LTCM would have been threatened, as would other hedge funds and investors who had made similar bets. All of them would have been forced to raise cash by selling assets, leading to further price declines, and so on. Corporations and households that had nothing to do with LTCM or the world of investing could have been negatively affected. So, at the end of the day, the men in black pinstripes at the Federal Reserve managed to save the world from the so-called masters of the universe. For Mr. and Mrs. average American, the world had come close to catastrophe — and most of them never even knew it. Hedge funds were supposed to be too small to matter, but, as it turned out, at least one of them had become too big to fail.

LEAD STEERS

The ability of hedge funds to become extensively over-leveraged is one problem with the notion that they are too small to matter in terms of raising issues for policy-makers. A second problem relates to the herd behaviour of financial markets and the ability of hedge funds to act as lead steers. We saw in Chapter 2 how mutual and pension fund managers will often follow the behaviour of other investors because of the costs and difficulties associated with the collection and analysis of economic information. Given these difficulties, many investors and traders will often allocate their capital in response to "pseudo-signals." This term refers to any source of information other than economic fundamentals that fund managers believe conveys information about future returns. Sometimes investors buy and sell assets based simply on movements in their price. At other times, they follow market gurus who are seen to have better information or analysis.

Within the context of this trend-chasing behaviour, one way that hedge funds can act as market leaders relates to their ability to single-handedly move the price of an asset. Under certain conditions, a lone hedge fund may be able to move the price of an asset through a combination of leverage and directional (rather than diversified) investing. In other words, by borrowing large amounts of money and placing many of its eggs in the same basket, a hedge fund can often create enough demand for an asset to bump up its price. When this happens, it can invoke a herd-like response from other investors who are buying and selling based on price movements. This ability to lead markets can also work in reverse through a strategy known as "short selling," something that hedge funds are famous for.

Short selling is a technique that hedge funds often use to profit from a fall in the price of an asset. It's designed to reverse the order of the old "buy low, sell high" maxim. Essentially, a fund manager who is seeking to "short" makes use of a specialized type of financial contract to sell an asset that he or she does not actually own. The terms of the contract mean that the fund manager doesn't have to deliver the asset until some time in the future. The fund manager is thus selling high in expectation that the price of the asset will fall by the time he or she has to deliver the asset. If the price of the asset does fall, the fund manager buys the asset at the lower price and then delivers the asset (previously sold at the higher price) and profits from the difference. So short selling still involves buying low and selling high, just in the reverse order. When a fund manager "shorts" an asset, it can have the same effect on an asset's price as selling it; that is, it reduces demand for the asset and causes its price to fall.

So, whether they are buying (going "long") or selling (going "short"), hedge fund managers can often single-handedly move an asset's price and initiate a herd-like response from other investors who are buying and selling on the basis of price movements.

Hedge funds can also act as lead steers because of the intellectual authority that many hedge fund managers possess. Because many of these managers are the elite of the financial world, other investors have a tendency to regard their pronouncements as the holy gospel. They pay attention when hedge fund managers express their opinions in the press. They devote time and energy to tracking their activities. When news leaks out that a certain hedge fund manager is buying a particular asset, it often leads to a rise in the asset's price as other investors attempt to emulate the wisdom of the master. As *Euromoney* magazine once noted, "The attention paid by investors and traders to the activities of hedge funds does . . . magnify their impact on the markets."[6] For example, in 1993, George Soros — the now-famous manager of one of the largest macro hedge funds, Quantum Fund — purchased between 2 million and 3 million ounces of gold at $345 per ounce and 10 million shares in Newmont Mining. When Soros's purchases became known, and with no other changes in the underlying economic fundamentals, the price of gold rose to over $350 an ounce. *The Economist* noted: "His reputation . . . has put Mr. Soros in the position that all gurus aspire to; his prophecies are now self-fulfilling."[7]

HEDGE FUNDS AND MARKET VOLATILITY

As we saw in the case of LTCM, hedge funds that are over-leveraged can cause a great deal of trouble when they're losing money. But when their ability to borrow money is combined with their ability to act as market leaders, it seems that hedge funds can also cause trouble when they're making money. One way they seem to be doing this is by increasing market volatility; that is, they are contributing to large swings in prices, swings that make it difficult for companies to plan for the future.

Before 1994, oil companies and other related firms were the main players in the buying and selling of oil futures contracts on the New York Mercantile Exchange. Oil futures contracts are a specialized type of financial contract, a derivative, which are used to manage risk. Since 1994, according to George Yates, chairman of the Independent Petroleum Association of America, the industry is "seeing more and more hedge funds buying crude oil futures contracts," to the extent that they now account for about 10 percent of the oil futures market.[8] Hedge funds buy these contracts purely for the purpose of speculation and, in doing so, they seem to have created a decline in efficiency and a rise in price volatility. The *Houston Business Journal* reported in 1998 that "[o]ver the last two years virtually every time the large speculators — primarily hedge funds — have held 'long' market positions, the price of oil has gone up, and whenever they have held 'short' positions, the price has gone down."[9]

Part of the problem is that the hedge funds seem to be basing their trades on isolated pieces of information, such as weekly oil inventories, which are only one of the many economic fundamentals used to determine the price of oil. When investors overemphasize some fundamentals and ignore others, it can lead to a decline in market efficiency because the prices of assets do not reflect their true fundamental values. And when this is combined with frequent trading, it means that asset prices can become highly volatile in a way that makes it difficult for companies to plan for the long term. Says Houston oil analyst Matt Simmons, the "fact that the price makes no economic sense does not seem to matter [to the hedge funds] — and it is destroying the industry."[10]

In a similar fashion, hedge funds have been accused by officials at the London Metals Exchange (LME) of increasing volatility in the price of metals. David Humphreys, chief economist at Rio Trinto, the world's largest mining group, argues that "With $120 billion under management compared with the combined value of LME warehouse stocks of less than $2 billion, it is clear that these funds have more than enough muscle to move metals prices substantially."[11] In fact, short selling by hedge funds was viewed as one of the key factors accounting for the price fall of aluminium, copper, nickel and other base metals in the summer of 1998, when these prices reached their lowest levels for several years.

These examples don't imply any wrongdoing or robber baron–style conspiracies to corner any markets. But they are evidence that, in certain circumstances, hedge funds are making the financial markets much less efficient.

HEDGE FUNDS AND CURRENCY CRISES

Where the market leadership role of hedge funds has received the most attention is in the case of speculative attacks against countries with a fixed exchange rate. During the European currency crisis of 1992, George Soros was accused by some politicians of causing the speculative attack against the British pound. Willy Claes, the Belgian foreign minister and president of the European Community's Council of Ministers, indirectly accused Soros of sinister motives in an interview with *Le Figaro*: "There is a kind of plot. In the Anglo-Saxon world, there exists organizations and personalities who prefer a divided Europe."[12] In the wake of the Asian currency crisis, some leaders within the Association of South East Asian Nations (ASEAN), led by Malaysian prime minister Dr. Mahathir, accused Soros of a deliberate plot to undermine their currencies. As motivation for the attack, Mahathir cited everything from a Jewish conspiracy to Soros's opposition to ASEAN's decision to admit Myanmar (formerly Burma) into their regional clubhouse.

While most observers ignored the Soros conspiracy theories (at least the part about sinister political motives), the events in Europe and Asia did raise the important question of whether hedge funds could in fact *cause* a financial crisis, a crisis that would not otherwise have occurred. If we think back to the models outlined in Chapter 3, particularly the more recent models of a self-fulfilling speculative attack, then, in theoretical terms at least, it's entirely possible for a large hedge fund to cause a financial crisis. How would this work?

Start with a country that has adopted the Washington consensus policy mix of capital mobility and a fixed exchange rate. Next, assume that the government has no intention of pursuing the expansionary monetary policies that can cause a fixed exchange rate to collapse. Remember, according to the logic of the impossible trinity, a country can't pursue capital mobility, a fixed exchange rate and an expansionary monetary policy all at the same time. If the government lowers interest rates to reduce unemployment (an expansionary policy), investors will take their money abroad, causing the value of the currency to fall and eventually leading to the collapse of the fixed exchange rate. But as long as a government with capital mobility and a fixed exchange rate doesn't pursue an expansionary policy, the fixed exchange rate should be sustainable.

But what happens if investors launch a speculative attack anyway? If they start to sell off the country's currency and other assets, the government will be forced to raise interest rates to defend the currency. But raising interest rates may be too politically difficult, because higher interest rates slow down the economy and cause unemployment to rise. This means that the government may eventually be forced to abandon the fixed exchange rate. So in this situation, it's possible for investors to launch a speculative attack that becomes self-fulfilling, causing a currency crisis that would not otherwise have occurred. If the speculative attack had never happened, the government wouldn't have been forced to choose between raising interest rates and giving up the fixed exchange rate.

Under normal circumstances, no single fund would be large enough to provoke a full-blown speculative attack, one large enough to become self-fulfilling and provoke a currency crisis. But this is where the ability of hedge funds to borrow large sums of money and to act as market leaders becomes really important. How would such an attack work in practical terms? Through a combination of leverage and directional investing, a fund manager might be able to short-sell a currency and/or assets priced in that currency in sufficient quantities to put downward pressure on the exchange rate. As the currency begins to fall, the actions of the hedge fund might begin to attract other trend-chasing investors who buy and sell based on movements in prices. As they begin to sell, the currency would drop even further. Now, to reinforce their sales of the currency with intellectual authority, the hedge fund manager could attempt to signal the market by either leaking out information about his or her sales or by making public pronouncements in the media that the currency in question is overvalued and that the government is no longer willing to defend its fixed exchange rate. This kind of statement would increase the chances that other investors would sell the currency based on the advice of the hedge fund guru. If the combination of short selling and making public pronouncements succeeded in generating a bandwagon effect, a speculative attack and collapse of the fixed exchange rate could become self-fulfilling. The falling currency would increase investors' fears that the government won't defend the fixed exchange rate, causing them to sell off more of the currency, causing its value to fall even further, causing investors to worry even more, and so on and so on.

Thus, hedge funds have the theoretical ability to cause a currency crisis that would not otherwise have occurred. They are able to initiate a self-fulfilling attack based on their ability to borrow huge sums of money and to act as market leaders. Conspiracy theories aside, this is pretty close to what actually happened in Europe. George Soros did launch a speculative attack on the British pound in 1992 and it did become self-fulfilling. He borrowed about $10 billion for this project, and he gave interviews with the press. By acting as a market leader, Soros was able to force a devaluation of the British pound by getting mutual funds and pension funds to reinforce his actions. Just ask the IMF: "While hedge funds acted as market leaders, the real financial muscle was provided by institutional investors."[13] At the end of the day (September 16, now dubbed "Black Wednesday"), Britain was forced to abandon its fixed exchange rate and George Soros became a household name for reportedly making over $1 billion on his leveraged bets.

But does this mean that Soros actually *caused* the European, or at least the British, currency crisis? We'll see shortly. But first, let's go to Asia.

As already mentioned, George Soros was accused by Malaysian prime minister Mahathir of doing to Asia what he did to Britain. Is Mahathir correct? Probably not. But all the evidence isn't in yet. One study that looked at the activities of ten of the largest hedge funds found that they didn't have large investments in Malaysia and that the funds managed by Soros only managed to break even in the aftermath of the crisis.[14] While this study appears to absolve hedge funds of playing any direct role in Malaysia, it doesn't adequately deal with what happened in Thailand. And Thailand is where the whole crisis started; Malaysia was a casualty of the panic that ensued when Thailand was forced to abandon its fixed exchange rate. Research by the IMF found that two very prominent hedge funds (it has never said which ones) did make some decent profits speculating against the Thai baht.

Does this mean that hedge funds caused the crisis in Thailand?

Well, this is where the evidence gets a bit murky. Remember, part of the problem is the fact that hedge funds are lightly regulated, so there isn't very much hard data available on their day-to-day operations. Arguing against the conspiracy theorists is the IMF: "Although they apparently sold ∶ . . . the baht in February of 1997, the bulk of hedge funds' forward sales to the Bank of Thailand appears to have occurred only in May at the tail end of the process. If herd behaviour contributed to the crisis, then the hedge funds were at the rear, not the front of the herd."[15] Arguing in favour of a hedge fund role in the speculative attack against Thailand is George Soros himself, who notes that "it must be admitted that hedge funds like mine did play a role in the Asian currency turmoil. Because hedge funds tend to be more concerned with absolute rather than relative performance, they are more likely to be actively involved in precipitating a change in a trend . . . For instance, by selling the Thai baht short in January 1997, the Quantum funds managed by my investment company may have sent a signal it may be overvalued."[16] So, while it doesn't seem likely that Soros or other hedge fund managers played as important a role in Asia as they did in Europe, the bottom line is that we simply don't know what role they did play, if any, because there isn't enough information available.

But even without all the information, there are still some strong theoretical reasons to suspect that Soros did not actually cause the British or Thai currency crises. I guess, as President Clinton might say, it depends what you mean by "cause." Whether or not you think hedge funds caused these crises really boils down to whether you think the fixed exchange rates in Europe and Asia would have lasted without any nefarious deeds by the hedge funds. As we saw in the last chapter, the collapse of the European and Asian currencies had more do with real imbalances related to the politics of fixed exchange rates and the bubbles that emerged in the countries' underlying economic fundamentals.

In Europe, the external shock of German reunification, which forced many countries to raise interest rates and slow down their economies, meant that Britain's fixed exchange rate was probably not long for this world anyway. With unemployment rising and the public showing less and less enthusiasm for the project of EMU, a speculative attack was bound to occur as investors began to realize that Europe's fixed exchange rates were becoming politically unsustainable.

In Asia, soaring asset prices and excessive borrowing had masked the fact that the economies of the region were hurting badly underneath. When the value of the U.S. dollar rose and pulled the Thai currency up with it, it hurt exports and began to rock the whole shaky edifice of the Thai economy. By the time the speculative attack occurred, mutual fund managers had already pulled out enough money to cause asset prices to fall. This revealed that the massive debts of Asian firms had been built on a foundation of sand. As in Europe, the fixed exchange rate was already on life support.

When Soros launched his attack against the British pound, he almost certainly brought the speculative attack forward in time. But it would have happened anyway. This means that hedge funds did not *cause* the crisis. And even if new evidence comes in to prove that Soros or any other hedge fund manager did help to initiate the run on the Thai baht, it seems clear that the Asian currency crisis also would have happened anyway. The crises in Europe and Asia were, ultimately, caused by the decision to adopt the politically unsustainable policy mix of capital mobility and a fixed exchange rate, and by the herd behaviour of mutual fund and pension fund managers, which created imbalances and sent false signals to economic actors.

One interesting point about hedge funds and currency crises is that when we speak about hedge funds in this context we are really talking about George Soros. In Chapter 3, we saw that Soros is one of the few market operators who recognizes how a bubble in asset prices can create a bubble in underlying economic fundamentals themselves. In fact, Soros wrote up a unique theory of financial market behaviour that incorporated this phenomenon in his first book, *The Alchemy of Finance*. Knowing that a bubble in economic fundamentals can make the onset of a crisis more difficult to predict may give Soros an advantage when it comes to identifying a profit-making opportunity. And when this knowledge is combined with his ability to lead markets, it means that Soros may be able to reduce the risk of contrarian investing by provoking a speculative attack rather than sitting back and waiting for it to happen. The bottom line is that if Soros's successes demonstrate anything, it's that investors would do well to pay greater attention to situations where a bubble in asset prices leads to a bubble in the underlying economic fundamentals.

FROM "HIGH CLOSING" TO "PUMPING UP THE TULIPS"

Directly manipulating individual stock prices is illegal. Manipulating entire stock markets and currencies is not. When pension fund managers at the Royal Bank of Canada manipulated a few individual stocks through the practice of high closing, they were nailed to the wall. When unregulated hedge funds tried to manipulate the entire Hong Kong stock market, they never looked back.

Most of the time, hedge funds act in the way that supporters of the industry tend to predict. In other words, they do act as contrarian investors who make the financial markets more efficient by investing against the herd. But sometimes hedge funds' ability to act as market leaders gives their managers an incentive to manipulate, rather than to invest against, the trend-chasing investors. This means that hedge funds have the potential to deliberately manipulate markets for their own economic benefit. The IMF argues that, "[w]ith greater concentration of wealth in the hands of professional fund managers, financial markets must cope with the effects of the attendant increase in the market power of market participants. Chief among these effects is the increased likelihood of market manipulation and even less efficient markets."[17]

Through a strategy known as "pumping up the tulips," a reference to the classic speculative bubble that emerged in Dutch tulip prices in the seventeenth century, a hedge fund manager can benefit from market manipulation in the following manner. First, by borrowing a ton of money and then investing it in an asset, the manager can unilaterally push up the asset's price and, thus, attract other trend-chasing investors. As these investors purchase the asset, its price rises further still and attracts even more trend chasers. Then, to reinforce the price movement with intellectual authority, the hedge fund manager can signal the market by simply leaking out information about the purchase. Finally, when the asset price has risen sufficiently, the fund manager simply sells the asset at the higher price and realizes the profit, all without any changes in the economic fundamentals. As we saw earlier, this strategy can also work in reverse through the use of short selling; that is, by profiting from pushing an asset's price down.

One prominent manager who is widely reported to make use of this strategy is Jeffrey Vinik, the former manager of Fidelity Investments' largest mutual fund — the Magellan fund — who now manages his own hedge fund, Vinik Asset Management LP. *Business Week* has said of Vinik, "At Magellan, [he] had a reputation of building up a large position in a stock, which pushed up the price. When the action attracted other investors, he would quickly unload his position."[18] As a hedge fund manager, Vinik has apparently reinforced this strategy through the use of his status as a market guru. He often takes a position of more than 5 percent in a company's outstanding stock, which requires him to publicly disclose the move through a 13D filing with the U.S. Securities and Exchange Commission. In July of 1997, for example, Vinik began purchasing shares in a company called Vivus. On

September 15, he disclosed a 7.2 percent stake when the stock was trading at $26, and "In less than two weeks, with no other news, Vivus soared to [$]38."[19]

Like Vinik, George Soros also seems to have employed this strategy, but on a much larger scale. In April of 1993, when Soros publicly announced large purchases of both gold and shares in Newmont Mining, *The Economist* remarked that his public announcement was "Not a bad ploy: the price of gold began to soar . . . presumably increasing the value of his investment."[20] However, of possibly greater significance, in terms of the ability of hedge funds to manipulate markets, is the reportedly real target of Soros's attempt at manipulating gold prices. As *The Economist* speculated at the time,

> [t]here is a persistent rumor that Mr. Soros' real interest in all this is not gold at all, but the bond markets. Suppose that he recently sold bonds short (i.e., promised to deliver in future bonds which he did not then own) when [bond] prices were at their peak. Now that [bond] prices have fallen, as gold prices rose, he stands to make a pretty profit. The trillions of dollars in the bond markets have been jostled by a few judiciously placed millions in gold.[21]

What was important about this manoeuvre was that it demonstrated how a single hedge fund manager, through his market leadership role and clever tactics, may have been able to manipulate the incredibly large international bond market.

In terms of large national markets, hedge funds also seem to have been involved in attempts at market manipulation in the wake of the 1997 Asian financial crisis. Reporting in *Fortune* magazine, MIT economist Paul Krugman notes that "a cabal of hedge funds apparently did try a squeeze play on Hong Kong's currency and stock market."[22] In August of 1998, Hong Kong began to make massive stock purchases in order to support falling prices. Finance officials claimed that they were fighting a deliberate conspiracy designed to instigate, and profit from, panicked selling conditions. But where did these panicked selling conditions come from?

Well, it seems that a number of hedge funds were shorting the Hong
Kong stock market; that is, they were using specialized financial
contracts to make a bet that the value of the Hong Kong stock market
would fall. This move on its own may have put a bit of downward
pressure on the market because, as you'll remember, "shorting" stocks
has the same effect as selling them. But the hedge funds weren't content to wait and see if the market kept on falling of its own accord.
Instead, they attempted to provoke its fall by attacking the Hong
Kong dollar.

Huh?

In the same way that Soros was rumoured to have manipulated gold
prices to affect the bond market, the hedge funds in Hong Kong were
trying to do the same thing to the stock market by putting downward
pressure on the currency. Downward pressure on a currency forces a
government with a fixed exchange rate to raise interest rates in defense
of the currency. Hong Kong has a fixed exchange rate, so the idea
was to put downward pressure on the currency and force the government to defend it with higher interest rates. Higher interest rates, of
course, generally cause stock markets to fall in value. So the hedge
funds would make profits on their original bets. Not too shabby, eh?
No wonder so many of our brightest minds go into high finance.

In a widely circulated letter, Donald Tsang, finance secretary of
Hong Kong, stated that "Regular patterns [of currency sales] suggested
a co-ordinated manipulative play involving very large funds," which
were rumoured to include George Soros's Quantum Fund and Julian
Robertson's Tiger Fund, two of the world's biggest hedge funds.[23] Also,
Tsang implicitly accused the hedge fund managers of spreading rumours
in the media that were designed to put further pressure on the Hong
Kong dollar. They apparently voiced their opinions to the press that the
Chinese currency was soon to be devalued and that the Hong Kong
dollar would drop along with it.

And if this weren't enough, a similar strategy also seems to have been
under way when the currencies of Australia, New Zealand and even
Canada came under heavy downward pressure in the summer of 1998.
In the wake of the Asian financial crisis, Canada and Australia managed

to weather the pressure on their currencies by simply letting their value drop. The only alternative would have been to sharply raise interest rates, something that would have protected the value of the currency but induced an unnecessary economic slowdown. In the Australian case, financial markets viewed the decline as a short-term buying opportunity rather than as an indicator of future trends and, as a result, the currency initially stabilized itself. But in late August, the Australian dollar came to the edge of a free fall, reaching a low of 56 cents against the U.S. dollar. Krugman reveals that "a lot of the plunge had to do with hedge funds shorting the currency." He goes on to state that "some people from the hedge funds actually told the Australians, in effect, that resistance was futile — that they were only a small piece of a coordinated play against Australia, New Zealand, South Africa and Canada — not to mention Hong Kong, Japan and China."[24] Protection for whole economies and markets has previously been viewed as unnecessary because, in contrast to individual assets such as stocks, they were perceived to be far too large for anyone to manipulate. But as this chapter has attempted to show, the rise of hedge funds and their ability to act as market leaders means that this may no longer be the case.

With hedge funds out of the way, we can now move from the international to the domestic. In Chapter 2, we saw how institutional investors have changed the way that capital mobility works by making the financial markets much less efficient. In the last three chapters, we saw the problems they can cause, both intentionally and unintentionally, for fixed exchange rates. In the next chapter, we'll take a look at their impact on the final pillar of the impossible trinity: the control of governments over monetary policy and their ability to implement the types of policies that their citizens want.

6

MUTUAL FUNDS, PENSION FUNDS AND DEFICITS — OH MY!

Nineteen ninety-five was the year that Canadians were informed their governments were no longer in charge — that their democratically elected representatives no longer had the power to deliver the kinds of policies voters wanted. Finance Minister Paul Martin tabled a budget that *Maclean's* magazine would later refer to as "The Remaking of Canada." The budget cut $25 billion (CDN) and 45,000 jobs out of the public sector over a three-year period. According to the forecasting firm Infometrica, this would amount to a net loss to the economy of over 80,000 jobs in the first year alone. Social spending, from health care and education to unemployment insurance and welfare, was to be cut dramatically. And whether they loved it or hated it, most pundits agreed that the deeds contained within the 1995 budget were a significant departure from the words of the 1993 election campaign.

In the campaign, "dignity of the worker" was the phrase to beat. Jean Chrétien's Liberals drew a clear and purposeful distinction between themselves and Kim Campbell's deficit-obsessed Conservatives by running on a platform of jobs and growth. The deficit would be reduced, but by stimulating the economy rather than by spending cuts. In the now-infamous Red Book, the emphasis was on "immediate measures to make our economy grow and create jobs" as opposed to the Conservative plan for "another five years of cutbacks, job loss and diminished expectations."

In an election that pitted jobs against spending cuts, Canadians voted overwhelmingly for jobs. Two years later, pollsters reported that jobs and the maintenance of the social safety net were still the top priorities in the minds of voters — not the deficit. But, by the time Paul Martin delivered the second budget of the first Liberal mandate, jobs and "the dignity of the worker" had been all but overwhelmed by spending cuts and the stated need to drastically "reinvent government." Deficit reduction through job creation had become job creation through deficit reduction — precisely the policy that voters had rejected.

In the United States, President Clinton had recently completed his own transition from a focus on jobs to one on deficit cutting. In the 1992 election campaign, he ran on a platform of jobs and growth, including a promise for a short-term stimulus package to jump-start the economy. In the early days of the administration, Clinton pollster Stanley Greenberg, through focus groups and polling, asked voters to name Clinton's most important campaign promises. The results, according to Bob Woodward of the *Washington Post,* were as follows: "The first answer was the promise to create 8 million jobs, the second health-care reform, the third welfare reform. All of these ranked above deficit reduction."[1] But as was soon to happen in Canada, Clinton's jobs-and-growth agenda was replaced by a focus on reducing the deficit.

It wasn't just in North America that deficit-slashing fever was taking hold. Around the world, democratic governments were taking a reluctant knife to the welfare states that their populations had cherished so deeply. From Australia and New Zealand to continental Europe, deficit reduction through spending cuts had become the only game in town.

Even in the European Union, the heartland of the welfare state, it seemed that social programs and job creation were no longer possible. Half a century ago, governments in Europe and North America abandoned the free market in favour of the Keynesian welfare state because of systemic factors. Most important among these were the heightened power and expectations of ordinary citizens. The power came from mass democracy, newly won in the aftermath of the First World War. The heightened expectations and the demand for something better rose from the rubble of the Great Depression and the Second World War. The villagers had suffered greatly and fought hard; they wanted some payback in the form of jobs and social programs. Now they had the ballot box to make sure the wealthy landowners gave them what they wanted.

The economic shift from the free market to the Keynesian welfare state as the world's preferred brand of capitalism was based on a fundamental shift in the political balance of power from Wall Street to Main Street through the advent of mass suffrage. So, fifty years later, if so many governments were now turning their backs on the popular welfare state, there had to be a systemic reason, a common denominator.

Shortly after Paul Martin introduced his 1995 budget, we were told what had happened.

MASTERS OF THE UNIVERSE: THE STORY OF EXTERNAL CONSTRAINTS

According to the media, the shift to the economic right, both now and over the last two decades, was a story of the growing power of the financial markets and the way that they had imposed a new external constraint on the policy choices of individual governments. *Maclean's* summed it up best. On the cover of their March 20, 1995, issue stood a lone individual perched atop a pillar of rock, steadying himself as the mountain around him crumbled away. Together with the banner headline "Shifting Ground," this image conveyed to us that the world had become a very different place. What was the specific cause of this earth-shattering change? *Maclean's* explained: "When money traders rule the world, the old rules crumble."[2]

Under the "old rules," governments were accountable to their citizens and had sufficient control over their economies to make this accountability meaningful. Under the new rules, governments were said to be powerless in the face of the global financial markets. Average people may have wanted jobs and growth, but the financial markets wanted deficit reduction and a roll-back of the welfare state. And with the political balance of power having shifted dramatically in their favour, the financial markets won the day.

Twenty years ago, financial markets were just that: markets where financial instruments — such as stocks, bonds and currencies — were bought and sold by all manner of individuals and institutions. By 1995, however, "the financial markets" (Yawn!) had become "The Financial Markets" (Oooo!), a powerful global force to which governments around the world had to increasingly bend their will. The sources of the financial markets' new power, we were told, were the usual suspects of globalization and technology, both of which enabled investors to rapidly move money from country to country in search of the economic policies that would generate the highest returns. Under the old rules — and they were *rules* — governments regulated the financial markets, preventing investors from moving their money abroad. These rules, in turn, gave governments the freedom to implement the kinds of economic policies that their citizens demanded. If investors didn't like these policies, it was their tough luck.

But globalization and technology had apparently changed all that. The end result was the brave new world of capital mobility. And it was this new-found mobility that greatly increased the financial markets' influence over government policy. When investors can move massive pools of money across borders at a moment's notice, governments are forced to compete for this capital by providing the types of policies that investors want. If they don't, investors vote with their feet by transferring billions out of the country. The result is, at best, a falling currency and, at worst, a full-blown financial crisis.

"Globalization" and "capital mobility" are useful terms if you're an academic who spends his Friday nights poring over reports from the IMF. (And yes, I do know that I'm a nerd.) For most people, however, and for the reporters who seek to inform them, these concepts are a little dry. They certainly don't sell magazines and newspapers. What sells is drama and conflict, and these require both good guys and bad guys. The exploits of Luke Skywalker make for a pretty boring day out at the movies if not for Darth Vader. So to tell the story of globalization and the new power of the financial markets, reporters sought out a villain. It wasn't enough to find the smoking gun; they wanted to know who was pulling the trigger.

Bay Street? Nah, not specific enough.

The big banks? Done to death. A new problem needs a new villain.

In their quest for a villain, the media were assisted by politicians who wanted to avoid being put into the slot themselves. On the contrary, they wanted to be portrayed as the underdogs, the democratic Davids fighting the valiant but ultimately hopeless battle against the financial Goliaths. As *Maclean's* reported, "the Liberal government has deliberately played on that growing anxiety about the erosion of Canada's domestic sovereignty in its bid to win broad political support for an austere cost-cutting budget. In a speech in Vancouver . . . Finance Minister Paul Martin declared that his hardline budget . . . was imperative for Canada's autonomy. 'My goal is to make sure that my kids don't have their sovereignty dictated to by somebody outside of this country,' he said, referring to the clout of foreign creditors."[3]

Across our southern border, the Clinton administration also wanted to deflect blame for their new focus on cost-cutting. Possibly the best known quote came from Clinton election advisor James Carville who quipped: "I used to think that if there was reincarnation, I wanted to come back as the president or the pope. But now I want to be the bond market: you can intimidate everybody." French Prime Minister Jacques Chirac had a similar goal. He was a little more direct, however, when he identified speculators as his villain of choice, describing them as "the AIDS of the world economy."

Foreign creditors? Bondholders? Speculators? Now here were villains the media could use. These elements had just the kind of conspiratorial ring to them to make a good story. It became fashionable in the media to imply that deficit cutting, volatile exchange rates and financial crises were all caused by someone else — that all the unwelcome changes wrought upon our societies were the fault of what *Business Week* called "a sort of shadow world government."[4] We were never told who these mysterious foreign bondholders, speculators or creditors were, or from what country their villainy emanated. Anything too specific would have weakened the shadowy puppet-master angle.

But as useful as foreign bondholders and speculators were as villains in the drama, there was still one problem, especially for magazine and television reporters. They needed a photo. A picture of a foreign bond-holder would probably just be a suit at a desk — too boring. No, they needed an image that was dramatic, something that would convey the proverbial thousand words and provide a quick summary of the power of the financial markets. The image the media settled on, and the one that constantly reappears whenever something "financial" happens, was the buzzing hive of a trading floor, where hyperactive currency traders scream orders and flash hand signals, while a Bloomberg screen scrolls out the latest price information over their heads. These are the images of the new financial order. Fast. High-tech. Global.

This image reinforced the message. "It is beginning to dawn on citizens of the world that their governments are no longer in charge . . . A new breed has risen to take the real reins of power, often face-less, always unelected and accountable only to the bottom line. The new global elite is composed of international money traders and there is no mistaking their clout," wrote *Maclean's* editor Robert Lewis.[5]

In story after story, traders were referred to as "hot money" and "the masters of the universe." They were young, wealthy, rash and full of bravado. "If the Liberals think they're setting the economic agenda, they're sadly mistaken up there in Disneyland on the Rideau," bragged one trader at the Toronto Dominion Bank.[6] It was easy to dislike these guys. Perfect! Even in the business press, currency traders seemed to be the cause of all the world's ills. "The dollar is crashing. Mexico is in meltdown. The European currency system is collapsing. One force is driving it all: Global money traders voting thumbs-down on deficits" noted *Business Week*.[7]

Currency traders and foreign bondholders helped to reinforce the idea that there was little that governments could do in the face of the new power of the financial markets. Bondholders were often described as "foreign" and thus beyond regulation. Currency trading was portrayed in much the way the Internet is, as a decentralized, technology-based network that is virtually impossible for a state to regulate. For a while, it seemed that politicians had found a perfect scapegoat to explain their reincarnation as economic conservatives. But in the pages of the business press and in many scholarly journals, the myth of the financial markets' new power did not go unchallenged.

THE IMPOSSIBLE TRINITY AND THE MYTH OF EXTERNAL CONSTRAINTS

Among academics, the notion that all-powerful financial markets have forced governments to pursue the conservative policies of very low inflation and cutbacks to social programs is often referred to as the "external constraints" view. Like the story told by politicians and the media, the external constraints view argues that the developed world's shift away from the Keynesian welfare state, which began in the late 1970s, is primarily a result of the growing power of the financial markets. Proponents of this view argue that governments were forced to give investors the policies they wanted or else face massive capital flight out of their economies.

The external constraints view has been challenged by both left- and right-wing economists, however.

Those on the left have challenged what Linda McQuaig dubbed "the cult of impotence" — the notion that governments are powerless in the face of capital mobility and the new muscle of the financial markets.[8] Their intent is to demonstrate that governments *do* have a choice and that politics, not economics, explains why economic policy-making has shifted sharply to the right. Conservatives, on the other hand, challenge the external constraints view in order to show that the shift to conservative policies didn't happen because governments were forced but because these policies make the most economic sense. For obvious reasons, there are large differences between what the left and right have to say, but they both start from some common ground.

The common ground that challenges the external constraints view is the "impossible trinity" that we discussed in Chapter 3. You will recall that the logic of the impossible trinity tells governments what they can't have; hence the term "impossible." What they can't have is capital mobility, fixed exchange rates and discretion in monetary policy all at the same time. If governments want capital mobility and a stable exchange rate, then they have to give up the option of stimulating their economy through lower interest rates. In other words, when governments adopt both capital mobility and a fixed exchange rate, they are forced to pursue the types of economic policies that investors demand.

But just as the impossible trinity tells governments what they can't do, it also tells them what they *can* do. If governments don't adopt a fixed exchange rate, and Canada and the United States haven't, then they should have full discretion over their monetary policy — meaning that it should be entirely possible for them to stimulate growth and reduce unemployment by lowering interest rates.

If the government did decide to stimulate job creation through lower interest rates, it would lead to a small rise in inflation. Investors, who hate inflation with a passion, would take their money abroad, and this would cause the value of the dollar to drop. No one likes inflation because rising prices make the products we purchase more expensive. For most people, however, a little bit of inflation is a price worth paying for the lower unemployment and higher overall wages that come from a faster-growing economy. The same applies to a falling dollar. A slightly falling dollar benefits most people because it helps to further stimulate growth and job creation by boosting our exports. Investors, of course, work from the exact opposite point of view. They make their money from investments rather than wages, and rising inflation and a falling dollar serve to erode the value of their investments over time.

The bottom line is that, despite the claims of politicians, most economists would agree that capital mobility was not the reason governments adopted policies of very low inflation and cutbacks to social programs: that the shift to the economic right over the past two decades had little to do with the growing power of the financial markets. If governments wanted to create jobs and maintain well-funded social programs, all they had to do was tolerate a slight fall in the value of the dollar. In Canada, the most prominent advocate of this view was Pierre Fortin, an economist at the University of Quebec at Montreal. In numerous articles and speeches, and even testimony before the House of Commons Finance Committee, he promoted the idea that Canada did have a choice — that growing out of the deficit through a discretionary monetary policy rather than spending cuts was possible because Canada did not have a fixed exchange rate.

Does this mean that governments didn't need to rein in the welfare state at all over the past couple of decades? Well, even some economists on the left wouldn't agree with that.

MILTON FRIEDMAN AND THE STORY OF INTERNAL CONSTRAINTS

In North America, the shift to the economic right began as far back as the late 1970s, when central banks in Canada and the United States drastically raised interest rates to fight soaring inflation. Before this, governments had maintained expansionary policies to achieve very low unemployment, and this policy had led to rising, but not soaring, levels of inflation. Looking back, both conservative and Keynesian economists seem to agree that the shift to more conservative monetary policies was made necessary by the emergence of "stagflation." Stagflation is a situation where *both* high inflation and high unemployment emerge at the same time.

In Keynesian theory, stagflation was supposed to be impossible. If unemployment went up, inflation was supposed to go down. If unemployment went down, inflation was supposed to go up. It all had to do with the amount of demand in the economy. Low unemployment creates more demand for products because people with jobs have more money to spend. And greater demand for products serves to push up their price, creating inflation. High unemployment, in contrast, reduces demand and keeps prices stable. So, because inflation and unemployment were supposed to move in opposite directions, Keynesians had difficulty in explaining why *both* inflation and unemployment had increased during the 1970s.

Then along came Milton Friedman, the de facto father of what came to be known as monetarist economics, the conservative rival to Keynesianism. According to Friedman, stagflation emerged because of the way that governments had been pursuing overly expansionary policies for far too long. This led to persistently high levels of inflation, which, he argued, had a tendency to become cumulative over time. In other words, high inflation that lasted for a while would eventually start to grow at an exponential pace. Why would this happen? Well, according to Friedman, high inflation would eventually become cumulative because workers and firms aren't stupid. If you're a worker and you know that prices are rising by 6 percent every year, you also know that a 6 percent annual raise means that you're just breaking even. In terms of what your paycheque will actually buy, you haven't gained a thing. So workers began to demand raises over and above inflation. To get a 2 percent raise with inflation running at 6 percent, they had to demand an 8 percent raise.

When workers began to incorporate the inflation rate into their wage demands, this created a huge problem for governments. It became much more difficult for governments to maintain low unemployment with expansionary policies. Governments had to expand their economies even more, over and above the existing level of inflation, just to achieve the same reduction in unemployment. So with governments pursuing ever-more expansionary policies that raised inflation, and workers demanding ever-rising wages to compensate for inflation, the whole process took on a kind of snowball dynamic that led to a combination of high inflation and high unemployment. Other one-time-only factors, such as the OPEC oil-price hike, also contributed to rising inflation. But the real heart of the problem was the way that

workers incorporated rising inflation into their wage demands, leading
to the emergence of stagflation.

Now, despite the aversion among Keynesians to conceding any
points to the father of monetarism, the truth is that Friedman was
correct; inflation at persistently high levels can become cumulative
over time. And part of the problem did stem from the difficulties
governments were having in controlling inflation by microeconomic
mechanisms. As we saw above, one way for governments to control
inflation is to pursue a contractionary monetary policy by raising interest rates, which reduces demand and slows the pace of economic
growth. Another way is to negotiate with unions and convince them
not to ask for too much. Using monetary policy to control inflation is
a macroeconomic method; using negotiations is a microeconomic one.
As one European social democrat argued, "As became clear in the late
sixties, the strategy to rely upon microeconomic policies to contain
inflation would come into conflict with the organizational logic of trade
unions."[9]

In the 1970s, unions were at the height of their power. They weren't
very interested in accepting any constraints on their wage demands.
This doesn't mean that unions did anything wrong; the job of a trade
union is to negotiate the best deal for its members. From the perspective of a trade union, there is virtually no such thing as too high a
wage or too low an unemployment rate, no matter how economically
unsustainable they can become. High wages are what their members
want, and unions are accountable to their members. The same logic
holds true for investors. For them, there is no such thing as too little
inflation, no matter how politically unsustainable the resulting high
unemployment can become. This is why I said in Chapter 2 that
capitalist democracies seem to work best when there is a balance of
power between Wall Street and Main Street. The economic discipline
of investors prevents inflation from getting too high and the political
discipline of workers prevents unemployment from getting too high.

In the 1970s, when investors were less mobile and unions were much
stronger, government policy tilted towards overly expansionary policies,
which led to rising inflation and, eventually, when workers and firms

began to incorporate inflation into their wage and price demands, to the emergence of stagflation. Stagflation benefitted no one and acted as an internal constraint on the ability of governments to maintain their expansionary policies. The result was that governments were forced to rein in inflation by pursuing contractionary monetary policies. So by the late 1970s, when inflation in North America was running at over 12 percent, governments responded by sharply raising interest rates.

At the end of the day, it seems that the initial shift away from expansionary policies in the late 1970s was triggered by the internal constraint caused by the problem of stagflation. Note that this need to impose some macroeconomic discipline is not inconsistent with Keynesian policies. While many on the popular left associate Keynesianism with expansionary policies, it's important to remember that Keynes advocated a balance between inflation and unemployment; when either exceeded tolerable levels, he argued, it would be necessary to implement offsetting (and, in the case of high inflation, contractionary) policies.

While some degree of consensus may exist between conservatives and Keynesians regarding the way that stagflation forced governments to implement contractionary policies, there is less agreement about whether these constraints ruled out the use of discretionary monetary policy altogether. Conservatives have long argued that, in the long term, monetary policy should have no real effect on the economy and can't be used to reduce unemployment. Keynesians disagree. But in the late 1970s, conservatives gained the upper hand because Friedman's explanation of stagflation had had the effect of temporarily discrediting Keynesian ideas in the minds of politicians. Stagflation occurred because governments went too far — further than Keynes himself would have advocated — and pursued expansionary policies that were economically unsustainable. But this didn't matter to politicians, who liked their explanations in black and white. If Milton Friedman was correct about stagflation, then he must have been correct in his entire critique of Keynesian economics.

Whether Friedman's entire critique of Keynesian economics is true or not (and it's not), his explanation of stagflation did give a huge boost to the ideas of monetarist economics. This was the case because Friedman had actually *predicted* the rise of stagflation. The elegance of Friedman's argument was that it delivered a double whammy to Keynesianism. On the one hand, it explained the rise of stagflation and revived the old conservative chestnut that monetary policy could not be used to reduce unemployment. On the other hand, it also managed to explain something that conservative economics had long failed to account for: that Keynesian techniques of using monetary policy to reduce unemployment had worked in the past.[10] Conservative economics had long argued that Keynes's ideas on government intervention were false. They argued that, in the long term at least, government intervention would have no real effect on the economy or on unemployment — at least, no positive effect. The problem with the conservative view, as is so often the case, is that the existing reality didn't match their theory because Keynesian policies *had* worked in the past. So because Friedman's stagflation theory included an explanation of why Keynesian policies had worked in the past, but then went on to show why they would no longer work in the future, it really made a big splash.

Basically, Friedman argued that Keynesian policies had worked in the past because workers were fooled. Expansionary policies reduced unemployment because workers didn't expect inflation and therefore didn't incorporate it into their wage demands. The effect was that wages would rise but this rise would not immediately translate into a rise in prices, so workers had more purchasing power than before. This encouraged them to spend more, boosting demand in the economy. At this point, Friedman revealed his trump card: the idea that you can't fool all of the people all of the time. He argued that when expansionary policies eventually produced inflation, and when inflation began to become a permanent feature of the economic landscape, workers would no longer be fooled and would eventually incorporate inflation into their wage and price demands. When this happened, it meant that governments would have to pursue ever-more expansionary policies in order to achieve the same effect on the economy. As we saw above, these policies eventually led to the emergence of stagflation.

Predicting stagflation in the context of an argument that also explained why Keynesian policies had worked in the past gave an enormous boost to Friedman's credibility and, in turn, to the credibility of his overall critique of Keynesianism. As Paul Krugman notes, "Friedman was right, on a very big issue. His insights deservedly raised his prestige and that of the [monetarist] school of economics to new heights, and gave his earlier, monetarist critique of Keynesianism new respectability."[11] This earlier critique of Keynesianism, which fit extremely well with the prejudices of conservatives and Wall Street, was the idea that monetary policy could not be used to fight recessions or to reduce unemployment — that all it could be used for was to achieve very low inflation.

In making this argument, Friedman focused on explaining why government intervention could not be used to stimulate an economy out of a recession. He argued that a recession would always be self-correcting and that, if the government tried to stimulate the economy in the midst of one, it would cause more problems than it solved. Why would a recession, or any episode of high unemployment, be self-correcting? Well, if you think back to Chapter 3, you'll remember that the conservative solution for dealing with unemployment goes back to the idea of the reduced-to-clear bin. If a store can't sell a product, then the only way to clear it off the shelves is to drastically lower its price. In the view of Friedman, and conservatives more generally, the same logic holds true for labour. If unemployment is high it's because there isn't enough demand for labour relative to the supply. To reduce unemployment, workers simply need to reduce themselves to clear, by drastically lowering their wage demands. And conservatives believe that workers will do this automatically and thus that instances of high unemployment will be self-correcting.

But if workers will automatically reduce their prices when the demand for labour goes down, why do recessions even happen? Why don't workers *immediately* lower their wage demands, causing the economy to immediately self-correct and unemployment to fall? To answer these questions, Friedman once again pointed to the problem of workers and firms being temporarily fooled. He argued that a recession would occur because workers and firms would mistake falling demand in the whole economy for a temporary fall in demand just for their own product or labour. So they wouldn't reduce to clear right away. Instead, they would keep their price or wage demands where they were and hope that the temporary fall in demand would quickly go away.

According to Friedman, a recession would self-correct as soon as workers and firms realized what was going on. Once they realized that demand was falling in the whole economy, they would lower their price and wage demands, causing shoppers to start buying, employers to start hiring and unemployment to start falling. The idea that workers and firms will automatically reduce to clear is why conservatives believe that recessions and other episodes of high unemployment will always be self-correcting. This is the first part of the conservative argument for why governments shouldn't intervene in the economy. The conservative view is that government programs such as unemployment insurance and welfare merely extend a recession because they prevent workers from lowering their wage demands. The second part of the conservative argument against government intervention is based on the widely accepted fact that monetary policy takes some time to actually work — that when a government tries to stimulate the economy by lowering interest rates, it takes a while to actually boost output.

Why does this mean that governments shouldn't try to fight recessions and reduce unemployment with lower interest rates? Conservatives argue that, because governments are unlikely to recognize the onset of a recession any earlier than the private sector, and because a recession would be self-correcting anyway, any attempt to stimulate the economy would merely produce inflation because it wouldn't have any effect until a natural recovery was already well under way. So, conservatives argue, governments shouldn't use monetary policy to fight recessions and to reduce unemployment.

Instead, Friedman argued that all governments could do was keep inflation very low. And the best way to do this, he maintained, was by targeting the money supply — the amount of currency in circulation. When a government pursues an expansionary monetary policy to stimulate the economy, it lowers interest rates by increasing the money supply. (When the supply of money increases, the price of money — the interest rate — goes down.) Friedman argued that the best way to achieve very low inflation was to focus on expanding the money supply at a very slow and steady rate, just enough to meets the demands of the economy but no more.

Strict monetarist policies of this type had a very short-lived history. Achieving low inflation by targeting the money supply was implemented in the United States and Canada only up until the recession of the late 1970s and early 1980s. As we've seen, some recession was necessary to rein in the high levels of inflation associated with stagflation, but the targeting of the money supply and the abandoning of Keynesian principles caused the recession to be much deeper and last much longer than was economically necessary. As Krugman argues, "in mid-1982, as the economy plunged more deeply than anticipated, even the pretense of monetarism was abandoned, never to be resumed."[12] In fact, calls for a return to the use of monetary policy to stimulate demand and end the recession came from such conservative institutions as the IMF and the Bank for International Settlements, as well as from the Group of Seven industrialized countries.

By the mid-1980s, Friedman's painful policy of targeting the money supply was quickly replaced by a return to the use of discretionary monetary policy. Governments had learned two valuable lessons over the previous decade, both of which centred on the original Keynesian idea that there had to be a balance between inflation and unemployment, and that they couldn't let either get too high. The first lesson was that they needed to avoid overly expansionary policies, which would eventually lead to stagflation. The second was that they had to maintain their discretion over monetary policy to fight recessions and prevent unemployment from getting too high. With this realization, Keynesianism had once again beat out its conservative rival, at least in the area of monetary policy. Friedman's claim that monetary policy had no effect on unemployment was disproven on two fronts. On the practical front, it was disproven by the experience of the recession, which had failed to self-correct as conservatives had predicted. Workers and firms didn't lower their wage and price demands enough, and the recession lasted too long.

On the theoretical front, Keynesians eventually came up with an explanation of why workers and firms had failed to reduce labour costs and goods prices and why the recession had failed to self-correct. The core of this explanation, advanced by economist George Akerlof, was that wages and prices were "sticky." He argued that it was difficult for firms to quickly reduce prices and wages because it required a lot of administrative hassle — hassle that would cost money. These administrative hassles are often referred to as "menu costs" by economists, named for a very straightforward example. Imagine a restaurant owner who is faced with the need to reduce her prices in a recession. She will need to spend a bunch of money to reprint her menus. Menu costs exist throughout the economy and come in many different forms. For workers, menu costs can include things like multi-year contracts that prevent the quick adjustment of wages.

But if the restaurant owner doesn't lower prices, won't she be driven out of business as customers flock to her competitors? Won't the discipline of the market — in this case, restaurant customers — force her to lower her prices when demand falls? According to Akerlof, the answer is, not necessarily. In conservative theory, restaurant customers, like all consumers, shop around for the best price. This is the discipline of the marketplace. If firms don't offer the best price, then customers won't go there. But in reality, most of us can't be bothered to spend too much time shopping around just to save a few bucks. When you pop out of the office for lunch, do you really care if you could have bought your hamburger for 20 cents less somewhere else? Do you really go from restaurant to restaurant to find the best price? Of course not. The time it would take to shop around is worth more to you than the little bit of money you might save as a result.

Apply this to the whole economy and you have the reason that firms and workers fail to reduce wages and prices in a recession as fully as conservative theory suggests. Menu costs (or employee contracts) make it difficult for firms to lower their prices and the wages of their workers. The fact that consumers really don't shop around in the extreme fashion described by conservative theory means that market discipline is not completely cut and dried. So prices and wages are "sticky" and the economy doesn't self-correct from a recession.

By the mid-1980s, governments had abandoned their flirtation with monetarism and, as both the experience of the recession and the new developments in Keynesian theory show, they were right to do so. The initial shift away from expansionary monetary policies during the early 1980s was based on the need to deal with the internal constraint of stagflation, rather than with the external constraint of the growing power of financial markets. In both the United States and Canada, inflation rates were brought down from about 12 percent to about 4 percent. Meanwhile, Friedman's theories rose and fell as a practical guide to policy. While his explanation of stagflation was accepted, his broader case against the use of discretionary monetary policy was quickly rejected in actual practice. In many ways, Friedman's explanation for stagflation merely updated Keynesianism by providing a sound rationale for avoiding overly expansionary policies. So at the end of the day, the shift to the right in terms of monetary policy during the 1980s was fairly short-lived. It wasn't until a few years later that conservative ideas really began to have an effect.

JOHN CROW AND THE POLITICS OF PRICE STABILITY

Canada's real shift to the economic right began in the late 1980s when John Crow became the governor of the Bank of Canada. Crow had spent his formative years abroad working at the IMF, which, for conservative economists, is the financial equivalent of the Vatican. So imbued was he with the gospel of monetarism and zero inflation that, upon his return to Canada, he sought to zealously spread the word. In 1987, when he was appointed by the Mulroney government as the governor of the Bank of Canada, he got his chance. In 1988 he announced his intention to pursue "price stability," which he defined as an inflation rate "clearly below" 2 percent. In doing so, he shifted Canadian monetary policy far to the right.

By the late 1980s, recovery from the recession was fully under way in Canada, and had begun to produce an uptick in inflation that approached the 4 to 5 percent mark. While most Keynesians would agree that the Bank of Canada needed to keep an eye on inflation and, if necessary, prevent it from rising any further, Crow went beyond preventing a re-emergence of stagflation in pursuing his goal of price stability.

Crow's pursuit of price stability is explained entirely by politics rather than economics. Inflation needs to be controlled, but there was no need to force it down to near zero with punishingly high interest rates. Nor did the growing power of the financial markets force Canada to embark on this new experiment with monetarist economics. It all came down to Crow's conservative leanings, and those of the Mulroney government that appointed him. To make the case for price stability, conservatives couldn't appeal to the external constraint of the financial markets or the internal constraint of preventing the re-emergence of stagflation. So without the option of saying that "there is no alternative," they had to rely on trying to explain why the policy would actually benefit average Canadians. The problem was, it didn't.

The case in favour of price stability is thin. It tends to focus on the long-term expectations of business and on such trivial benefits as greater certainty in accounting practices. According to this argument, price stability reduces business uncertainty about the future and thus encourages firms to undertake projects with longer-term horizons. However, as even proponents of price stability concede, it is very difficult to quantify these benefits or to determine the precise advantage of moving from low inflation to zero inflation. At the same time, critics have argued that the higher real interest rates associated with very low inflation have the opposite effect; that is, they can encourage firms to speculate rather than to invest in productive enterprises.

Keynesian economists have not only questioned the benefits of price stability but also argued that proponents of zero inflation have heavily underestimated its costs. Says Krugman, "There is some evidence that a push to zero inflation may lead not just to a temporary

sacrifice of output but to a permanently higher rate of unemployment."[13] Once again, the politics of economics becomes important
here. A 1996 study by economists George Akerlof, William Dickens
and George Perry found strong evidence of what economists call
"nominal wage rigidity."[14] Essentially, it's the old politics of the
reduce-to-clear bin; workers don't like to see their wages falling, and
when they do, they tend to resist it.

Consider the case of an economy where demand is falling and
employers need to reduce wages somewhat to stay in business. If there
is a little bit of inflation in the economy, say 5 percent, the firm can
lower wages in a way that workers are less likely to resist. Instead of
cutting wages, they can simply increase them by somewhat less than the
inflation rate. For example, a 2 percent raise when there is 5 percent
inflation is actually a 3 percent cut in real wages, or the purchasing
power of the workers' pay. But workers are less likely to resist this type
of pay cut because their "nominal wages," the actual numbers on their
paycheque, actually go up. But if inflation is running at zero, the only
way a firm can cut real wages by 3 percent is to cut nominal wages by
3 percent. This means that the actual number on a worker's paycheque
will drop. According to the evidence, workers are much more likely to
resist a cut of this kind. So, because it becomes difficult for a firm
to cut workers' pay, if the firm needs to cut costs, it is forced instead
to lay workers off. This situation, not surprisingly, leads to higher
unemployment.

The bottom line, as Krugman notes, is that "the belief that absolute
price stability is a huge blessing that brings large economic benefits
with few if any costs rests not on evidence but on faith. The evidence
actually points the other way: the benefits of price stability are elusive,
the costs of getting there are large and zero inflation may not be a
good thing even in the long run."[15] Crow's decision to aim for price
stability was a political and ideological decision rather than one justified
by economic necessity or any real benefits to the economy as a whole.

When Crow jacked up interest rates at the end of the 1980s, the
effect was devastating for the economy. Growth slowed, unemployment

rose and, as we'll see in a minute, the deficit soared. Nevertheless, in 1991, the Mulroney government signed a formal agreement with the Bank of Canada instructing it to reduce inflation to 2 percent by 1995 and thereafter to maintain it within a target band of 1 to 3 percent. Crow exceeded his target dates with punishingly high interest rates, managing to drop inflation below 2 percent four years earlier than mandated. Following this drop, Canada's inflation rate averaged 1.4 percent between 1992 and 1996.

Conservatives are forever comparing Canada to the United States and when they do, they usually argue that faster American growth and lower unemployment is all about the tax differences between the two countries. One of the biggest differences, though, has been in the area of monetary policy. The United States never adopted explicit inflation targets and didn't try to push inflation anywhere as near as low as Canada did. In fact, between 1992 and 1996, Canada's inflation rate was half of that which prevailed south of the border. This difference is one of the main reasons for the United States' lower rate of unemployment and faster growth. Is it any wonder that Americans love their central bank governor Alan Greenspan so much? As Paul Krugman noted in a 1996 piece in *The Economist*, "the Bank of Canada's anti-inflationary zeal . . . [cost Canadians] hundreds of thousands of jobs."[16]

Very low inflation led to a rapid increase in Canada's deficits and debt. As Crow pushed up interest rates to pursue near-zero inflation, unemployment rose to well over 10 percent, and this had a ripple effect throughout the economy. First, unemployed people pay less tax, so government revenues went down. Second, higher interest rates meant that the government had to pay much more in interest payments to service the existing debt. And third, with unemployment rising, governments had to pay out much more to people on unemployment insurance and welfare. At the time, there seemed to be a great deal of confusion about this increased spending on social programs such as unemployment insurance and welfare. From the media, one was left with the impression that the government had all of a sudden decided to start paying out much more through these programs — that the programs had become more generous.

This was not the case. Social programs, like unemployment insurance and welfare, used to be structured as what economists call "automatic stabilizers." An automatic stabilizer is any social program that helps to automatically regulate demand in the economy. If demand falls and unemployment rises, programs like unemployment insurance and welfare automatically pump more money into the economy because more people are on the programs. When demand rises and unemployment drops, there are fewer people on unemployment insurance and welfare, and government spending goes down. The key point is that government spending goes up and down automatically based on the state of the economy and the number of people on the programs. So when Crow's high-interest-rate policy led to a massive rise in unemployment, government spending automatically increased because there were far more people depending on these programs. Increased spending had nothing to do with profligate governments making these programs more generous and everything to do with the number of people who were on them because of rising unemployment. Crow's high-interest-rate policy contributed directly to the rise in Canada's deficits and debt.

By the early 1990s, Canada's economy was not in great shape. Government deficits and debt were soaring and unemployment was in the double digits all because John Crow wanted to achieve his goal of zero inflation. The deficit situation was becoming economically unsustainable and the unemployment situation was politically unsustainable. Both had to be addressed and there seemed to be two main options for doing so. The first was the conservative option, which focused on spending cuts. Cutbacks to social programs would reduce the deficit and, according to conservatives, help to reduce unemployment by lowering the unemployment benefits and welfare payments that prevented workers from lowering their wage demands to a level where employers would hire them. The second option was the Keynesian one, which focused on dealing with the monetary policy that had caused the deficit and high unemployment in the first place. This option involved lowering interest rates to stimulate the economy. A growing economy would cause unemployment to fall, the interest payments on the debt to be reduced, tax revenues to rise and spending on unemployment benefits and welfare payments to fall. If high interest rates had caused the deficit and high unemployment, then lower interest rates would reverse the situation and cure both problems.

The Chrétien Liberals campaigned on the Keynesian solution while the Conservatives focused on spending cuts. In the end, the Conservatives found out just how politically unsustainable unemployment had become when the Tories were virtually wiped out in the 1993 election. It clearly didn't help when Conservative leader Kim Campbell made her now-famous comment that there was little the government could do about unemployment. However, despite their focus on deficit reduction through job creation, the Liberal government, once in power, became more conservative than the Tories had ever been. In his 1995 budget, Paul Martin abandoned the Keynesian solution of stimulating the economy for the conservative focus on spending cuts.

As we saw earlier in this chapter, Martin blamed this conversion on the growing power of the financial markets, saying that they had left him with no choice. Critics argued that the power of the financial markets was a myth and that Canada did have a choice, that the Liberals could have reduced both the deficit and unemployment by stimulating the economy with lower interest rates. They argued that, because Canada didn't have a fixed exchange rate, its government could stimulate the economy and all that would happen was that the dollar would drop a little. No big deal. A lower dollar would stimulate the economy even further by boosting our exports. According to the critics, Paul Martin's shift to the right seemed to be a purely political decision, a case of the Liberals campaigning from the left and governing from the right.

I used to support this view. I used to believe that the Liberals did have a choice but, for whatever political reasons, decided to abandon their campaign promise to reduce the deficit by stimulating the economy rather than gutting social programs. Now I'm not so sure. My research on the rise of mutual funds and pension funds and their impact on behaviour in the financial markets is pushing me towards the conclusion that the Liberals may have had less of a choice than their critics contend. Before looking at the evidence, let's take a look at how mutual funds and pension funds could have theoretically increased the pressures on the government to give the financial markets the spending cuts they wanted.

DEFICITS AND THE POLITICS OF PRICE OVERSHOOTING

The theoretical case that mutual funds and pension funds increased pressures on the government to cut spending rather than lower interest rates stems from the way that fund managers' short-term focus and herd-like behaviour have increased the potential for market over-reaction and price overshooting. Recall that, in economic terms, price overshooting has led to a decline in market efficiency and to an increased potential for market volatility and financial crises. In political terms, it has led to a dramatic shift in the balance of power between the financial markets and government policy-makers. But how, specifically, does price overshooting increase the pressures on the government to give investors the types of policies they want? Under normal circumstances, if the government decided to tackle the deficit by lowering interest rates to stimulate the economy, investors would pull some of their money out of Canada and the value of the dollar would drop a little. This wouldn't be a problem because a slightly falling dollar would boost exports, leading to further economic growth.

In a textbook world, one where markets are efficient and investors look to the long term, this view would be correct. In a textbook world, the financial markets only "punish" a country in proportion to its perceived "crime" against investors; a misdemeanor in the form of a little economic stimulus should only result in a small drop in its currency. But when markets are prone to overreact, and prices to overshoot, a country may be punished by investors far out of proportion to its crime. If the government implements policies that investors dislike, rather than simply dropping a little, the currency could plummet. And while a slightly falling currency is no big deal, it is difficult for a government to stand by while its currency drops uncontrollably.

There are a number of reasons for this. If the Canadian dollar started to plummet, it would lead to a flood of our goods into the United

States. This would be okay for Canada, but it's virtually guaranteed that certain U.S. congressmen would kick up a stink about Canada gaining an unfair trade advantage. The government would also come under pressure from importers, whose costs would rise massively, and from the Canadian population as a whole because of the national shame that seems to be associated with a rapidly falling currency. So, as *The Economist* comments: "The risk of extreme price movements puts a greater premium on policies conducive to fiscal discipline and price stability."[17]

Reinforcing the pressures on governments that come from a plummeting currency is the way that price overshooting can affect other prices in addition to the value of the dollar. Most important here are long-term interest rates, which, in technical terms, refer to the yields on long-term government bonds. So far, when I've been talking about governments stimulating their economies by lowering interest rates, I've really been talking about short-term interest rates. In the past, central banks could influence both short-term and long-term interest rates because lowering or raising the former would usually have a similar effect on the latter. Today this is not always the case, because the global integration of national bond markets means that the expectations of investors now exert much more influence over long-term bond yields and, thus, over long-term interest rates. As *The Economist* put it: "Although central banks can set short-term interest rates, they can no longer control long-term rates. The effect of a change in monetary policy on bond yields depends on the market's assessment of its impact on the economy, adding to the unpredictability of it all."[18]

To understand what this actually means, let's consider a hypothetical example. In a situation where investors are already worried about the potential for a rise in inflation in a country (maybe because a more left-of-centre political party has just been elected), it's possible that any attempt by the government to expand the economy by lowering interest rates or by borrowing money to increase social spending will cause investors to panic. If they do, and they sell off the currency and government bonds of that country, it will cause the value of the currency to fall and the yield on bonds to rise, meaning that long-term interest rates will go up. When long-term interest rates go up, it can have the effect of cancelling out the government's attempt to stimulate the economy with lower short-term interest rates. Therefore, while the risk of a falling currency puts indirect pressure on the government not to stimulate the economy, rising bond yields can impose a more direct constraint by pushing up long-term interest rates, which slow the economy back down.

It's important to note that the pressures on governments to give investors the policies they want will vary over time. Sometimes investors seem to tolerate more government spending and higher deficits. But this doesn't mean that the underlying constraints aren't still there. What seems to happen is that fund managers pour money into a country when the government does something to increase the confidence of investors, such as pursuing a policy of very low inflation. Once invested, fund managers, especially foreign ones, have much less incentive to monitor the government — which they now "trust" — on an ongoing basis. Countries like Canada usually account for a very small part of a foreign portfolio and there is little incentive for the fund manager to spend a lot of time and resources keeping an eye on our government. Instead, foreign investors will often ignore the country until something significant happens to call the government's credibility into question. Before this happens, in the period where fund managers trust the government, constraints on a government's policy choices may appear to be much less because investors aren't paying sufficient attention. The government may be able to sneak through a few small measures that investors dislike, or even build up a large deficit. But this isn't the same as having real freedom of policy choice because governments may eventually have to pay for their sins once investors start paying significant attention again.

Fund managers will begin to pay attention if something big happens to make them question their trust in the government. If a more left-leaning political party is elected, for example, fund managers may start to pay close attention. They may worry that a left-of-centre government will try to reduce deficits by lowering interest rates rather than by cutting spending. A financial crisis in another country may also cause

fund managers to worry and take a closer look at policy. As a 1999
report by the IMF notes, "a crisis in one country can serve as a 'wake-
up-call,' inducing financial markets to reassess other countries'
fundamentals."[19] If foreign fund managers start to pay significant attention, they will be more prone to panic if the government implements
a policy that they dislike. And this means that the potential for panic
and price overshooting will impose a real constraint on the policy
choices of the government.

This is the theory. Now let's see what actually happened in Canada
in 1995.

PRICE OVERSHOOTING
AND THE 1995 BUDGET

The Liberal Party of Jean Chrétien, both in opposition and during the
1993 election campaign, argued that the deficit should be reduced by
stimulating the economy rather than by drastic cuts to social programs.
Both Chrétien and Paul Martin had explicitly stated that they would
order the Bank of Canada to place a higher priority on economic
growth than on price stability. But once in power, the Finance Minister
came under immediate pressure not to alter Canada's very low inflation
monetary policy. And in the space of a few short months, Paul Martin
came to believe that if the Liberals made any real changes to monetary
policy, the financial markets would rain punishment down upon them.
As journalists Edward Greenspon and Anthony Wilson-Smith reported
in their bestselling book *Double Vision: The Inside Story of the Liberals in
Power*, Paul Martin came to accept "the view of his new officials and
nearly every person that he knew in the private sector that it would be
better to stick with his party's monetary *bête noire* than risk a financial
market insurrection."[20]

Whether or not the financial markets would have inflicted strong
punishment on Canada at this time is open to question. But it does
seem to have been somewhat likely because investors were starting to
pay close attention to the new Liberal government that had just been
elected on a populist, anti–Bay Street platform. A 1999 report by the

Bank for International Settlements did seem to think that any attempt to lower interest rates more than the financial markets thought was appropriate could have led to a plummeting currency. And a plummeting currency would have forced the government to raise interest rates. The report noted that "movements in exchange rates can generate [a snowball effect] which may prove difficult to stabilize" and that the interest-rate hikes that would have been necessary to defend the currency "might well [have] last[ed] long enough to cause discomfort." It further noted that "Such occurrences have been experienced in Canada on a number of occasions in [the 1990s]" and that "in virtually every instance the episode was sparked by an attempt to lower short-term interest rates more aggressively than the market thought was warranted."[21]

In any case, Paul Martin was sufficiently convinced of the financial markets' power to renew the Bank of Canada's existing 1 to 3 percent inflation target band, meaning that the Liberals had given up their promise to re-focus monetary policy towards stimulating the economy. In fact, Bank of Canada governor John Crow wanted to continue his push for zero inflation, and pushed for the target band to be lowered to 0 to 2 percent. But the Liberals found Crow's position politically unappealing and economically inappropriate. At the end of the day, Crow resigned and was replaced by his deputy governor, Gordon Thiessen. Thiessen was more pragmatic than Crow, but was sufficiently committed to Bay Street's goal of very low inflation that his appointment as governor was enough to reassure investors and ward off any panic.

Once the Liberals had given up lowering interest rates to stimulate the economy, a struggle ensued in the Liberal cabinet over the extent of spending cuts that would be required for the 1995 budget. According to many insiders, one of the most decisive events in this struggle was the "demonstration effect" provided by the Mexican peso crisis. As you'll recall from Chapter 4, the Mexican peso crisis began in December 1994, only a couple of months before Paul Martin's historic deficit-cutting budget of February 1995. The peso crisis provided a strong example of market overreaction and the potential damage that

could be caused by a plummeting currency. Fund managers overreacted
to the Mexicans' attempt to devalue their currency and the value of the
peso fell dramatically.

This lesson was not lost on the Liberals sitting around the cabinet
table in Ottawa. "The Mexican experience was one of those practical
object lessons that politicians understand a hell of a lot better than the
theoretical arguments," recalled Peter Nicholson, an advisor to Paul
Martin on loan from the Bank of Nova Scotia.[22]

As if to reinforce this lesson, the "tequila effect" hit country after
country, eventually making its way to the Canadian dollar. Having
been burned by the devaluation of the peso, fund managers were now
paying greater attention to countries that were seen to be in a similar
situation, particularly those, such as Canada, with large deficits. As a
paper written for the Bank of Canada noted, "The Mexican financial
crisis focussed investor attention on countries experiencing large fiscal
and [trade] imbalances."[23] In the month following the onset of the peso
crisis, the Canadian dollar fell a cent and a half, forcing interest rates to
rise by 1.57 percentage points. To politicians, it seemed as though the
barbarians that had just ransacked Mexico were now at Canada's gate.
Edward Greenspon and Anthony Wilson-Smith made this comment
on the demonstration effect provided by the Mexican experience:
"Mexico would provide a lesson for nation-states in just how dependent they were on the vagaries — even potential irrationalities — of
the financial markets."[24]

When foreign fund managers started to pay close attention to
high-deficit countries like Canada, the issue of deficit reduction became
a test of credibility. Investors became as concerned with the "quality"
of deficit reduction as they were with the quantity. For example, in
Sweden, the February 1995 budget, while working to reduce the
deficit, included a significant number of tax increases. As Greenspon
and Wilson-Smith noted, "The Swedish budget had relied heavily on
tax measures rather than spending cuts, and the markets had responded
by pushing [Sweden's currency] down and interest rates up."[25] So,
where the peso crisis provided a lesson about the potential for market
overreaction and disproportionate punishment, the Swedish experience

emphasized the subjective nature of how investors would determine whether a particular government was "credible." As Paul Martin commented, Sweden "was not important for the fact that their interest rates went through the roof. What Sweden was important for was [to show] that the market would not give you credit for tax actions. A year earlier, the market didn't seem to care how you reduced the deficit. Sweden demonstrated that the market had evolved."[26]

So, by the time Paul Martin stood before Parliament to tighten the nation's collective belt, the Liberal government had learned its lesson. Mexico and Sweden had convinced our political leaders that they were no longer in charge.

In the United States, the Mexican peso crisis and resulting "tequila effect" had a similar impact on the currency. Despite strong economic fundamentals, the dollar's value negatively overshot in the months following the Mexican devaluation. The cause, according to *Business Week*, was simply this: "Stuffed to the gills with dollars after decades of heavy American trade deficits and borrowings, fund managers no longer want to hear vague assurances about America's fiscal health."[27] The peso crisis had helped to raise concerns among investors about all high-deficit countries, but in the American case another important factor was the narrow defeat of the Republican Balanced Budget Amendment in the Senate. Taken together, these factors served to focus and increase investors' concerns regarding the U.S. budget deficit. As economics reporter Chris Farrell comments, "the fundamentals suggest there should be no dollar crisis. The problem lies elsewhere — in the psychology of the foreign-exchange markets. The real fear is that with the balanced budget amendment defeated, U.S. policy-makers will be loath to grapple with difficult choices on the spending side."[28] As in Canada, the falling dollar in the United States lent support to those elements within the government, such as congressional Republicans, who were recommending more substantial spending cuts. The Republican House Speaker, Newt Gingrich, grasped the falling dollar as a symbol of the need for dramatic spending cuts.

At the end of the day, it seems that the increased potential for price overshooting associated with the rise of mutual funds and pension funds increased the pressure on the Liberals to reduce the deficit through spending cuts rather than economic growth triggered by lower interest rates. Because the Mexican peso crisis had focused the attention of investors on high-deficit countries like Canada, there were real constraints on the government's ability to lower interest rates at all. Had they done so, it is quite likely that the Canadian dollar would not just have dropped a little. Rather, with investors already nervous and focusing on deficit reduction as a test of credibility, the dollar was likely to plummet. This is not to say that the government had no options whatsoever. But it does mean that any attempt to stimulate the economy with lower interest rates would have to have been preceded by some measure to lessen the impact of panicking investors. In Chapter 9, we'll discuss what some of these measures could have been.

7

CORPORATE
BOARD GAMES

If 1995 was the year we found out governments could no longer focus on creating jobs and providing well-funded social programs, then 1996 was when we learned that our corporations were also unable to oblige. Once again, it seemed that globalization, technology and the need to compete had created a new set of rules. Academics called it "the flexibilization of labour." According to *Newsweek*, it was "in-your-face-capitalism." Whatever the name, the new rules were simple: "You lose your job, your ex-employer's stock price rises, the CEO gets a fat raise."[1]

At Petro-Canada's 1995 shareholders' meeting, for example, CEO James Stanford told the assembled crowd that the company had just *completed* a "very successful financial turnaround." He also mentioned, by the way, that they were about to dump 700 employees. The next day Petro-Canada's share price rose by 25 cents.[2]

In March of 1996, the *New York Times* spelled out the implications of the new capitalism in a week-long series called "The Downsizing of America." At kitchen tables across the country, the stimulative effects of morning coffee were buttressed by a collage of newspaper headlines stamped on the cover of the Sunday paper: "AT&T's call: 40,000 out." "IBM chief making drastic new cuts; 35,000 jobs to go." "Lockheed Martin to cut 15,000 jobs." Taken on its own, it would have been easy to think that each of these announcements was an isolated event. After all, mass layoffs were hardly unprecedented. But as one read through the article, it became clear that something new was afoot.

"While permanent layoffs have been symptomatic of most recessions, now they are occurring in the same large numbers even during an economic recovery that has lasted five years and even at companies that are doing well," reported the *Times*.[3]

Also new was the fact that it was not just blue-collar workers who were being affected. Middle-class, white-collar employees found themselves without jobs as well. Between 1991 and 1995, almost 2.5 million Americans lost their jobs to corporate restructuring. In the preceding decade, the employment rolls of Fortune 500 companies had already dropped from 16 million in 1980 to 12 million in 1990.[4] As always, tragedy bred comedy. At AT&T, where CEO Robert Allen had just announced his plans to lay off over 40,000 workers, a joke of the gallows-humour variety made the rounds: with so many employees having been shown the door, AT&T would soon stand for "Allen and Two Temps."

In Canada, a similar trend was under way. In 1995, General Motors Canada reduced its workforce by 2,500 at the same time as its profits increased by 36 percent. The same year, the Bank of Montreal saw its profits rise by 20 percent as it shed over 1,400 employees. Between 1988 and 1996, according to a report by the Canadian Centre for Policy Alternatives, thirty-three major Canadian corporations cut their employment rolls by almost 35 percent. Tellingly, these job losses — totalling 216,000 — occurred at a time when the combined revenues of these companies had increased by over $40 billion (CDN).[5]

Downsizing had become so widespread that it was no longer something that happened to "other people." Six degrees of separation had become one or two degrees at best. A poll by the *New York Times* found that nearly three-quarters of all American households were in some way connected to layoffs, with one-third having had a family member downsized, and many of the rest having a friend or neighbour who'd lost a job. For obvious reasons, the term "downsizing" came to take on a whole host of negative connotations. Even mentioning it in polite conversation around the office was considered to be a bit of a faux pas. And its effects on morale were not limited to those who found themselves on the receiving end of a pink slip. To assuage their feeling of guilt, those who pulled the trigger took a page from military training manuals where the act of killing is hidden behind a glossary of sanitized terms. Soldiers don't kill people, they neutralize them. When a bombing sortie accidentally wipes out a group of civilians, it's collateral damage. Likewise, in the business world of the 1990s, you no longer got fired; you got unassigned, separated or outsourced. Corporations didn't downsize; they restructured.

The notion of restructuring is a comfortable one because it seems to imply moving workers around rather than eliminating them; it suggests that those who are laid off will quickly find work elsewhere. Reinforcing this view is the fact that, downsizing notwithstanding, employment has actually increased in the economic boom of the 1990s. It has certainly increased by enough to absorb all of those displaced workers. What is less encouraging, however, is the nature of the replacement work. Specifically, while more jobs are being added than lost, many are part-time jobs or jobs in small companies that offer significantly lower pay and benefits. It is the nature of these new jobs that constitutes one of the further unique characteristics of in-your-face capitalism.

"Whereas twenty-five years ago the vast majority of people who were laid off found jobs that paid as well as their old ones, Labor Department numbers show that now only about 35 percent of laid-off full-time workers end up in equally remunerative or better-paid jobs," reported the *Times*.[6]

And it's not just the downsized who are finding themselves having to work more for less. In the same way that a financial crisis abroad helps to discipline governments at home, workers who keep their jobs are mindful that they could be next. They work longer hours, take fewer sick days and accept fewer raises and benefits in the hopes of avoiding a similar fate.

Where there are losers there are winners; and where there's an oppressed villager, there must be a wealthy landlord. So to tell the story of corporate downsizing, the media set off in search of a villain.

BLAMING CEOS

Standing at the podium before the swanky crowd of the Economic Club of Detroit, Robert J. Eaton, chief executive officer of the Chrysler Corporation, was pleased to be amongst his own. He had a beef to share, one that he felt would not be popular outside the rarified atmosphere of this pro-business environment.

"I'm going to complain about the ongoing demonization of corporate America by some of our prominent politicians and news organizations," he began.

The real problem was that these people had been telling his mother he was a bad man. Mrs. Eaton used to be proud of her little boy. He ate all his peas and worked hard. Hard enough to become the very-well-paid head of one of the country's largest corporations.

But now she was confused.

"That's because every time she opens a magazine or turns on the television, she's told that people like me are no good . . . She reads that people like me fire thousands of other people so we can impress Wall Street and get bigger bonuses for ourselves," explained Mr. Eaton.[7] It seemed that the media had found their villain.

Like any wanted poster, this one was complete with mug shots and a list of crimes. Unlike any wanted poster, it sold on magazine racks across North America. In big, bold letters the banner headline "CORPORATE KILLERS" adorned the cover of *Newsweek*'s issue of February 26, 1996. On the cover and throughout the accompanying article, readers were treated to photographs of the accused and reports of their six- and seven-figure salaries as well as their crimes against humanity: job cuts in the thousands and tens of thousands. If Mr. Eaton was displeased with the magazine's cover, he was downright pissed off at what reporter Allen Sloan had to say inside. Sloan acknowledged the twin pressures of globalization and the need to incorporate labour-saving technology, but charged that "Wall Street and Big Business have made a bad problem worse by being greedheads."

"How many CEOs of big, downsizing companies sacrificed some of their pay and perks to encourage a sense of community? Did they apologize publicly to the people they fired? Did they take any personal responsibility for mistakes that helped cause the problems they're solving with layoffs?" asked Sloan rhetorically.[8]

Soon after the publication of the *Newsweek* and *New York Times* articles, a number of prominent politicians jumped on the anti-CEO bandwagon. From the staunchly protectionist Pat Buchanan on the right to those damn bleeding-heart Democrats on the left, it was open season on executives, who, according to Buchanan, "on one hand, fired their workers and on the other, lined their pockets." Even the business press was getting in on the action. *Business Week*'s two cents on the issue was that "throughout its decade-long restructuring, Corporate America has primarily viewed workers as liabilities rather than assets."[9]

Et tu, Brute?

And while ostensibly mounting a spirited defense on behalf of the corporate downsizers, *The Economist* — that most pro-business of pro-business journals — chose as its cover for February 10 the illustrated mantle of a sweaty, snout-in-the-trough CEO with dollar signs for eyes. Ouch! Now that just hurts.

The media's focus on greedy CEOs as the cause of corporate downsizing is based on the conventional wisdom of a little-known area of economic theory called "corporate governance." Corporate governance refers, naturally, to the way that corporations are governed; that is, the nature of the relationship between those who own the company and those who manage it on a daily basis. When people talk about the

differences between the American, Asian and European models of
economic development, they're often talking about differences in
corporate governance.

In 1932, Adolf Berle and Gardiner Means, a lawyer and economist
respectively, sketched out the contours of the U.S. model of corporate
governance.[10] They argued that the old model of family-owned firms
was being replaced by the modern corporation, which was publicly
listed on the stock exchange. As firms grew and took on shareholders,
the U.S. model of corporate governance became characterized by the
separation of ownership and control; a large number of unconnected
shareholders owned the company, but control was delegated to a
small group of technically specialized managers. And while management
was supposed to be accountable to a board of directors elected by
shareholders, the boards were traditionally composed of management
nominees who tended to defer to the CEO.

Based on this separation of ownership and control, the U.S. model
of corporate governance was fundamentally dependent on the decentralized nature of the U.S. financial system. In Europe and Asia,
financial systems were much more centralized; firms raised money
primarily by getting loans from the large banks. American firms, in contrast, raised capital by selling stocks and corporate bonds to the broader
public. As American management professor Michael Useem notes,
the decentralized nature of the U.S. financial system meant that U.S.
corporations were characterized by the "scattering of stock among
thousands of small owners [which] undercut the capacity of shareholders to oversee their enterprises."[11] What this means in practical
terms is that CEOs were all-powerful because individual shareholders
were too small and too unconnected to challenge their authority. If
individual investors were unhappy with a company's performance, their
only option was to sell their shares.

For journalists and politicians seeking to explain the causes of
corporate downsizing, the Berle-Means model of small, unconnected
shareholders and independent managers naturally leads to a focus on
the decisions of individual CEOs. According to this logic, if CEOs are
all-powerful, any decision to downsize must be theirs and theirs alone.

Among critics of corporate downsizing, the decisions of individual CEOs to pay themselves large salaries while laying off thousands of workers represents nothing more than individual greed.

So if ever there was an oppressed minority in America, it seemed that, by 1996, elite CEOs were now it. Yes, they made gobs of money. Yes, they fired lots of people. But were they really the most nefarious axe-men to walk the earth since Genghis Khan?

In fact, they weren't.

CONCENTRATED POWER AND SHORT-TERM HORIZONS

When a highly paid executive such as Jeffrey Maurer, president of the United States Trust Company, complains that "it isn't all that pleasant these days to be the president or chairman of a large American company," the reaction of most of us falls under the boo-hoo-cry-me-a-river category.[12] We feel about as much sympathy as we do for an executioner who complains that his hand hurts from all that darn chopping. The only problem is, by ganging up on these poor down-trodden CEOs, critics may be venting their anger in the wrong direction. The fact of the matter is that CEOs are no longer the real power in North American boardrooms. The real power behind corporate downsizing and soaring executive salaries is, once again, mutual funds and pension funds.

"Clearly pension funds have become major, if not dominant, players in the Canadian economy. And while the media and government focus on the celebrity corporate elite, their power struggles and divorces, the nondescript pension fund managers are probably the most powerful arbiters of business," wrote *National Post* columnist Bill Tielman in 1999.[13]

Once again, it comes down to concentrated power and short-term investment horizons. Twenty years ago, when the ownership of U.S. stocks was scattered among a large number of individual investors, CEOs were all-powerful because owners were too small and unconnected to challenge their authority. But with the rise of mutual funds and pension funds, stock ownership has become concentrated to such an extent that CEOs can no longer ignore the demands of their large institutional shareholders. In the United States, for example, institutional holdings of corporate stock rose from 16 percent in 1965 to 46 percent in 1990, while individual holdings declined from 84 percent to 54 percent over the same period. By the late 1990s, institutional investors controlled well over half of all shares in large U.S. companies. And by concentrating share ownership, the rise of mutual funds and pension funds has fundamentally altered the balance of power between shareholders on the one hand and managers, workers and other stakeholders on the other.

Now, in the same way that this concentration of stock ownership has increased the ability of investors to exercise influence over corporate managers, so too has it increased their incentives to do so. As Michael Useem argues, institutional investors "turn their attention to corporate governance in part because their great holdings prevent them from readily selling their stake in underperforming companies."[14] Unlike individual investors, who can express their dissatisfaction with a company's performance through the mechanism of "exit" (selling their shares), institutions that own large blocks of shares run the risk of forcing down the stock price as they attempt to sell. Like any market, the stock exchange works on the principle of supply and demand. Trying to sell a large block of shares quickly increases the supply relative to the demand, leading to a fall in the price of the stock and a loss for the investor.

Another constraint on the ability of fund managers to sell their shares is the growing use of an investment strategy known as indexing. Indexing is a passive investment strategy under which a fund manager is mandated to hold shares in the companies that make up a specific stock market index, such as the TSE 300. As long as the fund is mandated to follow an indexing strategy, the fund manager is forced to hold stocks in the index even if they perform poorly. So, because of these problems associated with "exit," mutual funds and pension funds have a much greater incentive to exercise "voice" — that is, to intervene directly in the affairs of a corporation.

In Canada, corporate ownership has always been concentrated. But whereas the boardrooms of Canadian companies were once dominated by a handful of elite families, today power has increasingly been transferred to the mutual funds and pension funds that now own well over one-third of all Canadian stocks, up from only 1 percent two decades ago. John Bart, president of the Canadian Shareowners Association, has argued that the old "Family Compact" of corporate Canada has given way to a "Funds Compact" led by institutions such as the Ontario Teachers' Pension Plan Board and the Ontario Municipal Employees Retirement System.[15] In fact, the Ontario Teachers' Pension Plan alone owns over $18 billion worth of Canadian shares, representing an average of 3 percent of the top 300 companies listed on the Toronto Stock Exchange.[16]

The difference in concentrated ownership today, however, originates in the competitive nature of the investment industry and the fact that fund managers are often under intense pressure to perform strongly in the very short term. And because of these pressures, fund managers demand that companies focus exclusively on "shareholder value," which often translates simply to short-term stock performance. Commenting on the rise of these short-term pressures, Andrew Sigler, former chairman and CEO of Champion International Corporation, noted that the "dramatic change in corporate ownership from individuals to institutions currently works against the ability of companies to manage for the long term. Where once we had patient investors interested in our long-term growth and development, today we are under constant pressure from institutional investors to boost the price of our company's stock and 'provide immediate value to shareholders.'"[17]

This combination of concentrated power and short-term focus on the part of institutional investors explains many of the current trends in corporate restructuring. The first of these trends was the wave of hostile takeovers that became the hallmark of the 1980s as the "decade of greed."

GREED IS GOOD

No movie portrayed the business world of the go-go 1980s more memorably than *Wall Street,* starring Michael Douglas as the villainous

corporate raider Gordon Gekko. The most unforgettable and oft-
quoted scene was Gekko's speech to the shareholders of a company he
was trying to acquire through a hostile takeover. Decked out in the
Armani suit and slicked-back haircut usually reserved for James Bond
villains, Gekko sought to convince the assembled shareholders to sell
him their shares by informing them that "greed is good." The thrust of
Gekko's argument was that a short-term, bird-in-the-hand profit was
far better than any long-term payoff they might receive by backing the
company's management. While *Wall Street*'s Gordon Gekko may not
have been typical of the average real-life corporate raider, he was typical of how the media both focused on, and portrayed, the new breed
of vulture that circled the skies above corporate America.

Corporate raiders were excellent fodder for reporters looking to spice
up the normally dry pages of their newspaper's business section. Their
modus operandi seemed to originate more in the imagination of a
Hollywood screenwriter than in the sleepy business schools populated
by a generation of soon-to-be bankers. For these legendary corporate
raiders, money was made — and made quickly — through hostile
takeovers, in which the raider attempted to accumulate a controlling
block of a company's shares against the wishes of the firm's management. In many cases, these takeovers involved dramatic struggles
between the raider and management for the hearts and minds of the
company's shareholders. On one side of the struggle was the raider,
who was offering to buy the shares at a premium above their current
market value: an immediate profit for shareholders. Against this, the
company's management would plead for the shareholders not to sell
their stock to the raider. What they offered in return was the promise
of greater profits over the long term.

Raiders were also interesting because of what they did after they'd
acquired control. The standard tactic was for the raider to take over the
company and then attempt to realize an immediate profit by breaking
it up and selling off its assets. This was the premise of *Wall Street*'s plot,
where the evil Gordon Gekko was seeking to acquire and break up a
small airline. The movie showed this story as a classic struggle between
good and evil, between the short-term interests of the raider and the

long-term interests of the company. This perception was reinforced by the fact that workers and others in the local community, fearful of the company being broken up, would often side with management in attempting to ward off a potential takeover.

Greedy, get–rich–quick schemers have always existed. So the important question is, what changed in the 1980s to make their raiding operations so feasible? The short answer is the rise of institutional investors and the way that their concentrated power and short-term focus altered the structural context of the U.S. business environment. They brought about this structural change in three ways.

The first was by valuing stocks in a way that made a potential takeover much more profitable. As a representative for the U.S. Business Roundtable testified before Congress, "The pricing of a company's stock that's done by institutional owners is based on a short-term look at its earning potential, having nothing to do with its basic underlying assets . . . That differential between short-term earnings and underlying asset value is what all of the [takeovers] work on, buying at the lower price because of the market, breaking up and selling the assets at their underlying value."[18] In other words, because fund managers often took a short-term view when valuing a company's shares, many firms had a stock-market value that was below their break-up value; that is, the sum total of the assets owned by the company. And this meant that raiders were virtually guaranteed a profit if they could gain control of the firm and sell it off into parts. It also meant that they could offer shareholders a premium price for their shares.

The second way that institutional investors helped to facilitate the takeover wave of the 1980s was through their concentration of share ownership. Takeovers require a would-be raider to convince enough shareholders to sell their stock to give the raider control. This task is made much easier when shares are concentrated in fewer hands. At the same time, the short-term focus of institutional investors meant that when offered the chance to make a quick profit by a raider, they were much more likely to sell their shares and realize the immediate gain. Indeed, a 1989 report by the U.S. Business Roundtable confirmed that "Institutional investors are most likely to sell their shares for a premium in a hostile takeover situation."[19]

The final way that institutional investors contributed to the takeover phenomenon was by providing the financing that raiders needed to gain control of their target companies. In Wall Street parlance, hostile takeovers are often facilitated through a "leveraged buyout," or LBO. Leverage, as you may recall from the discussion of hedge funds in Chapter 5, is just a fancy way of saying "debt," and many of the buy-outs were financed through the use of debt. Popular at the time was for raiders to generate the funds they needed to purchase a target company's stock by selling "junk bonds." Junks bonds are very high-risk bonds, which credit rating agencies generally rank slightly below a day at the track — hence the name. In addition to junk bonds, raiders could raise money from investors by creating a specialized type of investment fund known as an LBO fund. These funds were set up with the express purpose of taking over a company and either breaking it up or downsizing it in order to realize a quick profit.

Institutional investors helped to facilitate takeovers by acting as major investors in the junk bonds and leveraged buyout funds that were used to finance them. In 1988, according to the U.S. Congressional Research Service, pension funds directly purchased 15 percent of all junk bonds, while insurance companies and mutual funds purchased an additional 60 percent of them. A survey by the trade journal *Pension and Investment Age* found that, in 1988, the top 200 public and private pension funds had invested $3.5 billion in leveraged buyouts.[20] And as the U.S. Business Roundtable commented at the time, "Without the funding mechanism of junk bonds and LBO funds, many of today's corporate takeovers would not be possible. Thus, pension funds play a second key role in fueling the takeover phenomenon, in addition to their willing-ness to sell to the highest bidder, by making these pools of financing capital easily available."[21]

While the media tended to focus on the more dramatic individual raiders and financiers, such as Carl Icahn and "Junk Bond King" Michael Milken, the driving force behind the takeover wave of the 1980s was the rise of institutional investors and the way that it con-centrated stock ownership and shifted the focus to shorter-term horizons, altering the structural context of the U.S. business environment. As American management professor Michael Useem argues, "During the mid-1980s, institutional holders played a major role in takeovers and buyouts. They rendered shares to would-be acquirers; they invested in takeover and buyout funds, and they gave votes to strategic block investors. These developments help to explain why mergers and acquisitions of publicly traded companies more than doubled between 1980 and 1988, and leveraged buyouts rose by a factor of ten."[22] In fact, the value of takeovers of all types rose from $12 billion in 1975 to over $260 billion in 1988.[23]

THE CEOS FIGHT BACK

Of course, CEOs didn't just sit quietly by and allow their companies to be taken over. After watching many of their colleagues lose their companies and jobs to the predatory corporate raiders, a number of them began to fight back.

The first way that CEOs fought back was by undertaking measures to make their firms less vulnerable to a takeover. As mentioned earlier, firms were vulnerable to takeovers because of the way that institutional investors valued their stocks. Since fund managers tended to focus on earnings rather than assets, many companies had stock-market values that were below their break-up values. To remedy this situation, a number of CEOs sought to prevent takeovers through measures that immediately boosted the value of their shares, thus making a takeover more expensive and less profitable. The most popular method for boosting share price was for a company to recapitalize, or refinance, itself by exchanging equity for debt. This means that a firm would borrow money and use it to buy back its own shares. When firms repurchase their own shares, it reduces the supply of shares relative to the demand for them, and this has the effect of immediately boosting the stock price.

The fact that the debt of U.S. corporations increased by $840 billion in the mid-1980s at the same time as their equity decreased by almost $300 billion illustrates the widespread nature of this trend.[24] However, while borrowing money to repurchase shares did have the effect of boosting a company's stock price in the short term, the higher debt loads incurred set the firm up for a fall in the long term by making it much more vulnerable to an economic downturn. A 1989 report by the U.S. Business Roundtable summarized the situation this way: "Because institutional investors are pressing for ever-quicker returns to shareholders measured by stock price, corporate managers are too often driven to focus excessively on short-term performance to the detriment of the long-term best interests of the corporation and the economy as a whole. In today's takeover-driven securities markets, corporate managers engage in stock repurchases, recapitalizations and leveraged transactions resulting in higher debt in order to ward off hostile bids."[25]

The second way that corporate managers responded to the threat of takeovers was through the development of various legal defense mechanisms. Most important here was the adoption of "shareholder rights plans," also known as "poison pills." Despite their name, shareholder rights plans are designed to *limit* the power of shareholders in a way that helps management to prevent a hostile takeover. Poison pills come in a variety of forms, but the standard practice in the late 1980s was for management to put a provision in the company charter (the corporate equivalent of a constitution) that allowed shareholders who owned stock before the start of a takeover to purchase additional stock at a substantial discount. The effect of this provision was to discourage raiders by diluting their voting power and, thus, their ability to gain control of the firm.

In the early 1980s, there wasn't a single American firm that had a poison pill in place. But by the end of the decade over two-thirds of the largest U.S. companies had adopted some form of shareholders' rights plan. In addition to putting these provisions in company charters, firms would often adopt "golden parachute" severance packages for managers that would only come into effect in the event of a takeover. This meant that if a company was taken over and the management laid off, the firm would be forced to pay the managers extremely generous severance packages — so generous that they would make any takeover much less profitable. Another anti-takeover defense mechanism was the use of "greenmail" payments to corporate raiders. Basically, the management of a targeted firm would pay the raider to go away by offering him or her a large premium on the shares the raider had already purchased.

Corporate managers also turned to governments for assistance in warding off the raiders. They lobbied for legislation to reinforce poison pills with laws that allowed company directors to reject a takeover bid even if it might benefit shareholders in the short term. Like fund managers, those who sit on a company's board of directors are subject to the requirements of "fiduciary duty." Directors are the representatives of shareholders within a company; fiduciary duty generally requires them to make decisions that are in the best interests of the shareholders. In the case of a takeover, where shareholders are being offered a premium for their shares by a corporate raider, the directors are often legally bound to accept the offer.

To free directors from the risk of lawsuits from shareholders if they rejected such a takeover offer, state governments passed laws to loosen the requirements of their fiduciary duty. One method was for the government to pass an "other constituencies" clause. Such a clause expanded the definition of a director's fiduciary duty to include the interests of "stakeholders," which include any group that has an interest in the company (such as employees, the local community, etc.). "Other constituency" provisions allowed directors to reject a hostile takeover bid if they deemed that it would not best serve the public interest. By 1990, over 80 percent of U.S. states had adopted these types of regulations (there were none a decade earlier). States used these rules to prevent the job losses and economic dislocations that could result from a local company being taken over and sold off for parts.

By the late 1980s, the combination of poison pills, the onset of an economic slowdown and the reduced willingness of investors to extend financing to raiders led to the end of the takeover boom. And it was the collapse of this boom that marked the beginning of the current trend towards corporate restructuring and employee downsizing.

THE RISE OF SHAREHOLDER ACTIVISM

For institutional investors, the takeover wave of the 1980s was a god-send. If a raider took over a firm, the manager of a pension or mutual fund that owned shares in it was sure to make an immediate profit by selling the shares at the raider's premium buying price. If corporate managers tried to prevent a takeover by using debt to boost the stock price, the fund manager still made an immediate profit by hanging on to the shares. Takeovers, and the threat of them, were the stick that forced management to focus exclusively on delivering immediate value to shareholders. So when this stick was removed with the collapse of the takeover boom at the end of the 1980s, institutional investors began to look for new ways to promote "shareholder value."

One answer to this quest was the clout inherent in their ownership of large blocks of corporate shares. While this concentration of stock ownership, as we have seen, made it difficult for fund managers to sell shares in underperforming companies (since the sale itself might force down the stock price), it also made it easier for them to exercise influence over corporate managers. The specific mechanism that allows fund managers to influence CEOs is their ability, as shareholders, to vote on different aspects of corporate policy. When a firm wants shareholder approval for certain types of management decisions, the CEO proposes a resolution for shareholders to vote on. These resolutions are a type of referendum on management policy. Shareholders can also propose their own resolutions. Corporate votes work on the principle of one share, one vote; the more stock you own, the more votes you get. These resolutions are usually voted on at a company's annual general meeting; shareholders who aren't there in person can let their vote be known with a form known as a "proxy." Sometimes a special resolution is voted on by mail. For institutional investors who owned large blocks of shares, exercising their proxy votes and proposing shareholder resolutions became the new tools for influencing corporate managers and promoting shareholder value.

The use of proxy votes by institutional investors was given a boost by three developments in the late 1980s and early 1990s. The first was a 1988 regulatory ruling by the U.S. Department of Labor, which stated that proxy voting was part of a fund manager's fiduciary duty. To comply with the ruling, a number of pension funds began to develop specific procedures for voting on company resolutions. The second development was the success of anti-Apartheid activists in using proxy votes and shareholder resolutions to stop American companies from doing business with South Africa. For fund managers, the success of the anti-Apartheid ethical investment campaign convinced them that proxies could be a powerful force for influencing how corporations operate.

The final development that encouraged the use of proxy votes was a 1992 change in U.S. Securities and Exchange Commission (SEC) rules on investor communication. Prior to this rule change, if ten or more of a company's shareholders discussed a shareholder resolution, they were required to go through the costly procedure of sending a notice to all shareholders and filing a report with the SEC. Under the new rules, any number of shareholders can communicate orally without restriction as long as they are not seeking to cast votes for others. This rule change is significant because it made it much easier for U.S. fund managers to coordinate their activities when trying to influence corporations through proxy votes.

Not all fund managers got involved in trying to influence corporate policy directly. The most active of the institutional investors in this period were the pension funds of public-sector employees. There were a number of constraints that prevented the fund managers of private-sector pension funds and mutual funds from being active shareholders. The first constraint was the fear of retaliation. Private pension funds are set up by a company for the benefit of its employees. If the managers of these funds attempt to influence the policy of another corporation, the potential exists for the target company to retaliate using the clout of its own pension fund. As Claude Lamoureux, head of the Ontario Teachers' Pension Plan, observed, "It is a little foolish (and career shortening) for a private fund manager to, in essence, attack another company."

For external fund managers, whose business is managing pension funds on behalf of a number of companies, the fear of alienating potential customers provided a different sort of constraint on their ability to directly promote shareholder value by directly intervening in corporate decisions. If you're an external fund manager, you may not want to vote proxies against the management of General Motors because you may hope to someday win the contract to manage the GM pension plan. This fear of alienating potential customers can also apply to mutual fund companies. Remember that many mutual fund companies are really asset management companies that have both retail and wholesale divisions. The retail side of the business sells shares in mutual funds to the general public. The wholesale side provides external fund management services for private-sector pension plans. So, many mutual fund managers have an interest in not alienating any companies whose pension plans might be potential clients for their wholesale division.

Despite these constraints, institutional investors, particularly the large public pension funds, did become increasingly active in trying to promote shareholder value through the use of proxy votes and shareholder resolutions. And their concentrated power meant that they often had the clout to get what they wanted. By the mid-1990s, they were using this power to restructure corporations in ways that made the CEO much more accountable to the short-term interests of shareholders. This process of making CEOs more subservient to investors involved three main steps.

STEP 1: CORPORATE BOARD GAMES

In their push to promote shareholder value, the first thing pension funds set their sights on was the structure of corporate boards. Boards of directors are to CEOs what the Senate is to the House of Commons. They are, in theory at least, the supposed realm of experienced wisdom and sober second thought, there to watch over managers but to intervene only in extreme circumstances. They are elected by shareholders to represent their interests and to ensure, by voting on management policy, that the CEO and management are accountable to the firm's owners.

But as we saw earlier, this notion of elected boards and accountable management was more fiction than fact — though the analogy of the Canadian Senate is probably a near-perfect fit. In reality, most corporate boards were classic old boys' clubs. CEOs often appointed themselves chairman of the Board and nominated their buddies, often other CEOs or ex-politicians, for election as directors. The result was that boards of directors had become the sleepy lapdogs of corporate CEOs. They would pretty much approve whatever decisions management put forth. And by appointing each other as directors on their own boards, CEOs would often enter into informal back-scratching arrangements, with everybody approving everybody else's decisions.

The whole insiders-only set-up of corporate boards was designed to make CEOs all-powerful by ensuring that shareholders would have no opportunity to challenge their decisions. The advantage of this system was that the day-to-day affairs of the firm could be left to the experts, free from short-term pressures applied by transient shareholders. Right or wrong, the only reason management got away with this set-up was because shareholders were small, unconnected and far too unorganized to assert themselves against management. Most shareholders didn't even bother to vote on company resolutions, let alone propose their own resolutions.

Of course, all this changed with the rise of institutional investors and the resulting concentration of share ownership. To right the wrongs of corporate governance, fund managers began to wield their new-found tools of proxy votes and shareholder resolutions. They began to demand reforms to the structure of company boards and other mechanisms that had served to insulate management from accountability to shareholders. Topping their list of demands was the separation of the roles of CEO and chairman of the Board. No longer would shareholders tolerate a CEO wearing both hats. They also demanded the nomination of directors who were independent of the CEO, to do away with the cronyism of the past and to make sure that boards would pay heed to their interests. A final thrust of this corporate governance reform movement was to demand that companies remove, or at least water down, the poison pills that protected management from the threat of a hostile takeover.

Taken together, these demands for reform were promoted by fund managers as a form of "best practice" for corporations. At the vanguard of the corporate governance reform movement were the public pension funds, the most prominent of which was the California Public Employees Retirement System, known as CalPERS among its close friends. From the late 1980s onward, CalPERS promoted best practices in corporate governance across the United States. Typical of the CalPERS strategy was its 1988 decision to back the management of Texaco during a hostile takeover bid in exchange for the company appointing independent directors to its board. In a similar manoeuvre, CalPERS teamed up with the New York Employees Pension Fund to pressure General Motors to accept a resolution making at least half of its directors independent from its management.

Further north, pension funds such as the Ontario Teachers' Pension Plan and the Ontario Municipal Employees Retirement System have promoted similar reforms in corporate governance through direct contacts with managers and, when necessary, through the use of proxy votes. "We are in the midst of a gradual revolution in corporate governance. The key factor in this revolution is . . . the emergence of active institutional shareholders who participate fully in the governance process," said Ontario Teachers' head Claude Lamoureux. In 1995, the Ontario Teachers' Pension Plan voted proxies in 317 publicly listed companies, with about a third of these votes going against management. Commented Matthew Barrett, former CEO of the Bank of Montreal, "there is no doubt in my mind that the most powerful force for change has been the rise of the institutional investor . . . In effect, institutional investors have become the gear mechanism that transmits the demands of the marketplace to the boardroom. They can and do decide the fate of major corporations."[26]

In addition to the efforts of individual pensions funds, the promotion of best practices in corporate governance has become more centralized and strategic through the formation of various shareholders' rights organizations, such as the Council of Institutional Investors in the United States, the National Association of Pension Funds in the United Kingdom, and Fairvest Securities Corporation in Canada. Funded primarily by institutional investors, shareholders' rights organizations monitor firms' adherence to best practices in corporate governance and publish "hit lists" of those who don't measure up. They also monitor and evaluate company resolutions and advise shareholders on how to vote their proxies, as well as coordinating shareholder pressure on poor performers.

By the mid-1990s, the corporate governance reform movement had achieved most of its aims. The campaign to promote "best practices" was so successful that it became part of North American corporate culture. CEOs began to reform their boards proactively to avoid being placed on a hit list of poor performers. And as boards were altered to give institutional investors more direct power over corporate policy, this shareholder influence was increasingly "locked in." However, while reforms to corporate boards were a necessary condition for promoting greater shareholder value, it wasn't sufficient to ensure that fund managers would get the short-term stock performance they demanded. For this to happen, a few examples would have to be made.

STEP 2: WALK SOFTLY AND CARRY A BIG STICK

As any good Mafia don will tell you, power is meaningless unless you're willing to back it up. If you want to be a tough guy and compel obedience among those around you, sometimes you have to knock a few heads together. In corporate America, institutional investors knew that their newly achieved influence on company boards simply wasn't enough. So, in the early 1990s, they began to knock a few CEOs' heads together.

If a firm's management was lagging in its effort to provide immediate value to shareholders, fund managers would either dictate policy to them or take the more extreme measure of having the board of directors dump the CEO. In 1992, CalPERS and other pension funds reacted to declining profits and share values at General Motors by pressuring the board of directors to install a new CEO, who then cut the company's North American workforce by 23 percent. As management professor Michael Useem observed, "the new CEO installed by the GM board well understood his mandate to reduce operating costs and restore shareholder value."[27]

General Motors's former CEO, Robert Stempel, wasn't the only executive-suite casualty. In 1993, institutional investors directly intervened to dump underperforming CEOs at IBM, Westinghouse, Eastman Kodak, American Express, Apple Computer, Eli Lilly and Scott Paper to name a few. And as *The Economist* reported, "The abrupt departures at GM, IBM, Westinghouse and American Express were all prompted by enraged institutional shareholders, who demanded that board directors act quickly to restore confidence in firms that were floundering."[28]

Direct intervention in corporate policy has also become a favourite tactic for a new type of "value" investment fund. The managers of normal value investment funds seek to identify and invest in firms that the market has underpriced and then wait patiently for the stock price to go up. The new type, such as Heine Securities, the Lens Fund and Relational Investors, are nowhere near as patient. They identify firms that haven't yet restructured and then pressure the CEO to undertake measures that will realize immediate increases in shareholder value. This comment by Nell Minow of the Lens Fund in 1996 shows how successful these measures can be: "Rather than invest in a stock and hope it goes up, we spur management and the board to do a better job. We have invested in seven companies in our history. All had major restructurings, all but one replaced the CEO . . . and all of them responded to our requests that they do better."[29]

One example of how these funds operate is found in the role played by mutual fund manager Michael Price of Heine Securities in the banking merger between the Chase Manhattan Corporation and the Chemical Banking Corporation. In 1995, Price disclosed that his funds had become the largest single shareholder in the Chase Manhattan Bank, with 6 percent of Chase's stock. Seeking to realize an immediate gain, Price pressured Chase's management to either break up or sell off the bank. Within a few months of Price's demands, Chase announced a merger with the Chemical Bank, which created the largest bank in the United States. As is typical in these kinds of mergers, shareholders realized an immediate benefit, while employees realized that they were out of a job. The outcome of the Chase–Chemical merger? About a billion dollars in costs were saved, 12,000 employees lost their jobs, and Price's mutual funds achieved a one-day premium of $84 million and an overall gain of $275 million — a 70 percent return in just six months.

Another example of this new type of "value" fund is the AmeriMex Maquiladora Fund set up by U.S. and Mexican investors. The fund's mandate is to target U.S. firms and encourage them to relocate their production facilities to lower-cost export processing zones (the "maquiladoras") on Mexico's northern border.

In Canada, the same trends have been taking place, but in a much quieter way. Notwithstanding the claims of Molson's Joe Canadian, Canadians *are* more polite and less confrontational than their American counterparts. So, too, are our fund managers. Rather than dumping CEOs or seeking to publicly embarrass them through the publication of hit lists, Canadian fund managers such as Claude Lamoureux tend to exercise their influence in a more subtle manner. "We've tended to be fairly quiet about it," says Lamoureux, "but if we think that a company is not running the way that it could be, we'll talk to the management or the board quietly, not with guns blazing, but to see if these boards would implement some of our ideas." Of course, it's not always all sunshine and lollipops, even in the Great Polite North. As Lamoureux opines, "We like to act quietly, but on occasion you have to be pre-pared for war."

Changing the structures of corporate boards was the stick that fund managers wielded to intimidate CEOs. Occasionally they would use this stick to dump a CEO and set an example for the rest. But to fully bring CEOs over to their side, the stick from behind had to be rein-forced by the carrot dangled in front.

STEP 3: KISS AND MAKE UP

Like any leadership battle within a political party, once you've defeated your opponent, it's usually a good idea to kiss and make up. To make nice with corporate managers in a way that would bring them onside to the cause of shareholder value, fund managers promoted the use of stock options to tie the interests of CEOs directly to the company's stock price. Stock options are a type of derivatives contract that allows their owner to purchase stock, at some point in the future, at a pre-set price. When the company's stock price moves up to or beyond this price, the owner converts the options into stock and can sell them for a profit.

At the behest of institutional investors, CEOs today are increasingly paid in stock options to link their overall pay more directly to their ability to deliver immediate value to shareholders. As *The Economist* reported, "Now, almost every big firm uses equity [through stock options] as a form of management incentive, up from around half ten years ago."[30] In 1998, stock options accounted for 53.3 percent of the total compensation given by America's top 100 companies to their CEOs, up from 26 percent in 1994 and only 2 percent in the mid-1980s.[31] For an individual CEO, this shift to pay-for-performance is significant because stock options now account for about two-thirds of an average CEO's compensation package, up from only one third in the 1960s. And this means that, if a CEO wants to boost his or her pay, the most effective way is to focus on short-term measures that will have a nearly immediate effect on the stock price.

THE RISE OF THE SHORT-TERM CORPORATION

Whether through the carrot of stock options or the stick of being replaced, today's CEOs are under enormous pressure to deliver share-holder value in the form of an immediate improvement in stock price performance. So, despite the media's focus on greedy CEOs, the real powers behind mega-mergers, mass layoffs and soaring executive salaries are mutual funds and pension funds. The managers of these funds are under enormous pressure to make sure their portfolios perform strongly in the short term. And through their concentrated power, they've been able to transfer these pressures to those who run our largest corporations. Today, it's the institutional investors, not the CEOs, who determine the fate of large corporations. Gerry McGoey, the former chief financial officer of BCE Inc., has commented that the managers of pension funds "have far more clout than the Old Establish-ment ever did."[32]

But why, specifically, does the short-term focus and growing clout of institutional investors translate into corporate downsizing and mega-mergers? Because the easiest way to boost your stock price in the very short term is by cutting costs rather than increasing productivity or market share. Laying off workers and selling assets, through mergers or otherwise, are about cutting costs. Firms can use the cost savings from these measures to buy back their own shares. As we discussed earlier, this repurchasing by a company of its own shares serves to decrease the supply of the company's stock relative to the demand for it. The result is an immediate increase in the share price.

This method of using layoffs and asset sales to fund stock repurchases has become widespread. In 1998, U.S. firms announced share repur-chases worth $220 billion, compared to only $20 billion in 1991.[33] According to a recent study by George Fenn and Nellie Lang of the U.S. Federal Reserve Bank, the primary purpose of these repurchases has been to return cash to shareholders.[34] More often than not, "share-holder value" is just a sanitized term for short-term stock performance based on downsizing. "Companies aren't put together to create jobs. The number one priority is creating shareholder wealth," explains Bob Bertram, senior vice-president of the Ontario Teachers' Pension Plan.[35]

Downsizing, cost-cutting and stock repurchases have become the new one-size-fits-all strategy of corporate turnaround specialists such as "Chainsaw" Al Dunlap and Louis Gerstner. In 1994, when Gerstner replaced ousted CEO John Akers as the head of IBM, he immediately set about applying this magic formula so beloved by fund managers. Within a year, Gerstner had laid off almost half of IBM's workforce — over 180,000 employees. He also repurchased over $10 billion worth of IBM stock, giving a quick, massive boost to the share price. For his efforts, "the Holy Terror" (as Gerstner was described by *Fortune* in reference to his devout Christian leanings) received almost $70 million worth of stock options.

In Canada, the pressure to boost stock prices through downsizing has been equally intense. Fred Telmer, CEO of Canadian steel maker Stelco

Inc., understands this pressure well. In an interview with the *Globe and Mail* he noted that fund managers are under tremendous pressure to perform strongly in the short term and that they, in turn, pressure corporate managers to boost stock prices, often through imprudent job slashing. In 1995, after Stelco had already reduced its payroll to 12,356 workers from a 1980 high of over 26,000, Telmer was being pressured for further cuts, cuts that he felt would not be in Stelco's long-term best interest. "A lot of people [were] saying, 'Why aren't you getting on with this? When are you going to get rid of all those people?'" he said. Telmer understood, however, that Bay Street knew little about the business of making steel; that sacking all those employees would cost a bundle in severance packages and leave the firm with too few employees to actually run the company. In the end, he managed to convince shareholders that the thousands of workers already laid off were enough and that they would just have to trust him.[36]

Other Canadian companies have not been so lucky. According to a study by the Conference Board of Canada, over half of corporate Canada underwent some form of downsizing between 1995 and 1997. And as *Maclean's* business columnist Deirdre McMurdy observes, this pressure to downsize is being strongly reinforced by the growing use of stock options. "The excessive use of stock options reinforces the already intense focus on share prices. North American investors have become accustomed to quarterly — if not instant — gratification from their holdings. And that has greatly contributed to this decade's mania for corporate downsizing and narrow focus. Layoffs and asset sales, for example, have become one of the most efficient ways to boost stock price in recent years," said McMurdy.[37]

While everybody in business and finance knows that institutional investors are the driving force behind the recent trend towards corporate restructuring, they don't often say it in public. Trends such as downsizing and mergers are usually attributed to the pressures of the product market, rather than the financial market. CEOs and business pundits generally argue that companies need to restructure in order to be competitive in the new global economy — unless firms streamline themselves and reduce labour costs, their competitors will produce better quality products more cheaply and the firm will eventually be driven out of business.

Now, while there's no doubt some truth to this argument, it doesn't explain why mass layoffs seem to be a primarily North American phenomenon. If all corporations around the world need to compete with each other for customers, why haven't firms in Europe and Asia been downsizing to the same extent? The answer is that institutional investors are nowhere near as powerful in these countries as they are in North America. Firms in Asia and continental Europe still rely much more heavily on banks than on the stock market for financing. And this means that they aren't subject to the same short-term pressures that fund managers put on North American CEOs. As *The Economist* notes, "In Japan and much of continental Europe . . . firms often accept broader obligations that balance the interests of shareholders against those of other 'stakeholders.'"[38]

In the end, the pressure to downsize has more to do with improving a firm's short-term *financial* performance than with making the company more globally competitive. But if downsizing isn't absolutely necessary from a business point of view, does it at least work? As you can probably tell by the title of the next section, the answer is somewhat less than a resounding yes.

SHORT-TERM GAIN, LONG-TERM PAIN

While layoffs and asset sales have helped to improve corporate *financial* performance in the short term, the evidence on their long-term benefits is much more open to question. "What [fund managers] are trying to do is build value so they can show a profit," says Stephen Jarislowsky, who sits on the boards of a number of Canadian corporations and who runs an investment counselling firm in Montreal. "It can do alot of good in the short-run but it can hurt in the long run . . ."[39]

A study conducted by Watson Wyatt Worldwide validates Jarislowsky's view. In a survey of 148 firms that had undergone downsizing, the study found that "relatively few companies accomplished their goals." While 62 percent reduced their costs, only 37 percent increased profits, only 17 percent improved their competitiveness and only 40 percent increased their productivity. Marc Mentzer, a commerce professor at the University of Saskatchewan, found similar results in his study of 250 large Canadian firms over an eight-year period. What Mentzer's study revealed was that "There is no clear relationship between downsizing and profit."[40]

To illustrate why the downsizing strategy often fails to deliver, consider the impact of corporate turnaround expert Al Dunlap. When Dunlap took over as the head of Scott Paper in 1994, his focus was on cost-cutting to increase shareholder value. Dunlap laid off a third of the company's employees, cut spending on research and development, sold off millions in assets, closed a number of factories and put an end to charitable donations. Within two years, Scott's share price had increased exponentially. In the end, though, Scott Paper, which had been the top-selling paper company in the world when Dunlap took over, had lost market share on its core businesses of paper towel, toilet paper and facial tissues, and was eventually merged with its former competitor Kimberly-Clark.

To explain the long-term pain that can result from a short-term strategy of downsizing and cost-cutting, Stephen Roach, a chief economist at investment bank Morgan Stanley, makes a useful distinction between efficiency (which benefits shareholders) and productivity (which benefits the economy as a whole). "Downsizing means making do with less — realizing efficiencies by pruning both labor and capital. Sustained productivity growth, however, hinges on getting more out of more — deriving increased leverage from an economy's (or a company's) expanding resource base."[41] In other words, while layoffs and asset sales may offer a one-time improvement in efficiency and the share price, they can often leave corporations without the resources necessary to increase productivity and market share over the long term. As Roach argues, "Instead of focusing on investment in innovation and human capital — the heavy lifting required to boost long-term productivity — corporate strategies have become more and more focused on downsizing and compressing labour costs. The result is increasingly hollow companies that may be unable to maintain — let alone expand — market share in a rapidly growing economy."[42]

If downsizing is bringing few economic benefits, its impact on society more generally is even less encouraging.

THE RISE OF THE SHORT-TERM SOCIETY

Corporations are more than just economic and legal entities. They're the places most of us work. They determine where and how we work, how much money we have and the hours we have on and off the job. For many of us, work is more than what we do for a living; it's about who we are and about how society views us. When corporations and the nature of work change, so too does much of society.

In sociological and political terms, the most important impact of the downsizing phenomenon is the way that it has contributed to a growing polarization within society. As we saw at the beginning of this chapter, downsizing involves the shift away from a workforce characterized by secure, full-time employment with decent pay and benefits to one that is increasingly dominated by part-time and contract work, with lower pay, fewer benefits and less job security. At the same time, those who keep their jobs often work longer hours, accept fewer raises and benefits and suffer from decreased morale because of the fear that they could lose their jobs at any time, for reasons that have little to do with their merit. As a 1999 article in *USA Today* reported, "Worker insecurity — that gnawing anxiety that your job could be eliminated even if you're a good worker — persists despite the best economic conditions in half a century."[43] In fact, according to a survey by the Chicago-based consultants International Survey Research, job insecurity peaked in 1997 and, while it dropped somewhat by 1999, was still three times higher than during the middle of the recession in the early 1980s.[44] The fear of asking for a raise, engendered by wave after wave of downsizing, is one of the key factors behind continued low inflation despite a booming economy and falling unemployment.

And just in case anyone thought that the downsizing phenomenon was simply about such pecuniary matters as job losses and declining wages, each installment in the *New York Times*'s "Downsizing of America" series went on to catalogue the social effects of mass layoffs. It was a sad tale indeed. Increased workloads were leaving people with less time to spend with their families and in their communities. The result was a divorce rate 50 percent higher than average among families where one earner — usually the husband — had lost his or her job and couldn't quickly find an equivalent one. Sociologists were reporting a decline in community participation and less involvement in parent-teacher associations, town meetings, civic clubs and church events.[45]

On the other side of the tracks, the 1990s has witnessed an exponential growth in the salaries of CEOs and senior corporate managers. For average employees, downsizing has led to stagnating wages, low benefits and little job security, while, for corporate managers who are paid with stock options, it has led to soaring salaries as the financial markets reward firms that are seen to be cutting costs. In the 1990s, executive pay has increased massively because of corporate downsizing and the bull market in North American equities. Among 365 of the largest U.S. companies, CEO pay climbed by 35 percent in 1997, while worker pay rose by only 2.6 percent. American CEOs today make approximately 365 times the average pay of workers; in 1965 the figure was 44 times.[46]

Beyond simple measures of growing inequality, what is also new in the 1990s is growing evidence that mobility between classes is slipping. A number of recent studies have followed the same sample of individuals over many years. In the past, most studies of inequality relied on U.S. Census Bureau surveys that took an annual snapshot of income distribution. The new studies trace long-run mobility using data from, for example, a University of Michigan survey that has followed a nationally representative sample of 5,000 families since 1967. A key finding of these new studies was a stratification of the economy in the 1990s; workers at the bottom became less likely to move up in their lifetimes.[47] It is becoming increasingly rare for individuals to rise from the factory floor to the upper echelons of a firm's management, because many of the downsized jobs are first-line managerial jobs that used to be the first step in upward mobility. But as Henry Schacht, former CEO of the Cummings Engine Company, notes, "today those stairs don't exist."[48]

The middle rungs of the corporate ladder are being removed by downsizing, making it much more difficult for people to make the leap from lower to upper income levels. High levels of inequality are always a source of political tension, but in the United States the population has tended to accept inequality in return for a higher *potential* for upward mobility. Today, however, as William J. McDonough, president of the Federal Reserve Bank of New York, notes, "You can't take solace anymore in the American dream of working hard and migrating up through society . . . That still exists in our society, but we're kidding ourselves if we don't realize that the degree of stickiness of people in lower earnings levels is a new problem."[49]

The rise of institutional investors has fundamentally altered the landscape of corporate North America. The concentration of stock ownership in their hands, and the short-term view they tend to take, are the driving force behind mega-mergers, mass layoffs and soaring executive salaries. For a privileged few these trends have led to rising wages and better lives. For many of the rest, however, they've led to stagnating incomes and social problems. Whether these trends are offset by the benefits of the rise of mass investment and of mutual fund returns is the subject of the next chapter.

8

THE POLITICS OF THE NEW INVESTMENT CULTURE

The prize for the best encapsulation of the political implications of the mass investment revolution probably goes to this statement from *The Economist*: "If you had to create capitalism from scratch, and you wanted to make it popular, the first thing you would do is invent mutual funds."[1] Mutual funds have brought more and more individuals into the financial markets over the past decade in a way that creates the perception that much of the North American population is benefitting from the current bull market in North American equities.

There is no question that mass investment is a real phenomenon. As I write this chapter in 2000, almost 60 percent of American households owned stock, compared with 25 percent in 1987 and only 3 percent in 1929. In Canada today we see a similar situation: almost half of the population now has some stake in the financial markets. Also important, in terms of creating the perception that stock market gains are being widely distributed, is the fact that in 1996, 18 percent of U.S. households with annual incomes below $35,000 owned mutual funds, while 41 percent of households with incomes between $35,000 and $50,000 owned mutual funds. Here in Canada, over half of those who contribute to mutual funds through RRSPs have annual incomes of less than $40,000 (CDN).

With mutual fund ownership increasing and broadening, more and more individuals now appear to have a direct material interest in the conservative economic policies that benefit investors, such as very low inflation, cutbacks to social programs, low capital gains taxes and the focus on shareholder value within corporations. And even though these policies negatively affect most people in their roles as citizens and workers, the immediate benefits to their mutual fund returns may serve to artificially alter their political outlook. The *Washington Post* argues: "As more and more Americans gain a stake in stocks, their views undoubtedly will change on such matters as business regulation, taxes, anti-trust policy, trade and even foreign affairs."[2]

Perhaps even more important to the perceived intersection of the interests of Wall Street and Main Street is the contribution mutual fund returns have made to the rising net worth of many households even as their real incomes have declined. In Canada, real incomes, after rising by an average of 2.9 percent per year between 1961 and 1989, actually declined by an average of 1 percent per year between 1989 and 1997. Add this up and it means that the real incomes of Canadians fell by over 7.5 percent over this period. Part of this decline is the result of lower returns from bank deposits and other interest-bearing investments; the total decline in wages and salaries in Canada during the 1990s was about 3.5 percent.

But even though incomes have been declining, household net worth (assets minus debts) has continued to rise. Between 1961 and 1989, household net worth grew by 2.9 percent per year, a figure that corresponds to the rise in incomes during that time. The growth of household net worth has been slowing in the 1990s, but it hasn't stopped. Household net worth grew at about 1.3 percent per year during the last decade of the century, with most of this growth coming from capital gains on rising stock values. These grew at double the rate of gains from real household assets such as homes and land. By 1997, net financial wealth accounted for about 45 percent of total household net worth, up from only 35 percent in 1980.[3] This means that falling wages, on average, are being somewhat offset by rising returns from mutual funds and other financial vehicles. As *Globe and Mail* economics reporter Bruce Little observed, "There are millions of Canadians whose incomes from working have fallen, but who do have mutual-fund investments, employer pension plans or personal pension plans on which they have made compensating gains."[4]

In the United States, similarly, the median American wage has declined by almost 3 percent between 1989 and 1996, but household net worth has roughly doubled, to a national total of $35 trillion in 1999.[5] It was only $16.8 trillion in 1987. And while higher values for tangible assets such as homes and cars account for some of this gain, most of it has come from financial assets, including approximately $8 trillion in stock gains.[6] So, south of the border, too, falling wages have been offset by rising stock prices and mutual fund returns.

The revolution of mass investment has put more and more North Americans into a curious situation in terms of the economic policies that they believe will best serve their interests: the same policies that benefit individuals in their role as investors are also hurting them in their roles as workers and citizens. *Newsweek* put it like this: "Growing numbers of Americans have been cast into a psychological twilight zone. As workers, they often fear the harsh management of the 1990s, with its constant 'restructurings'; as mini-capitalists, they crave 'shareholder value.'"[7] The same psychological "twilight zone" applies to government policies. Very low inflation helps to maintain the value of investments, but at the same time the higher real interest rates which low inflation requires create higher unemployment and lower wages. Cuts to capital gains taxes allow people to keep more of their investment profits, but they also help to deny governments the resources to provide well-funded social programs.

WHAT'S GOOD FOR FIDELITY IS GOOD FOR AMERICA

Despite these contradictions, conservatives have latched onto the revolution of mass investment as a justification for governments pursuing the types of economic policies that have traditionally been demanded by Wall Street and Bay Street. They point to the increase in mass investment as a sign that the interests of the financial community and those of ordinary citizens coincide: that because we're all investors now, free markets and conservative economic policies benefit the bulk of the population.

This claim is a variation on an old theme. In the postwar era, the interests of business were often promoted through the argument that "what is good for General Motors is good for America." Today, given the growing dominance of the financial community and the shift from corporations to mutual funds as the source of the average person's retirement security, conservative policies are now being justified through the argument that "what is good for Fidelity Investments is good for America." The rise of mass investment is having important political effects as it creates the perception among policy-makers and the wider population that this view is correct.

An increasing number of media articles, with titles such as "All Capitalists Now" and "Why We're All Married to the Market," have pushed the notion of a new investor democracy by promoting the general view that "financial markets do not just represent the rich; most people have some savings, whether in a small savings account, a mutual fund or their future pension."[8]

Moving from the general to the specific, we see that this line of reasoning has been used to justify a number of conservative policies. *The Economist* has employed it in attempting to justify the growing influence of investors on government policy. In a stretch of reality that would make any spin doctor proud, one article argued that "in some ways, capital markets, driven by the decisions of millions of investors and borrowers, are highly 'democratic.' They act like a rolling twenty-four-hour opinion poll [on government policies]."[9] The message here is that individuals should not be concerned that they are losing their ability to influence government policy through their role as citizens because it is more than offset by their ability to discipline governments through their role as investors.

The revolution of mass investment became an important factor in helping the Clinton administration to justify its post–peso crisis bailout of Mexico at U.S. taxpayers' expense. As *Time* magazine argued,

> What many Americans discovered last week was that for all the
> beltway rhetoric pitting Wall Street against Main Street, Wall Street
> long ago intersected with Main Street. At risk in [Mexico] were not
> only U.S. banks and giant investment firms but mutual funds held
> by tens of millions of little-guy investors who bet their savings on
> double-digit yields in emerging markets like Mexico. "This wasn't
> about bailing out Wall Street" a congressional staff member said of
> [the rescue package], "but about mutual and pension funds and that
> means average Americans."[10]

In Canada, a similar strategy was employed to promote the further deregulation of the investment industry by raising the allowable foreign content (the amount of money that can be invested outside of Canada) for funds held in tax-subsidized RRSPs. This policy makes it easier for investors to put pressure on the government, since it would allow them to take more of their money out of the country. Yet a lobby group for the Canadian mutual fund industry argued that

> [i]t is not just wealthy Canadians who are saving for retirement.
> It is average Canadians who realize that the government may not
> be able to support them in their golden years . . . A change in the
> foreign property rule would go a long way to ensure that Canadians'
> retirement nest eggs are not too concentrated in one basket and that
> these nest eggs can take advantage of growth industries in other
> countries.[11]

The bottom line is that these "what's good for Fidelity is good for America" arguments are gaining ground because of the way that mass investment has created a perception that the interests of Main Street are now linked to those of Wall Street and Bay Street. But as we will see below, this view does not conform to reality.

THE LIMITS OF INVESTOR DEMOCRACY

On average, the real incomes of North Americans declined somewhat in the 1990s. On average, these losses were partially offset by gains from the current stock-market boom. Therefore, according to conservatives, on average, the policies that benefit the financial community should also be benefitting most people. Averages are not always the best way to see what's going on in a country because they can mask very different experiences. If you have your head in an oven and your feet in a freezer, your average temperature might appear to be just fine. Similarly, if a small portion of the population controls the bulk of the wealth while a large number of people are badly off, the average can make it look as if everyone is doing okay. And so it is with the financial assets of North Americans.

The revolution of mass investment means that over half of the North American population now has a stake in the stock market. While an optimist would note that the glass of stock ownership is half full, a pessimist might point out that it is also half empty — that half of the population has no stake in the stock market whatsoever. Also, of the half that does have such a stake, over 40 percent (which is 20 percent of the entire population) own only negligible amounts of stock. As a recent study by economists James Poterba and Andrew Stamwick reveals, this means that about 70 percent of U.S. households still own few or no stocks either directly or through mutual funds.[12] Commenting on these findings, *Business Week* observed that "juicy market returns do little for the average person. Instead, they fatten the wallets of the top quarter of households, which owns 82 percent of all stocks."[13]

In Canada, a survey conducted by Marketing Solutions Inc. in 1996 found evidence of a similar concentration in the benefits of mutual fund returns among upper-income earners. According to the survey, 70 percent of those making over $70,000 a year owned mutual funds, while only 14 percent of those earning less than $20,000 did so. Thus, as Marketing Solutions manager Dan Richards notes, "High [mutual fund] ownership among wealthier families flies in the face of conventional wisdom that mutual funds appeal largely to unsophisticated investors with lower incomes."[14]

What this means in practical terms is that the "intersection between Wall Street and Main Street" is more about perception than reality. If half of all households are receiving zero benefits from the stock market, and another 20 percent are receiving very small benefits, then declining incomes are *not* being offset by stock gains for the bulk of the population. The greatest declines in incomes are being experienced by the bottom 70 percent of the income pyramid. This large segment of the population, the bulk of society, has the most to lose from higher unemployment, stagnating wages, corporate downsizing and cutbacks to social programs. Furthermore, it is benefitting the least from the current stock-market boom. At the end of the day, even such conservative journals as *Business Week* and the *Investor's Business Daily* recognize that the notion of an investor democracy is an outright myth. The latter has remarked that "the general prosperity fed by the stock market is not providing more wealth for most families and doesn't offer them a way to improve their lot."[15]

So, if the idea of a new era of worker capitalism is simply not supported by the numbers — the economic "fundamentals" — then how do we account for the persistence of this myth among policy-makers, the media and the wider population? The answer seems to be that, while the revolution of mass investment has not actually ushered in a new investor democracy, it *has* ushered in a new investment *culture*, one that gives a false impression of what's actually going on.

THE MASS MARKETING OF GLOBAL FINANCE

Like the information revolution, the revolution of mass investment has become entrenched into our popular culture. It is a part of our everyday lives that seems entirely natural and inevitable. Leading the charge in creating this investment culture has been a change in the way that financial services companies market their wares. To target the mass retail market, mutual fund companies in the 1990s began selling investments as if they were consumer products. American Express, for example, offered customers who purchased designated mutual funds with their AmEx cards one point under the company's reward program for every $10 invested. Bank of Montreal once teamed up with McDonald's restaurants to market its mutual funds: at each McDonald's location, customers received an investment self-test and an information package about the bank's mutual funds.

A further development in the mass marketing of investment is the way that mutual funds are increasingly being sold in "supermarkets" of mutual funds or other financial services. The concept of the financial supermarket was introduced, in 1984, by a San Francisco discount broker named Charles Schwab. Called "Onesource," Schwab's scheme allowed investors to choose a range of funds from different companies and to switch among them without any transaction costs. It has since attracted over $1 billion per month and spawned numerous pretenders such as the one run by Fidelity Investments (Fidelity's is the second largest supermarket, offering 621 funds from 91 different companies).

But the most important aspect of the mass marketing of investment has been the huge growth in mutual fund advertising. These days, you can hardly get through an episode of *Traders* without someone informing you of how much fun it is to invest. In Canada, mutual fund companies spent $70 million in 1997 attempting to lure in new investors, up from only $6.4 million in 1991. And a recent study by Toronto-based Ascot Marketing suggests that this may be only the beginning: "a major advertiser such as General Motors of Canada Ltd. spends more than $100 million annually on campaigns, so at $70 million in spending, the growing mutual fund industry is just getting rolling."[16] In the United States, brokerage firms alone increased their spending on advertising by 95 percent in 1999, to a total of over $1.2 billion.

By mass marketing themselves as a form of "user-friendly" consumer product, mutual funds are helping to make investing as natural as consuming — part of the average person's normal routine, like buying clothes or food. As one mutual fund public relations manager remarked, "investing should be one of the basics; you put money away every month."[17]

INVESTMENT AS CONSUMPTION

In addition to being marketed as a form of consumer product, mutual funds are also actually being transformed into a form of *consumption*, in which individuals seem to benefit from the process of investing as much as they do from the potential returns. According to *The Economist*, "Besides reaping the material rewards that come with greater choice and higher returns, many people have discovered that managing their own finances can be tremendous fun."[18] For average people, mutual funds, like cell phones and other forms of conspicuous consumption, offer an accessible way to participate in an activity associated with being successful. For many people, nothing better signifies success and con-tributes to a feeling of self-worth than calling one's financial advisor — on the cell phone, of course. Investing, no matter how few shares you actually own, conveys a feeling of control, of being part of something larger than yourself. World events suddenly matter to you because of the way that they might affect your investments.

Also contributing to this feeling of empowerment is the tremendous growth in the number of mutual funds available. The increased choice allows ordinary people, through their role as investors, to exercise a greater degree of control in their everyday lives. In the United States, for example, the number of mutual funds on offer rose from 564 in 1980 to over 6,300 in April of 1997. But even more important than the simple rise in the number of mutual funds available is the emergence of numerous theme and specialty funds, which, like consumer products, facilitate "self-actualization" by allowing individuals to construct and express their identity through the process of investing.

Those who want to signify a cosmopolitan or risk-taking image can do so by investing in any of a wide range of regional, international, global and emerging-market funds. To allow consumers to demon-strate a knowledge of, or connection to, a particular industry, there exist numerous sector funds, such as those specializing in the resource, health, entertainment or high-technology sectors. In the United Kingdom, the Singer and Friedlander Group invites investors to "share in football's fortunes" with its new Football Fund, which, according to a former captain of the Liverpool football team, "provides an easy way for supporters and investors alike to become real owners and not just fantasy managers."[20] Funds such as these are helping to construct an investment culture in which the benefits of mutual funds go beyond the simple returns that await people in the future. Now, individuals are being tied into the financial markets through the *process* of investing itself.

Mutual funds now even offer individuals a way to express more overtly political forms of identity. The *Globe and Mail* reported in 1997 that the "Mouvement des Caisses Desjardins has launched a new mutual fund that invests exclusively in Quebec stocks and bonds, in a move aimed largely at placating patriotic customers who want to keep more of their money at home."[21] For the more socially progressive, the emergence of ethical mutual funds — including general ethical funds, labour-sponsored venture-capital funds and green funds — provides individuals with a financial outlet for their activist tendencies. Like the Che Guevara and Malcolm X products associated with "liberation marketing" strategies, funds of this type help to safely channel forms of everyday protest into directions that are compatible with the interests of the financial community. At the same time, by offering individuals an alternate mechanism through which they can exercise control, express their identity and even demonstrate resistance, self-actualization through the process of investing may help — albeit to a much lesser extent than the process of consuming — to offset the loss of control that many feel in their workplace and in society at large.

INVESTMENT SKILLS AS LIFE SKILLS

Mutual funds are also contributing to the creation of an investment culture through teaching. Unlike a simple bank deposit, which involves handing over your money and forgetting about it, investing in mutual funds requires a much higher degree of attention on the part of individuals. And this need for greater attention has brought with it a demand for education on basic financial skills. To meet this gap, an entire sub-industry has emerged to teach individuals the basics of investing. This trend began in decentralized fashion when individual firms began offering investment seminars primarily for the purpose of building relationships with current and potential customers. The aim was more one of marketing than of true education. But over time, the motivation of mutual fund companies became more sophisticated as they began to realize that educated investors are much more likely to invest in more complex instruments that generate higher commissions. At the same time, newspapers began to print articles and even establish separate sections on personal finance and investing; the increased demand for these pieces led to an explosion in the number and type of "how-to-invest" books available, some of which targetted specific groups, such as women.

In recent years, the promotion of investment skills has become more centralized and strategic, with the notion of "financial literacy" gaining currency among financial industry associations, securities regulators, government departments and consumer groups. This trend is widespread and seems to be picking up speed across the English-speaking world. In 1997, the U.S. Congress passed the "Savings Are Vital to Everyone's Retirement Act" and directed the Department of Labor to promote financial literacy through public service announcements, public meetings and seminars, educational materials and an Internet site. In the same year, the U.S. Senate Appropriations Committee directed the SEC "to provide a program to inform investors of the risk and rewards of the market, including the need for diversification."[22] In response, the SEC initiated its 1998 "Facts on Saving and Investing" campaign with a week of nationwide activities devoted to investor education.

Starting from the premise that "America faces a financial literacy crisis," the SEC campaign includes investment education seminars, a National Roundtable on Saving and Investing (which brings together leaders from government, the financial sector, consumer groups and the media to discuss financial education strategies) and a National Investors Town Meeting (a two-hour live broadcast available nationwide via satellite). In Canada, the Canadian Securities Institute has established the Investor Learning Centre of Canada and has held an "Investor Education Week," which included the mass distribution of investor education kits across the country. In Britain, the Association of Unit Trusts and Investment Funds offers one-day courses on investing, produces educational fact sheets and, in September of 1996, launched its "Getting Personal with Finance" campaign to "increase public awareness of [mutual funds] . . . and in particular to reach those who do not read the 'money' sections of national newspapers."[23]

The most interesting aspect of these public- and private-sector campaigns to promote financial literacy is the way that they have recently begun to target children. As with the adult-oriented campaigns, the targetting of children began as a marketing strategy. Companies introduced various children's mutual funds, such as Stein Roe's Young Investor fund and AIG's Children's World fund in the United States, Invesco's Rupert the Bear fund in the United Kingdom, and, in Canada, the Canadian Imperial Bank of Commerce's Mutual Fund Youth Portfolio and GT Global's "FUNds for Kids" program. Pointing to the motivation behind the GT Global program, Laura Curtis, manager of Communications and Public Relations, notes, "we decided that there was a void in the education system where one of the life skills, that being financial literacy, was not being addressed and that as a mutual fund company we could play a part in filling that void."[24] In the "how-to" publishing industry, an increasing number of financial education books for children have emerged, with titles such as *First Class: The Original Financial Guide for High School Students* and *The Money Tree Myth: A Parents' Guide to Helping Kids Unravel the Mysteries of Money*.

Investment education for children is on its way to becoming institutionalized as personal finance teaching makes its way onto curricula across the nation. In Canada, the Bank of Montreal runs a "My Money Investment Club" for kids, which includes the mass distribution of a "Simple Steps Investment Kit" to schools with a guide for teachers on how to teach investment skills and an investment board game. In

April of 2000, the Investor Learning Centre of Canada ran a seventeen-
school cross-country pilot project to bring financial literacy education
to Canadian high schools. The pilot included a five-hour course making use of a newly created, fifty-five-page text, titled *Investing in Your
Future*. With the pilot completed, the Investor Learning Centre hopes
that the program will be adopted more broadly.

In the United States, the Jump$tart Coalition for Personal Financial
Literacy has produced a benchmark survey of the financial literacy of
American high-school students and a set of guidelines for teaching basic
investment skills. It also acts as a centralized clearing house for all manner of teaching materials on the topic of personal finance. In the United
Kingdom, the National Westminster bank started a "Face 2 Face with
Finance" program in over two thousand English and Welsh secondary
schools with over 150,000 participating students. The Personal Finance
Education Group (PFEG), a coalition of investment industry representatives, educators and consumer groups, lobbied to have investment skills
put on the UK National Curriculum, which was up for review in the
year 2000. The PFEG has even developed a "Learning Framework for
Personal Finance" designed to fully integrate personal finance education
into curriculums by linking it to traditional subjects such as maths and
ethics. In mid-1998, twenty-four schools in Manchester, Kent and
London began a pilot program that was expanded nationally in 1999.

Over the course of the 1990s, investment skills have increasingly
become life skills. Like driving a car or using a personal computer; investing is now something that you simply have to know how to do. When
I was in high school, a mere fifteen years ago, business education was
much more centred on production than finance. Business skills, as taught
in those after-school Junior Achievement clubs, was all about inventing,
manufacturing and marketing an actual product. Today, the focus has
shifted to investing — to making money without making things. In many
ways this trend is emblematic of the broader shift in our society from the
dominance of business to that of the financial community.

While the promotion of financial literacy education is without question a good thing, it does produce an unintended side effect in terms
of conditioning people's views on economic policy. In a seemingly

conscious and strategic recognition of the political implications of financial literacy programs, a project manager for Britain's Personal Finance Education Group argues that "teaching personal finance is an essential part of making responsible citizens for the future."[25] "Responsible citizens," of course, are defined as those who accept the conservative focus on self-reliance and individualism in all things economic. To promote this focus, financial literacy programs promote specific lessons such as "the magic of compound interest," "dollar-cost averaging" and, most importantly, "the necessity of investing." Lessons such as these help to naturalize notions of self-reliance and to promote acceptance to cutbacks in government-provided social programs. As the U.S. Investment Company Institute notes, one of the key themes of the SEC's "Facts on Saving and Investing" campaign is the notion that "Financial security starts when you take *personal responsibility* for your financial well-being."[26]

More precise lessons in these educational materials help to demonstrate the virtues of specific conservative policies. Lessons on the need to diversify your portfolio (especially outside your home country) demonstrate the need for deregulation to allow fund companies to invest greater amounts abroad. Lessons associated with picking the right stocks and developing a lifelong financial plan help to convince individuals of the benefits of shareholder value and very low inflation. All this is not to imply any sort of conspiracy or deliberate attempt to influence the political outlook of voters. In most cases, the motives of the educators are fairly altruistic. But to pretend that financial literacy classes are having no political effects is to be naive in the extreme. If the Canadian Auto Workers started running after-school programs that dealt with the benefits of sharing, you can be sure that it would not go unnoticed by the columnists at the *National Post*.

INVESTMENT AS EVERYDAY LIFE

The most significant aspect of the new investment culture is the way that investing has become an entrenched part of our daily lives. The action in the stock market is put on display everywhere we go. We are becoming conditioned to the idea that investing is something we need to think about every single day. And in the process, more and more of us are gaining a familiarity with the world of finance through our day-to-day interactions with the stock market. As *The Economist* observed, the rise of mutual fund ownership "is having a huge effect — not just on America's stock market, but also on the nation's culture. Ask the man in the street what the Dow has been up to lately and there is a good chance that he will be able to tell you, because some of his own money is at stake."[27]

Our ability to track investments has vastly increased as the popular media has begun to institutionalize coverage of developments in the financial markets. Turn on CTV Newsnet and you are sure to receive a quick update on market events. Open the newspaper and you'll find page after page of mutual fund tables and daily changes in stock prices. *Newsweek* has commented that "[m]agazines like *Worth* and *Smart Money*, Web sites like thestreet.com and cable networks like CNBC and CNNfn cover the market like pro sports, ready with the highlight reel at the end of the day."[28] Readership of eleven U.S. business and personal finance magazines has soared from under 4 million in paid circulation in 1982 to over 7 million in 1997. On America Online, members routinely request over 70 million stock quotes a day.

Familiarity and constant interaction with the workings of the financial markets help to naturalize investing and self-reliance as a way of life and, more indirectly, cause individuals to evaluate the world around them through the lens of an investor. The opening sequence of the TV show *Traders* is a series of shots that swing between world events and the value of stocks. The impression is that world events matter, but only to the extent that they affect your RRSP. Investing in international or emerging-market mutual funds serves to intertwine people's lives with events around the globe. The seeming inevitability of a certain type of economic globalization may become more entrenched as individuals pay greater attention to, and interact more regularly with, the international events that might affect their investments.

In addition to the barrage of market information available to us, the emergence of twenty-four-hour investment hotlines and on-line trading facilitates further interaction with the market because it is now possible to alter your portfolio at almost any time, from almost any place. In the latter case, the Bank of Montreal's "Investore" has recently developed a mobile trading bus that visits shopping centres and remote communities complete with fund information, financial news, trading via satellite and even investment games for kids.

Investing is becoming so much a part of people's everyday lives that it is even beginning to encroach upon leisure time. For adults, the growth of investment clubs has served to transform financial literacy training and investing, especially among women, into a form of social activity. Promoted by organizations such as the (U.S.) National Association of Investment Clubs and the Canadian Shareowners Association, investment clubs generally meet once a month to learn new investment skills, track their investments and alter their portfolios, all while sharing coffee and cakes at a member's home. One of the most prominent investment clubs — the Beardstown Ladies' Investment Club — has even published a bestselling investment "how-to" book. And just as the shift in our schools from business to financial education reflects larger economic developments, so too is the rise of investment clubs among women a sign of the times. In years gone by, the equivalent to today's investment clubs also would have been focused on real products. Investment clubs are to the 1990s what Tupperware and Mary Kay cosmetics parties were to the 1950s and 1960s.

For teenagers, Competitive Edge Enterprises has created an investment board game, "Mutual Mania," which is now being marketed in Canadian toy stores. And don't forget GT Global's annual "FUNd Fair," which has been continued under the auspices of AIM Mutual Funds. This encroachment of investing upon the leisure aspect of people's everyday lives will further reinforce the extent to which individuals come to regard investing in general and conservative economic policies in particular as a way of life, a part of the natural order of things.

THE BUBBLE IN NORTH AMERICA'S "POLITICAL FUNDAMENTALS"

Is the new investment culture really having an effect on how voters evaluate which policies will best serve their interests? Well, the ultra-conservative American think tank the Cato Institute seems to think so. In a detailed study titled *The Rise of Worker Capitalism*, the executive director of the American Shareholders Association, Richard Nadler, argues that "[t]he growth of share ownership is changing the values and perceived political interests of voters — increasing the body politic's support for investor-friendly policies." In the study, Nadler shows how investing is changing people's outlook on policies such as the capital gains tax and social-program funding.

According to the study, "Shareholding workers support policies that cut taxes on savings for important life-cycle events such as education, health care and retirement. Conversely, workers who have investments exhibit rising skepticism toward government-run entitlements . . . Portfolio owners are shown to be more likely than non-owners to support a capital gains tax reduction. This effect is found in almost every demographic group, suggesting that investment influences opinion independently of the income, race, or other characteristics of the investor. The growth of share ownership, in other words, is changing the perceived political interests of voters — increasing the electorate's support for investor-friendly . . . policies."[29]

The study also cites other influences on the outlook of voters: "That working investors are internalizing attitudes long associated with the capitalist class is also evident in their reading habits." Pointing to the growing readership of such financial press staples as the *Wall Street Journal*, *Investor's Business Daily*, *Forbes*, *Business Week* and *Fortune* as well as the expanding ratings of finance-oriented television such as CNN Financial News, CNBC and Bloomberg, Nadler argues that "although the impact on workers' attitudes is impossible to quantify, the editorial content of [the financial press] certainly varies from the fare in the *Philadelphia Inquirer*, the *Washington Post*, and the *Los Angeles Times*."[30]

If the mass investment phenomenon were really as widespread as conservatives imply, then these changes in voter outlook would be justified. But when almost 70 percent of the population has little or no stake in the stock market, it seems that the new culture of investing is creating the political equivalent of a speculative bubble. According to conservatives, speculative bubbles in the financial markets should only occur when the information on fundamentals that is available is false or inadequate. In their view, this is the only reason that investors display herd behaviour and asset prices get away from the economic fundamentals underlying the assets. It seems that a similar logic is at work with the way that the culture of investing is altering how average voters evaluate which policies will best serve their interests. False or inadequate information about the benefits that ordinary people are actually receiving from the current stock-market boom has created a similar kind of bubble in North America's political outlook. Support for conservative policies seems to be based more on the *perception* of an investor democracy than on the reality of the underlying "political fundamentals." And this means that the political marketplace is not currently exercising the discipline it should over government policy-makers. Policy-makers have been lulled into believing that the conservative policies demanded by the financial community will be politically sustainable over the long term.

The conservative view holds that bubbles will always correct themselves when more accurate information emerges. The same may be true for the current bubble in North American political values. As more and more people begin to realize that the notion of an investor democracy is an inaccurate one, political views may quickly correct. And if a correction occurs in the stock market at the same time, there could be significant implications for politicians. As the *Washington Post* has speculated, a market crash "might be bitterly resented and could invite stories about how conniving Wall Street duped gullible Main Street."[31]

9

MAKING WHAT'S GOOD FOR FIDELITY GOOD FOR NORTH AMERICA

After reading this book, you might be left with the impression that the revolution of mass investment and the rise of mutual funds and pension funds is an out-and-out bad thing. You might figure that the only solution is to follow the advice in the title of Mark Heinzl's recent book: *Stop Buying Mutual Funds*. Heinzl made this suggestion for the much more limited reason that mutual fund managers consistently fail to beat the market average, and, as a result, that you're better off buying things like index funds, which invest in the market average — at much lower fees. This is a separate question, one that only concerns people in their role as investors. The more important reason for doing something about the mutual fund industry is its effects on people in their roles as workers and citizens. But this doesn't mean that we should stop buying mutual funds, or that we should ban the industry or regulate it to death. That would be throwing the baby out with the bathwater.

While you certainly haven't heard much about it in this book, mainly because you hear so much about it in every other book on the industry, the revolution of mass investment and the rise of mutual funds and pension funds is actually a good thing. They *do* help to make the financial markets more inclusive by making investing accessible to a much broader segment of the population. The real problem with mutual funds and pension funds is that they have grown so much and so fast that regulators haven't been able to keep up with the new developments in the industry, and with the often nasty side effects it is producing. In many ways, the situation is similar to the rapid rise of the Internet, or of recent advances in biotechnology. In each case, the first task is to identify the problems being produced, which is what I have attempted to do in this book. The second task is to propose solutions, which is why all books of this type have, or should have, a final "so-what-would-you do?" chapter. So. To keep the benefits of mutual funds while trying to do away with the many problems that they cause, here's what I would do.

MAKING THE FINANCIAL MARKETS MORE EFFICIENT

As we've seen in this book, the short-term outlook and herd-like behaviour of mutual fund and pension fund managers have caused many of the negative trends that have come to characterize the new global economy. Measures that can be used to prevent these negative trends fall into one of two broad categories. The first consists of measures to make the financial markets more efficient by reducing the degree to which fund managers behave in this short-term-focused, herd-like way. The second category consists of measures to insulate governments and corporations from this behaviour.

The first category will need to include both government intervention and industry participation, with threats of the former helping to encourage the latter. If the money management industry can come up with ways to reduce the short-term pressures on fund managers, then there will be less of a need for government intervention. If they can't, governments will need to intervene in several ways.

Governments could create incentives, penalties and/or regulations that encourage individuals and pension fund trustees to take a longer-term view. This could mean measures that prevent individuals from being able to quickly redeem their shares in mutual funds such as early withdrawal penalties or regulations. It could also mean regulations mandating longer-term contracts for the management of pension funds.

To encourage individuals and trustees to take a longer term view when deciding where to invest in the first place, financial literacy education is a necessary, but certainly not sufficient, measure. Instead, governments must consider more radical approaches. In some cases, too much information is not always a good thing. Daily valuations of funds and the publication of other short-term performance numbers help promote a short-term view among individual investors. Governments could restrict fund companies to using longer-term numbers in their advertisements and other promotional materials. Another option would be to restrict fund rating companies to only evaluating performance based on long-term criteria. A final method, which is admittedly much harsher and thus the least preferable, would be to create a public fund rating agency.

Through cooperation with the industry, regulators must also find ways to mandate longer evaluation periods for fund managers, through tax incentives and/or regulations. It would also be useful to de-emphasize paying and evaluating fund managers on the basis of relative performance. A case exists for mandating a system where fund managers are paid solely on their ability to deliver absolute returns.

At the end of the day, these are merely suggestions. But if governments cannot cooperate with each other and with the money-management industry to find ways to reduce the short-term focus and herd-like behaviour that pervades it, then the only alternative is more intrusive regulation to insulate government and corporate borrowers from the effects of this behaviour. Some of these measures are considered below.

PREVENTING FINANCIAL CRISES

Making the financial markets more efficient will go a long way towards preventing the kind of market overreaction that can give rise to speculative bubbles and the crashes that they help to bring about. But while these measures are necessary, they aren't sufficient. Countries need to take a page from defensive driving manuals. Not doing anything wrong simply makes you a good driver. A defensive driver goes a step further and assumes that other drivers will do something wrong, and so takes the necessary precautions. In the world of high finance, governments must assume that the financial markets won't always operate efficiently, and take the precautions necessary to deal with the results.

These precautions could take many forms, especially when it comes to preventing the type of currency crisis that emerged in the 1990s. First and foremost, governments need to avoid adopting the Washington consensus policy mix of capital mobility and a fixed exchange rate, which is politically unsustainable and far too prone to crisis. If Canada adopted a fixed exchange rate, as some pundits at the *National Post* and various conservative think tanks have suggested, it would only be a matter of time before we had our own currency crisis.

While most economists agree that fixed exchange rates are not viable in the democratic countries of the industrialized world, many believe that they can still be a useful way for developing countries to reduce excessive inflation and build much-needed confidence among investors. They do caution, however, that the fixed exchange rate should only be temporary, and must be abandoned before it begins to create the conditions that can provoke a speculative attack. Under normal circumstances, I might be inclined to agree with this view. But, as financial markets become increasingly prone to overreaction, the fixed exchange rate option looks less and less viable. As we have seen, if fund managers overreact to the adoption of a fixed exchange rate and pour excessive amounts of investment into a country, it can create a bubble in both the value of the currency and in the underlying economic fundamentals of the country. This in turn can convince the government that the fixed exchange rate really is politically sustainable, meaning that it is less likely to abandon it before problems develop.

In addition to avoiding fixed exchange rates, what other precautions can governments take? At present, the most widely promoted measure is the old conservative cure-all of greater "transparency," which essentially means that governments must be completely open with all information about the fundamentals of their economy. To the extent that they recognize the existence of herd-like behaviour in the financial markets at all, conservative commentators tend to blame it on a lack of transparency. While I agree that promoting transparency is useful, it simply isn't enough to prevent herd behaviour. As we saw in Chapter 2, herd behaviour by fund managers has much more to do with the performance pressures that cause fund managers to ignore economic fundamentals rather than any lack of available information about these fundamentals. More useful are measures that focus on the institutional investors themselves.

One such measure, proposed by Stephany Griffith-Jones at the UK-based Institute of Development Studies at Sussex University, is for developed countries to implement "risk-weighted cash requirements" on investment companies.[1] A risk-weighted cash requirement is similar to the reserve requirements that are currently imposed on banks. Banks are required to keep a certain percentage of their funds in reserve — i.e., not lend them out — in case there's a rush of depositors demanding their money back. This regulation is key to preventing bank runs. It means that banks should always be able to meet their depositors' demands for cash without having to sell off their assets at panic prices. Similarly, risk-weighted cash requirements for investment companies would ensure that fund companies always had enough cash on hand to meet demands for redemptions by individual investors. So, in a crisis, there would be less pressure on fund managers to sell a country's assets to meet the demand for redemptions; this in turn would help to reduce the herd behaviour that can lead to market overreaction.

Another useful measure, this time for the countries that *receive* investment money from mutual funds and pension funds, is the creation of holding-period taxes on capital inflows. These are exit taxes that make it more expensive for investors to withdraw their funds from a country in the very short term. The longer a fund stays invested in the country, the lower the exit tax. The important thing with holding-period inflow taxes is not that they prevent investors from leaving, but that they discourage short-term investors from investing in the first place and thus help to prevent the build-up of a speculative bubble that can quickly turn into panicked outflows. Chile had such taxes in place prior to the 1994 Mexican peso crisis. Their success is demonstrated by the fact that Chile was one of the few countries to avoid the "tequila effect" as the crisis in Mexico spread from country to country.

Financial crises can be prevented. On their own, governments can avoid adopting fixed exchange rates, and can insulate themselves from short-term-focused, herd-like behaviour on the part of fund managers through inflow taxes and other measures to reduce their reliance on hot money. In cooperation with other governments and with international financial institutions, developed countries can reduce herd behaviour by more closely overseeing and regulating the fund management industry. In both cases, it is simply a matter of political will.

REGULATING HEDGE FUNDS

Thinking back to Chapter 5, you'll remember that a hedge fund is an unregulated type of mutual fund that works on behalf of the very wealthy. In the world of high finance, hedge fund managers exercise a great deal of power because they can borrow huge sums of money, and because they act as market leaders.

Hedge funds are another area where governments may be able to improve the efficiency and legitimacy of markets through regulation. In the wake of both the Asian financial crisis and the near-collapse of LTCM, financial regulators began to look for ways to prevent hedge funds from manipulating markets and from posing a threat to the global financial system as a whole. Studies were conducted, with an eye to potential regulation, by the (U.S.) President's Working Group on Financial Markets, the Basle Committee on Banking Supervision (a division of the Bank for International Settlements, the world's club for central bankers) and the International Organization of Securities Commissions.

All three emphasized the need to prevent hedge funds from borrowing such excessive amounts of money that they pose a threat to the global financial system as a whole when things go wrong. So far, however, the bulk of the recommendations have focused on the banks and investment firms that lend to hedge funds. One proposal is for banks to be more transparent about how much they are lending to hedge funds, which would make it easier for regulators to determine when things have gone too far. The problem is that this does little to shed light on the activities of the hedge funds themselves. As we saw in Chapter 5, these funds are virtually unregulated and are not required to file the same reports as other institutional investors. If we are ever going to fully determine what hedge funds are doing and what issues they might raise for regulators, then we need to have better information. The IMF identified (but did not recommend) some measures to accomplish this. Most important is the need to expand the U.S. reporting requirements on large trades and positions that currently apply to mutual funds and pension funds to cover hedge funds as well.

In their recommendations to restrict lending to hedge funds by banks, regulators seem to be leaning towards the use of voluntary self-restraint among lenders. They apparently hope that the near-collapse of LTCM has scared many lenders straight, and that the problem will be solved by "market discipline" rather than government intervention. To put it bluntly, this won't work. The key problem with voluntary and market-discipline-based measures is that they aren't binding. Voluntary regulations will always come into conflict with the need for firms to make a profit. If one firm breaks the rules to gain an advantage, then all firms have to break the rules to stay competitive.

Even the banks and firms that lend to hedge funds seem to recognize this problem. As the *Wall Street Journal* suggested in 1998, "several bankers conceded that once the current [Long-Term Capital Management] crisis passes, it will take only one bank offering special breaks to hedge funds to begin the cycle all over again — that is, unless stricter regulation is imposed."[2] If regulators are going to focus on lenders rather than on the hedge funds themselves, they will need to legislate more prudent behaviour rather than simply recommending it. This means regulations to force lenders to ask for more collateral from the hedge funds.

Regulating lenders would help to prevent episodes where hedge funds become over-leveraged to the extent that they can pose a threat to the global financial system as a whole. (LTCM, for example, had borrowed about $28 for every $1 it actually had.) But regulating lenders rather than hedge funds won't be enough to prevent episodes of market manipulation, many of which rely on leverage of only five or ten to one. To deal with this problem, governments need to look at regulating the hedge funds themselves. One option here is to subject them to the same regulations that currently apply to other institutional investors, such as mutual funds. Even hedge fund manager George Soros himself has recently argued that "hedge funds should be regulated like all other investment funds."[3]

It would also be useful, in terms of preventing the price volatility and instances of market manipulation that are associated with hedge funds, for exchanges to impose "penal margin requirements" on funds that misuse large investment positions. Penal margin requirements force hedge funds to put up large amounts of collateral in a way that can prevent them from borrowing the funds they need to manipulate markets. The London Metals Exchange (LME), for example, currently has this type of penalties for funds that attempt to profit from "pumping up the tulips" or manipulating a market upwards. Recently the LME has been exploring the potential for imposing similar penalties on funds that attempt to manipulate markets by short selling where they profit from pushing prices down. In extreme circumstances, governments could also impose temporary bans on short selling altogether. This is what Hong Kong did when evidence emerged that hedge funds were trying to manipulate its currency and stock market.

One problem with regulating hedge funds and preventing some of their nastier side effects is that many of them operate offshore. Clearly, making regulations on hedge funds effective will require cooperation among governments to prevent the funds from fleeing to unregulated jurisdictions. But as George Soros notes, "if the regulatory authorities cooperate, this should not present any insuperable difficulties."[4]

Cooperation between governments is also necessary to develop broader regulations that protect entire national markets from manipulation and volatility. "If someone sold stocks in a U.S. company short, then spread rumors about problems with its products and feuds among its managers, he would soon face criminal prosecution. But as far as anyone can tell, it is perfectly legal to sell a country short, then spread damaging rumors about its future policies," points out Paul Krugman.[5] In the past, no one thought that it was necessary to regulate protection for whole economies and markets because they were seen as too large to manipulate. However, as we saw in Chapter 5 in the case of Hong Kong and Australia, this may no longer be the case.

ECONOMIC POLICY: RESTORING THE BALANCE BETWEEN BAY STREET AND MAIN STREET

Capitalist democracies need to be both economically and politically sustainable.* This means that governments need to achieve a balance between the interests of Bay Street and those of Main Street. What does this mean in terms of actual government policy for Canada? Well, in the case of fiscal policy (the amount that governments tax and spend), economic sustainability means avoiding deficits, with the possible exception of cases where they can be used to stimulate the economy in the event of a severe recession. Political sustainability requires well-funded social programs to prevent poverty and reduce inequality, and to ensure that the rising tide of economic growth really does lift all boats. Health care and education are important here in order to promote equality of opportunity for all Canadians. But equally important, if less popular in our current climate, is the need to restore at least some of the funding that's been cut from social assistance programs.

Prior to the 1995 budget, the Canada Assistance Program, which transferred money and tax points to the provinces to help fund their social assistance programs, was structured as a "cost-shared" program.

---

* They also need to be environmentally sustainable. But this is a can of worms best left to other authors.

The federal government split the cost of these programs on a fifty-fifty basis with the provinces. This cost-sharing structure meant that the program acted as an "automatic stabilizer" for the Canadian economy. When the economy slowed and unemployment rose, more people drew on these programs, meaning that they would automatically inject more money into the economy and help to stimulate growth. When the pace of economic growth picked up and unemployment fell, fewer people would draw on the programs and government spending would automatically drop.

After Paul Martin's 1995 budget, the Canada Assistance Program was rolled into the Canada Health and Social Transfer, a block grant of money for health care, education and social assistance that was fixed at a set limit. So federal funding for social programs no longer goes up and down with the swings of the economy. This new structure has reduced the ability of social assistance to act as an automatic stabilizer.

In our presently booming economy, automatic stabilizer programs may seem much less necessary than they were in the past. But they may be necessary in the future if an economic downturn occurs. When the Toronto government quietly cut the budget for snow-removal services in the summer months, no one seemed to notice or care. But along came winter and mayor Mel Lastman had to deflect a public outcry by implying that a natural disaster had occurred and calling in the Canadian Forces for snow-shovelling duty. Social assistance programs remain necessary even during our current boom, as rising levels of homelessness make abundantly clear. Cutting these programs during an economic boom is like cutting snow-removal services in the summer. Everything appears to be OK until a storm comes along. A boom that is producing ever-expanding fiscal surpluses is precisely the time to restore social programs to well-funded levels. And as long as we avoid returning to deficits, the financial markets will impose no constraints whatsoever on how we decide to divide up the current fiscal surplus.

More relevant to the power and interests of the financial markets is the issue of monetary policy. An economically sustainable monetary policy is one that prevents the re-emergence of high levels of inflation as we saw in the late 1970s. A politically sustainable monetary policy is

one that does not sacrifice jobs and growth on the altar of price stability. Canadian monetary policy has tilted away from the more politically
sustainable levels of inflation that are currently being pursued by Alan
Greenspan in the United States. Over the course of the 1990s, Greenspan kept inflation hovering slightly below 3 percent. The Americans
have seen the fruits of this policy in faster growth and lower unemployment. Monetary policy isn't the only factor accounting for the
strength of the U.S. economy, but it definitely plays a very large part.
To achieve a more balanced monetary policy, one that more closely
parallels the successful policy of Alan Greenspan, our own government
needs to adjust the Bank of Canada's inflation target range up slightly,
to a band of 2 to 4 percent, meaning that it would aim for an inflation
rate of around 3 percent, matching U.S. policy.

On the political front, there are some encouraging signs that elite
opinion may be moving in this direction. As I write this chapter at the
end of the summer in 2000, the business pages of the *Globe* and
the *Post* reveal that the Department of Finance is beginning to question
the Bank of Canada's excessive focus on price stability. In a memo dated
June 21, 2000, Deputy Minister of Finance Kevin Lynch advised Paul
Martin to raise the issue with Bank of Canada Governor Gordon
Thiessen. *National Post* columnist Terence Corcoran reported that "[t]he
drift of Mr. Lynch's comments is that Canada could risk a little more
inflation to squeeze a little more growth out of the economy by holding interest rates down while U.S. rates rose." Admittedly, Mr. Lynch
is not advocating a shift in the Bank of Canada's inflation target bands,
but simply suggesting that the recent increases in productivity mean that
the economy can probably grow at a faster rate without provoking a
rise in inflation. He thinks that the Bank should test this by not matching American interest-rate hikes. But this suggestion does show that the
Department of Finance seems to be more willing to risk a slightly
higher rate of inflation if it means we can achieve stronger growth and
lower unemployment. At the very least, efforts by conservatives within
the Bank and various think tanks to promote an even lower target band
of 0 to 2 percent have been halted in their tracks.

If the federal government develops the political will to match the

U.S. inflation rate, could it actually carry this policy out? What would be the reaction of fund managers? How would the Canadian dollar be affected? On both left and right there seems to be a consensus that the financial markets would panic and cause a sharp drop in the value of the Canadian dollar. Regarding the aforementioned memo from the Deputy Finance Minister, Corcoran commented, "The Lynch memo is not the kind of confidence-enhancing document currency traders take home at night to tuck under their pillows for security." If this is true — and it is — it stands to reason that traders and investors would be even less pleased by an announcement that the Bank of Canada was going to shift its inflation target range from 1 to 3 percent to 2 to 4 percent. Speculating on how financial markets would react to such a move, Canadian Auto Workers' economist Jim Stanford notes that the "implementation of such a program . . . would immediately spark a crisis of confidence on the part of capital."[6] And as we saw in Chapter 6, this means that, rather than simply dropping a little, the Canadian dollar could plummet.

Raising the Bank of Canada's inflation target slightly is made even more difficult by the fact that Canada has an *explicit* inflation target band. The United States has never adopted explicit inflation targets. Instead, the financial markets simply trust Alan Greenspan not to let inflation rise to economically unsustainable levels. If the United States decided to allow a little bit more inflation, it would be seen as a difference of degree. If Canada attempts to allow a little more inflation, it would be seen as a difference in kind, since it would require a specific change in policy. Such a change would be an "event" that would cause foreign investors to pay much closer attention to Canada, provoking large capital outflows.

Adding to this problem would be the actions of Bay Street and domestic conservatives, who would portray the shift in monetary policy as some sort of "crisis." They would argue that the shift to a 2 to 4 percent band was simply the thin edge of the wedge, a signal that governments were about to pursue policies that were far less friendly to investors. This would have the effect of making foreign fund managers even more nervous, causing them to pull even more money out of Canada. And as fund managers pulled more money out and the dollar fell, confidence would drop still lower, and the whole process would feed on itself, leading to a massive drop in the value of the dollar.

The bottom line is that any shift in monetary policy aimed at matching the more sensible levels of inflation currently being pursued in the United States would have to be preceded by measures to insulate governments from precisely this kind of short-term-focused, herd-like behaviour on the part of investors. The most widely promoted measure along these lines is the notion of a currency transactions tax, informally known as the "Tobin tax" after the Nobel prize–winning economist who proposed it, James Tobin.

PROS AND CONS OF THE TOBIN TAX

As originally proposed by Tobin, this tax aims to "throw sand in the wheels of international finance" to help prevent financial crises and to give governments greater freedom of choice in their monetary policy. The idea is to target the focus on short-term horizons that seems to give rise to market overreaction and price overshooting by charging a very small tax on every currency transaction. For investors focusing on long-term horizons who trade less frequently, the Tobin tax would be a negligible cost. But for short-term currency traders who trade frequently, the cost would be high enough to discourage the more extreme kinds of short-term-focused behaviour. As a side benefit, the Tobin tax would also raise billions of dollars in revenue that could be used for more socially productive purposes. The strength of this tax is that it would discourage short-term speculation while having no real effect on productive investments. But I'm beginning to think that this could also be one of its weaknesses.

The key problem with the Tobin tax is that it seems to target the wrong kind of short-term focus. It would regulate the behaviour of currency traders rather than mutual fund and pension fund managers. Because currency traders seek to make profit from very small changes in the value of a currency, they trade frequently, so it's only natural that the media and some economists view them as the cause of the short-term focus within the financial markets. Mutual funds and pension funds trade far less frequently. They generally buy and hold various assets, including stocks, bonds and currencies, hoping to profit as their value rises over, at least, the medium term. However, as we have seen in Chapter 2 and throughout this book, mutual and pension fund managers are driven to focus on the short term because they are evaluated and paid based on their ability to deliver strong returns on a quarterly or even monthly basis. But this short-term focus on the part of fund managers is not the same as the short-term outlook of currency traders, who buy and sell based on the small daily movements in the value of a currency. Fund managers care more about the month-to-month level of the currency and the larger swings in its value. If a currency has been rising over the course of a few weeks, then they are likely to join in the frenzy. And if a currency starts to drop significantly, they are prone to panic. The short-term horizons of fund managers mean that they need to do what everyone else is doing, regardless of what the fundamentals indicate, in order to avoid underperforming the average. But it is the mutual funds and pension funds that control the greatest amount of money in the global economy, far more than can be brought to bear by the currency traders.

The seeming difficulty with the Tobin tax is that it targets the wrong short-term horizons. Market overreaction and price overshooting, of the type that restricts the policy choices of governments and is present during financial crises, is caused primarily by large one-time outflows rather than by a high frequency of transactions and this is the difference between the short-term horizons of currency traders and those of fund managers. In debates over the Tobin tax, supporters and critics alike have failed to make a distinction between the volume of flows and the frequency of transactions. If two traders each have a thousand dollars and they trade it back and forth at a rapid frequency, the "volume" of transactions will be in the tens of thousands of dollars even though we are only talking about two thousand actual dollars.

In other words, while the frequency of daily currency transactions is high, we are really talking about a small volume of capital being counted over and over again. This frequency of transactions gives rise to the day-to-day volatility in the value of currencies. It does not, however, lead to the massive medium-term price overshooting that limits governments' policy choices and contributes to financial crises, because the amount of capital that traders can actually move out of a country in one shot is much smaller than the large volumes that can be removed by the mutual funds and pension funds. The problem with the Tobin tax is that it targets the kind of short-term focus that causes day-to-day volatility but not the kind that leads to massive one-time outflows.

An analogy may be helpful for illustrating the difference. If we imagine an ocean coastline where the water represents international capital flows and the beach represents a country, we can see two types of capital flows, each occurring at different time horizons. The waves represent the short-term flows of the currency traders; they bring the same flows in and out twenty-four hours a day. The tides represent the medium-term-but-prone-to-panic flows of the mutual funds and pension funds; they bring a greater volume of flows but at longer intervals.

In the same way that both the waves and tides affect the location of the water's edge, currency traders and institutional investors both affect the value of a currency. The difference is that the "tidal flows" driven by the institutional investors carry much greater volumes and have a much greater impact on the value of a currency than the "waves" of the currency traders. Whether the tide is in or out, the waves keep the edge of the water in constant motion, just as currency traders account for the small daily movements in the value of a country's currency. But when it comes to restricting the policy choices of governments and contributing to financial crises, what matters are the large tidal inflows that can give rise to speculative bubbles and the equally large outflows that can send a currency into a downward spiral. While the actions of currency traders, like waves, are more frequent and noticeable, they do not carry the volume of capital required to send a currency into freefall. As the IMF notes, "it is not so much short-term volatility as significant and sustained misalignments of asset prices from values consistent with fundamentals that are of concern, because of the macroeconomic imbalances and economic distortions to which they can give rise."[7]

By targeting the short-term horizons of traders, the Tobin tax would have the effect of calming the waves while leaving the tidal flows untouched. And this means that the Tobin tax is unlikely to achieve its intended goal of increasing the policy choices of governments and helping to prevent financial crises. This is not to say that the Tobin tax should not be implemented. But, if the Canadian government is ever going to adjust its monetary policy along the lines of the more successful U.S. model (by raising the Bank of Canada's inflation target range to 2 to 4 percent), then other measures will be necessary to prevent the financial markets from overreacting and the Canadian dollar from plummeting.

OTHER MEASURES

To prevent investors from withdrawing excessive amounts of money in response to a shift in Canadian monetary policy, the government needs to implement measures that focus on both domestic and foreign fund companies. One measure that would help to prevent panicked outflows by domestic investors is to strengthen the foreign content limits on tax-exempt savings plans such as RRSPs. Lowering the allowable amount of foreign content in Canadian investors' portfolios would limit the amount of money that domestic investors could move abroad and the amount that the dollar would drop. Unfortunately, after heavy lobbying from the mutual fund industry, Paul Martin moved in the opposite direction in the 2000 budget by expanding the existing limit from 20 to 30 percent, meaning that investors can now take even more of their money abroad. Back in the days of the 1995 budget, Paul Martin used to complain that the ability of investors to move their money abroad had forced him to cut social programs when he really didn't want to. But by raising the foreign content limit, he is increasing the ability of investors to put constraints on government policy choices. As a report by the Senate Banking Committee revealed, "Relaxing or eliminating the [foreign content limit] will also add an

additional measure of discipline on public-sector issuers of securities."
Translation: Relaxing the foreign content limit will strengthen the
ability of investors to restrict the policy choices of the government.[8]

Strengthening the foreign content limit (by reducing it back to 20
percent or lower) would help to prevent domestic fund companies from
pummelling the dollar if the government implements policies that Bay
Street dislikes. To prevent foreign investors from doing the same thing,
a useful measure would be regulations requiring them to hedge their
exchange-rate risk. If a government decides to tolerate a little more
inflation to stimulate growth and reduce unemployment, investors will
pull their money out and the value of the dollar will drop. For foreign
investors, a falling currency reduces the value of their Canadian investments because they are priced in Canadian dollars; if the dollar goes
down, the value of the investment goes down with it.

Forcing foreign fund managers to hedge against a potential fall in the
Canadian dollar would reduce this risk. This hedging could prevent a
slightly falling currency from gathering momentum and turning into
a plummeting currency. And by reducing the potential for price overshooting, mandatory hedges would limit the pressures on the government to give investors the policies that they demand. Currency hedges
could be mandatory if politicians made them a term of issue for
government bonds. In fact, if governments cooperated to make currency hedging mandatory around the world, it would achieve the
desired goal of the Tobin tax because it would force an end to currency
speculation, and exchange rates would be made to reflect their true
underlying fundamentals to a much greater degree.

RESTORING THE BALANCE
BETWEEN BAY STREET AND
MAIN STREET: CORPORATE POLICY

Lengthening the horizons of mutual fund and pension fund managers
would go a long way towards preventing the mass layoffs and other
short-term policies currently being pursued by many of our corporations. For this to happen in a consistent, across-the-board fashion,

governments have to intervene with the cooperation of the industry. Unfortunately, many on the left have been promoting more piecemeal methods for influencing the investment decisions of fund managers, including the use of "ethical" mutual funds and the idea that trade unions could attempt to exercise more influence over their members' defined-benefit pension funds.

Frankly, there are so many problems inherent to these piecemeal approaches that they are not worth discussing as serious policy options. A thoughtful and detailed critique of these strategies is outlined in the recent book *Paper Boom*, written by Canadian Auto Workers' economist Jim Stanford.[9] The key problem with both strategies is the same one that plagues all consumer boycott strategies; they have to rely on individuals being able to sustain a personal loss over a long period of time. To support certain specific causes, such as ending Apartheid in South Africa, consumers and individual investors were willing to buy more expensive products and to accept lower investment returns. But to expect individuals to sustain this permanently in all their investments is unrealistic. If you doubt this, ask yourself how many "green products" the average person is buying and how much of an impact green consumerism is having on the environment. If average people are interested in changing the investment behaviour of the fund management industry, primarily by reducing the short-term performance pressures on fund managers, then the only solution is to ask the government to intervene.

If governments are unable to lengthen the short-term horizons of fund managers, then the alternative is enacting regulations to insulate CEOs from the short-term demands of their institutional shareholders. Probably the most useful measure that the government could undertake in this regard is to impose limits on the use of stock options in executive pay. As we saw in Chapter 7, stock options create a huge incentive for corporate managers to focus primarily upon short-term stock performance in ways that can lead to unnecessary layoffs. Remember the words of *Maclean's* business columnist Deirdre McMurdy quoted previously: "The excessive use of stock options reinforces the already intense focus on share prices. North American investors have become accustomed to quarterly — if not instant — gratification from their holdings. And that has greatly contributed to this decade's mania for corporate downsizing and narrow focus. Layoffs and asset sales, for example, have become one of the most efficient ways to boost stock price in recent years."[10]

Limiting the use of stock options in executive pay would go a long way to reverse these trends.

THE POLITICAL HORIZON

Prosperity is, and has always been, about both economics *and* politics. The economics of prosperity boils down to productivity, to increasing the amount of output per worker or, put most simply, to growing the overall size of our economic pie in relation to the size of the population. It is fundamentally dependent on technology and on the way we organize our economy at the international, national and firm levels to incorporate new technologies in the most efficient manner possible. This also means that productivity is fundamentally dependent on how we organize our financial system. For technology and other resources to be used efficiently, prices in the financial markets must reflect their true value in order to send efficient signals to economic actors about how to allocate and organize their resources, including technology.

But economics alone does not ensure prosperity for the bulk of society. This prosperity will depend as much on politics as it does on economics. Our economic pie can be large but, for most of the population, prosperity also depends on how the pie is divided. This is why in first-year political science courses politics is always defined as the process of "who gets what." In our current economic climate, the information revolution, productivity and growing the economic pie seem to have completely overshadowed politics and economic distribution. Politicians, economists and the media focus almost entirely upon indicators of economic growth, on the various aggregates and averages that show us the daily state of how our economy is doing. GDP, the dollar, inflation, job growth and stock prices, rather than median wages, benefits, and the distribution of wealth, are what dominate both headlines and budgets. But averages and aggregates never tell the full story about prosperity. A country made up of rich and poor is, in the aggregate and on average, a middle-class society. But in reality, it is a country that is becoming increasingly polarized along economic lines.

This focus on economics rather than politics, on indicators of growth rather than on indicators of distribution, is the key reason decision makers and members of the media are often surprised to learn that the bulk of our population is not made up of middle-class citizens. Because most of the people they know live similar lives to themselves, they are often surprised to learn that half of the population doesn't shop on-line and doesn't own mutual funds. It's also the reason that they often don't understand what all the fuss is about when they see the growing ranks of protestors in front of provincial legislatures and international trade meetings. Capitalist democracies are about both capitalism *and* democracy, and this means that they need to be both economically and politically sustainable.

There are two reasons we need to fix how our mutual funds and financial markets work. We need to deal with the concentrated power, short-term horizons and trend-chasing behaviour of those who manage mutual funds and pension funds because these funds are making our financial markets much less efficient. In economic terms, this threatens productivity and economic growth because it increases the potential for bubbles, busts and a focus on the very short term. In political terms, it threatens economic distribution because the pressure it puts on governments and firms to downsize has served to upset the balance of power between Wall Street and Main Street in ways that are unlikely to be politically sustainable over the long term.

Signs that the global economy is becoming less and less politically sustainable are all around us. From the swelling ranks of the homeless in Toronto to the growing protest movements that are disrupting trade conferences around the world, the signs of dissatisfaction are increasingly daily. And while some of the economic critiques advanced by the protestors may lack precision in their explanation of causes, their efforts point to the growing dissatisfaction with the many negative effects of the new global economy and with their impact on economic distribution. If globalization and the new economy are fundamentally about technology and finance, then computer wunderkind Bill Gates and financier George Soros are, without dispute, two of our best and brightest. In his recent book, *The Crisis of Global Capitalism*, Soros argues that free-market policies have gone too far and are producing economic inequalities that are becoming politically unsustainable. In the fall of 2000, Bill Gates shocked a conference of tech wizards by noting that markets and technology alone would never solve the problems of the world's poor. What was needed, he said, was government intervention. In public, many politicians and members of the business community may write off the growing number of protestors as a rabble of misguided malcontents. But in private, politicians and advertisers long ago learned that each letter of complaint and each political protestor is merely the visible tip of a much larger public-opinion iceberg.

In the end, it is this iceberg that may become the next unseen power in the global economy.

NOTES

1/MR. SMITH GOES TO BAY STREET

1. Robert Samuelson, "Why We're All Married to the Market," *Newsweek* (27 April 1998), p. 47.
2. "Scared of Heights?" *The Economist* (28 March 1998), p. 18.
3. Richard Nadler, *The Rise of Worker Capitalism*, Policy Analysis No. 359 (Washington, DC: Cato Institute, 1999), p. 5.
4. Hans Blommestein and Norbert Funke, "Introduction to Institutional Investors and Institutional Investing,"*Institutional Investors in the New Financial Landscape*, ed. Organisation for Economic Co-operation and Development (Paris: OECD, 1998), p. 15.
5. World Bank, *Averting the Old Age Crisis* (Oxford: Oxford University Press, 1994).
6. Cited in Investment Company Institute, "Public Confidence in the Social Security System," *Fundamentals* (October 1996).

7. Cited in Michela Pasquali, "Young face their financial future," *Globe and Mail* (15 August 1996).

8. Marcia Vickers and Gary Weiss, "Wall Street's Hype Machine," *Business Week* (3 April 2000), p. 114.

9. E. Philip Davis, *The Role of Institutional Investors in the Evolution of Financial Structure and Behaviour*, Special Paper No. 89 (London, LSE Financial Markets Group, 1996), p. 6.

10. Organisation for Economic Co-operation and Development, *Institutional Investors Statistical Yearbook 1997* (Paris: OECD, 1997), p. 9.

11. Ibid.

12. Peter Drucker, *Unseen Revolution: How Pension Fund Socialism Came to America* (New York: Harper and Row, 1976), pp. 2–3.

13. David Hale, "Experiment in democracy," *Financial Times* (4 February 1994).

14. Richard Nadler, *The Rise of Worker Capitalism*, Policy Analysis No. 359 (Washington, DC: Cato Institute, 1999), p. 1.

2/LONG-TERM MONEY, SHORT-TERM BEHAVIOUR

1. Karen Howlett, Janet McFarland and Dawn Walton, "Stock rigging appears widespread," *Globe and Mail* (1 July 2000).

2. Cited in the *Globe and Mail* (24 June 2000), p. B7.

3. These quotes are drawn from the following sources: Karen Howlett, Janet McFarland and Dawn Walton, "Stock rigging appears widespread," *Globe and Mail* (1 July 2000), p. B4; Sandra Rubin and Garry Marr, "Regulators to follow OSC's lead," *National Post* (24 June 2000), p. D1; David Olive, "RT was a case of people playing with fire," *National Post* (24 June 2000), p. D7; and *Globe and Mail* (24 June 2000), p. B7.

4. Robert Shiller, *Irrational Exuberance* (Princeton, NJ: Princeton University Press, 2000), p. xii.

5. Thomas A. Hockin, "Institutionalisation, Retailisation, and Shifting Responsibilities: The Canadian Experience," in *Institutional Investors in the New Financial Landscape*, ed. Organisation for Economic Co-operation and Development (Paris: OECD, 1998), p. 142.

6. International Monetary Fund, *International Capital Markets: Developments, Prospects, and Policy Issues* (Washington, DC: IMF, 1995), p. 167.

7. Figures in this section on the growth of institutional investors were drawn from the following sources: Pam Woodall, "Who's in the Driving Seat? A Survey of the World Economy," *The Economist* (7 October 1995); Task Force on the Future of the Canadian Financial Services Sector, *Change, Challenge,*

Opportunity: Report of the Task Force (Ottawa: Government of Canada, 1998); Hans Blommestein, "Impact of Institutional Investors on Financial Markets," in *Institutional Investors in the New Financial Landscape*, ed. Organisation for Economic Co-operation and Development (Paris: OECD, 1998); Hans Blommestein and Norbert Funke, "Introduction to Institutional Investors and Institutional Investing," in *Institutional Investors in the New Financial Landscape*, ed. Organisation for Economic Co-operation and Development (Paris: OECD, 1998); "Schools Brief: Institutional Investors," *The Economist* (6 November 1999), p. 83; Investment Company Institute, *Mutual Fund Fact Book 1998* (Washington, DC: ICI, 1999); Milton Berlinski and Simon Western, "Perspectives on the US Asset Management Business," in *Institutional Investors in the New Financial Landscape*, ed. Organisation for Economic Co-operation and Development (Paris: OECD, 1998); Floyd Norris, "A Deal Reaffirms the Strength of the Individual Investor," *New York Times* (6 February 1997); World Bank, *Private Capital Flows to Developing Countries: The Road to Financial Integration* (Oxford: Oxford University Press, 1997); Investment Company Institute, "Institutional Markets for All Mutual Funds: 1998," Press Release (ICI Web site, 1999); Michael Useem, *Investor Capitalism: How Money Managers Are Changing the Face of Corporate America* (New York: Basic Books, 1996); M. Christian Murray, "Few Big Cos. Have Most 401(k) Assets," *National Underwriter* (26 October 1998), p. 4; Richard Minns, "The Social Ownership of Capital," *New Left Review* 219 (September/October 1996), pp. 42–61; Investment Funds Institute of Canada, "Monthly Statistics, December 1999," Press Release Toronto (17 January 2000).

8. International Monetary Fund, *International Capital Markets: Developments, Prospects, and Policy Issues* (Washington, DC: IMF, 1995), p. 165.

9. International Monetary Fund, *International Capital Markets Part I: Exchange Rate Management and International Capital Flows* (Washington, DC: IMF, 1993), p. 32.

10. William O'Barr and John Conley, "Managing Relationships: The Culture of Institutional Investing," *Financial Analysts Journal* (September/October 1992), p. 23. See also William O'Barr and John Conley, *Fortune and Folly: The Wealth and Power of Institutional Investing* (Homewood, Illinois: Irwin, 1992).

11. Hans Blommestein, "Impact of Institutional Investors on Financial Markets" in *Institutional Investors in the New Financial Landscape*, ed. Organisation for Economic Co-operation and Development (Paris: OECD, 1998), p. 51.

12. Brian Barry, "A Survey of Fund Management: All Capitalists Now," *The Economist* (25 October 1995), p. 20.

13. Merril Stevenson, "Only Perform: A Survey of Investment Management," *The Economist* (27 November 1993), p. 25.

14. International Monetary Fund, *International Capital Markets: Developments, Prospects and Policy Issues* (Washington, DC: IMF, 1994), p. 18.

15. World Bank, *Private Capital Flows to Developing Countries: The Road to Financial Integration* (Oxford: Oxford University Press, 1997), p. 129.

16. D. Scharfstein and J. Stein, "Herd Behavior and Investment," *American Economic Review* 80 (1990), pp. 465–79.

17. E. Philip Davis, *Institutional Investors, Unstable Financial Markets and Monetary Policy*, Special Paper No. 75 (London: LSE Financial Markets Group, 1995), p. 3.

18. Hans Blommestein, "Impact of Institutional Investors on Financial Markets" in *Institutional Investors in the New Financial Landscape*, ed. Organisation for Economic Co-operation and Development (Paris: OECD, 1998), p. 55.

19. Barry Eichengreen and Donald Mathieson, *Hedge Funds and Financial Market Dynamics*, IMF Occasional Paper (Washington, DC: IMF, 1998), pp. 11–12.

20. World Bank, *Private Capital Flows to Developing Countries: The Road to Financial Integration* (Oxford: Oxford University Press, 1997), p. 126.

21. Thomas Willett, *International Financial Markets as Sources of Crisis or Discipline: The Too Much, Too Late Hypothesis*, Working Paper (Claremont, CA: Claremont Institute for Economic Policy Studies, 1998), p. 27.

22. Quoted in "Hot Money," *Business Week* (20 March 1995); *Maclean's* (20 March 1995).

23. Joeseph Stiglitz, "Symposium on Bubbles," *Journal of Economic Perspectives* 4, No. 2 (1990), p. 13.

3/MUTUAL FUNDS AND FINANCIAL CRISES

1. Pam Woodall, "Who's in the Driving Seat? A Survey of the World Economy," *The Economist* (7 October 1995), p. 18.

2. On the classic model of a speculative attack against a fixed exchange rate, see Paul Krugman, "A Model of Balance of Payments Crises," *Journal of Money, Credit, and Banking* 11 (1979) and Robert Flood and Peter Garber, "Collapsing Exchange Rate Regimes: Some Linear Examples," *Journal of International Economics* 17 (1994).

3. Barry Eichengreen and Michael Mussa, *Capital Account Liberalization: Theoretical and Practical Aspects*, Occasional Paper 172 (Washington, DC: International Monetary Fund, 1998), pp. 41–42.

4. Barry Eichengreen, *Towards a New International Financial Architecture: A Practical Post-Asia Agenda* (Washington, DC: Institute for International Economics, 1999), p. 133.

5. On second-generation models of (self-fulfilling) speculative attacks against fixed exchange rates, see Maurice Obstfeld, "Models of Currency Crises with Self-fulfilling Features," *European Economic Review* 40 (1996) and Gulcin Ozkan and Alan Sutherland, "A Currency Crisis Model with an Optimizing Policymaker," *Journal of International Economics* 44 (1998).

6. Barry Eichengreen, *Towards a New International Financial Architecture: A Practical Post-Asia Agenda* (Washington, DC: Institute for International Economics, 1999), p. 140.

7. Maurice Obstfeld and Kenneth Rogoff, "The Mirage of Fixed Exchange Rates," *Journal of Economic Perspectives* 9 (1995) and Michael Klein and Nancy Marion, "Explaining the Duration of Exchange-Rate Pegs," *Journal of Economic Development* 108 (1997).

8. There is an exception here. Fixed exchange rates can be sustainable, in the face of a negative shock, if the two countries involved (the country which fixes its exchange rate and the country that it is fixed to) are sufficiently similar that the shock affects them both in the same way. In economics, the similar conditions required are laid out in what is called "optimum currency area theory." In the cases considered in this and the next chapter, the countries involved don't qualify as exceptions.

9. Rudiger Dornbusch, Ilan Goldfajn and Rodrigo Valdes, "Currency Crises and Collapses," *Brookings Papers on Economic Activity* 2 (1995).

10. Karl Polanyi, *The Great Transformation: The Political and Economic Origins of Our Time* (Boston: Beacon Press, 1944).

11. Ibid, p. 145.

12. Ibid, p. 25.

13. Barry Eichengreen, *Globalizing Capital: A History of the International Monetary System* (Princeton, NJ: Princeton University Press, 1996), p. 42.

14. Karl Polanyi, *The Great Transformation: The Political and Economic Origins of Our Time* (Boston: Beacon Press, 1944), p. 176.

15. Barry Eichengreen, *Globalizing Capital: A History of the International Monetary System* (Princeton, NJ: Princeton University Press, 1996), pp. 191–92.

16. George Soros, *The Crisis of Global Capitalism: Open Society Endangered* (London: Little, Brown and Company, 1998), pp. 49–50.

17. Hyman P. Minsky, "The Financial-Instability Hypothesis: Capitalist Processes and the Behaviour of the Economy," in *Financial Crises: Theory, History, and Policy*, ed. C. Kindleberger and J.P. Laffargue (Cambridge, England: Cambridge University Press, 1982).

4/THREE CRASHES AND A BOOM

1. Kathleen McNamara, *The Currency of Ideas: Monetary Politics in the European Union* (Ithaca, NY: Cornell University Press, 1998), p. 176.
2. George Soros with Byron Wien and Krisztina Koenen, *Soros on Soros: Staying Ahead of the Curve* (New York: John Wiley & Sons, 1995), p. 302.
3. Group of Ten, *International Capital Movements and Foreign Exchange Markets: A Report to the Ministers and Governors by the Group of Deputies* (Rome: Group of Ten, 1993), p. 11.
4. E. Philip Davis, *Pension Funds, Retirement Income Security and Capital Markets: An International Perspective* (Oxford: Clarendon Press, 1995), p. 292.
5. George Soros with Byron Wien and Krisztina Koenen, *Soros on Soros: Staying Ahead of the Curve* (New York: John Wiley & Sons, 1995), p. 83.
6. Paul Krugman, "Are Currency Crises Self-Fulfilling?" *Macroeconomics Annual 1996* (Cambridge, MA: MIT Press, 1996), pp. 366–67.
7. Jeffrey Sachs, Aaron Tornell and Andres Velasco, "The Collapse of the Mexican Peso: What Have We Learned?" *Economic Policy* 22 (1996), p. 21.
8. Timothy Kessler, "Political Capital: Mexican Financial Policy under Salinas," *World Politics* 51 (1998), p. 60.
9. Ibid, p. 63.
10. Paul Krugman, "Dutch Tulips and Emerging Markets," *Foreign Affairs* (July/August 1995), pp. 38–39.
11. Ibid, p. 39.
12. Ibid, p. 41.
13. Jeffrey Sachs, Aaron Tornell and Andres Velasco, "The Collapse of the Mexican Peso: What Have We Learned?" *Economic Policy* 22 (1996), p. 21.
14. Ibid, p. 33.
15. Diana B. Henriques, *Fidelity's World: The Secret Life and Public Power of the Mutual Fund Giant* (New York: Simon & Schuster, 1995), pp. 357–58, and Craig Torres and Thomas T. Vogel Jr., "Some mutual funds wield growing clout in developing nations," *Wall Street Journal* (14 June 1994), p. A1.
16. Craig Torres and Thomas T. Vogel Jr., "Some mutual funds wield growing clout in developing nations," *Wall Street Journal* (14 June 1994), p. A1.
17. Ibid.

18. David Hale, "The Markets and Mexico: The Supply-Side Story," in *Mexico 1994: Anatomy of an Emerging Market Crash*, ed. S. Edwards and M. Naim (Washington, DC: Carnegie Endowment for International Peace, 1997), p. 221.

19. Karen Pennar, "Why Investors Stampede," *Business Week* (13 February 1995).

20. E. Philip Davis, *Institutional Investors, Unstable Financial Markets and Monetary Policy*, Special Paper No. 75 (London: LSE Financial Markets Group, 1995), p. 15.

21. Paul Krugman, *The Return of Depression Economics* (New York: W.W. Norton, 1999).

22. Moises Naim, "Mexico's Larger Story," in *Mexico 1994: Anatomy of an Emerging Market Crash*, ed. S. Edwards and M. Naim (Washington, DC: Carnegie Endowment for International Peace, 1997), p. 305.

23. Paul Krugman, *The Return of Depression Economics* (New York: W.W. Norton, 1999).

24. Yung Chul Park, "East Asian Liberalization, Bubbles, and the Challenge from China," *Brookings Papers on Economic Activity* 2 (1995), p. 361.

25. Walden Bello, "The End of a 'Miracle': Speculation, Foreign Capital Dependence and the Collapse of the Southeast Asian Economies," *Multinational Monitor* 19, No. 1-2 (1998), p. 5.

26. Paul Krugman, "What Happened to Asia?" Unpublished paper, Harvard Institute for International Development, http://web.mit.edu/Krugman/www/ (March 1998).

27. Steven Radelet and Jeffrey Sachs, "The Onset of the East Asian Financial Crisis," Unpublished paper, Harvard Institute for International Development (March 1998).

28. Paul Krugman, "Balance Sheets, the Transfer Problem, and Financial Crises," Unpublished paper, Harvard Institute for International Development, http://web.mit.edu/Krugman/www/ (January 1999), p. 6.

29. Michael Pomerleano, "The East Asia Crisis and Corporate Finances: The Untold Micro Story," Mimeo (Washington, D.C.: The World Bank Group, 1999), pp. 30-31.

30. Paul Krugman, "What Happened to Asia?" Unpublished paper, Harvard Institute for International Development, http://web.mit.edu/Krugman/www/ (March 1998).

31. Walden Bello, "Asian Financial Crisis: The Movie," *The Ecologist* 29, No. 1 (1999), p. 7.

32. Steven Radelet and Jeffrey Sachs, "The Onset of the East Asian Financial

Crisis," Unpublished paper, Harvard Institute for International Development (March 1998).

33. Ibid, p. 10.

34. Ibid, p. 12.

35. Ibid, p. 17.

36. Paul Krugman, "What Happened to Asia?" Unpublished paper, Harvard Institute for International Development, http://web.mit.edu/Krugman/www/ (March 1998).

37. Walden Bello, "Asian Financial Crisis: The Movie," *The Ecologist* 29, No. 1 (1999), p. 7.

38. Paul Krugman, "What Happened to Asia?" Unpublished paper, Harvard Institute for International Development, http://web.mit.edu/Krugman/www/ (March 1998).

39. Barry Eichengreen and Donald Mathieson, *Hedge Funds and Financial Market Dynamics*, Occasional Paper (Washington, DC: International Monetary Fund, 1998), p. 19.

40. International Monetary Fund, *World Economic Outlook: May 1999* (Washington, DC: IMF, 1999), p. 61.

41. For figures on the decline in the U.S. savings rate and the rise in debt, see International Monetary Fund, *World Economic Outlook: May 1999* (Washington, DC: IMF, 1999) and Robert Samuelson, "Hell No, We Won't Save!" *Newsweek* (27 April 1998).

42. International Monetary Fund, *World Economic Outlook: May 1999* (Washington, DC: IMF, 1999), p. 59.

43. Tracey LeMay, "Families struggling: report," *National Post* (10 March 1999), p. D4.

44. Wynne Godley and Bill Martin, *America's New Era*, Occasional Paper No. 7 (London: Phillips and Drew Research Group, October 1999).

5/HEDGE FUND FOLLIES

1. Susan C. Ervin, "Hedge Funds in the 1990s: Private Risk Taking, Public Consequences?" in *The Financial Services Revolution: Understanding the Changing Role of Banks, Mutual Funds, and Insurance Companies*, ed. C. Kirsch (New York: McGraw-Hill, 1997), p. 380.

2. Steven A. Lonsdorf, Testimony before the House Committee on Banking and Financial Services, *Hedge Fund Operations*, Hearing before the House Committee on Banking and Financial Services, 105th Congress, 2nd Session, 1 October 1998, p. 296.

3. International Monetary Fund, *World Economic Outlook: May 1997* (Washington, DC: IMF, 1998), p. 4.

4. "The Risk Business," *The Economist* (17 September 1998):

5. William McDonough, Testimony before the House Committee on Banking and Financial Services, *Hedge Fund Operations*, Hearing before the House Committee on Banking and Financial Services, 105th Congress, 2nd Session, 1 October 1998, pp. 18–19.

6. Rosemary Bennett and David Shirreff, "Let's Bash the Hedge Funds," *Euromoney* (April 1994), p. 30.

7. "Good Guru Guide," *The Economist* (25 December 1993), p. 21.

8. M. Perin, "Insiders Decry Speculators Role in Fluctuations," *Houston Business Journal* 29, No. 31 (29 December 1998).

9. Ibid.

10. Ibid.

11. Quoted in P. Solman and K. Gooding, "LME moves to stop manipulators," *Financial Times* (15 October 1998).

12. Cited in Robert Slater, *Soros: The Life, Times, and Trading Secrets of the World's Greatest Investor* (New York: Irwin, 1996), p. 214.

13. International Monetary Fund, *International Capital Markets* (Washington, DC: IMF, 1993), p. 11.

14. S. Brown, J. Park and W. Goetzmann, *Hedge Funds and the Asian Currency Crisis*, Working Paper No. 6427 (Cambridge, MA: National Bureau for Economic Research, 1998).

15. Barry Eichengreen and Donald Mathieson, *Hedge Funds and Financial Market Dynamics*, Occasional Paper (Washington, DC: IMF, 1998), p. 18.

16. George Soros, *The Crisis of Global Capitalism: Open Society Endangered* (London: Little, Brown and Company, 1998), p. 142.

17. International Monetary Fund, *International Capital Markets: Developments, Prospects, and Policy Issues* (Washington, DC: IMF, 1995), p. 167.

18. D. Sparks, "The Juggernaut Who's Fattening Short-Sellers," *Business Week* 13 (October 1997), p. 98.

19. Ibid.

20. "George Soros: Talkative," *The Economist* (7 August 1993), p. 66.

21. "A Golden Lever," *The Economist* (1 May 1993), p. 83.

22. Paul Krugman, "I Know What the Hedges Did Last Summer," *Fortune* (December 1998).

23. Paul Krugman, "The Return of Dr. Mabuse," *New York Times Magazine* (November 1998).

24. Paul Krugman, "I Know What the Hedges Did Last Summer," *Fortune* (December 1998).

6/MUTUAL FUNDS, PENSION FUNDS AND DEFICITS — OH MY!

1. Bob Woodward, *The Agenda: Inside the Clinton White House* (New York: Pocket Books, 1994).
2. "Shifting Ground," *Maclean's* (20 March 1995).
3. Ibid.
4. William Glasgall, Bill Javetski, Rose Brady and Robert Neff, "Hot Money," *Business Week* (20 March 1995).
5. Robert Lewis, "Who Elected Them?" *Maclean's* (20 March 1995), p. 2.
6. Quoted in "Shifting Ground," *Maclean's* (20 March 1995).
7. William Glasgall, Bill Javetski, Rose Brady and Robert Neff, "Hot Money," *Business Week* (20 March 1995).
8. Linda McQuaig, *The Cult of Impotence: Selling the Myth of Powerlessness in the Global Economy* (Toronto: Viking Press, 1998).
9. Ton Notermans, *Social Democracy and External Constraints*, Working Paper No. 5 (Oslo: Arena, 1995), p. 18.
10. This point is made in Paul Krugman, *Peddling Prosperity: Economic Sense and Nonsense in the Age of Diminished Expectations* (New York: W.W. Norton and Company, 1994).
11. Ibid, p. 45.
12. Ibid, p. 54.
13. Paul Krugman, "Stable Prices and Fast Growth: Just Say No," *The Economist* (31 August 1996).
14. George Akerlof, William Dickens and George Perry, "The Macroeconomics of Low Inflation," *Brookings Papers on Economic Activity* 1 (1996).
15. Paul Krugman, "Stable Prices and Fast Growth: Just Say No," *The Economist* (31 August 1996).
16. Ibid.
17. Pam Woodall, "Who's in the Driving Seat? A Survey of the World Economy," *The Economist* (7 October 1995), p. 25.
18. Ibid, p. 15.
19. International Monetary Fund, *World Economic Outlook: May 1999* (Washington, DC: IMF, 1999), p. 69.
20. Edward Greenspon and Anthony Wilson-Smith, *Double Vision: The Inside Story of the Liberals in Power* (Toronto: Seal Books, 1996), p. 65.
21. William R. White, *Evolving International Financial Markets: Some Implications for*

Central Banks, Working Paper (Basle, Switzerland: Bank for International Settlements, 1999).

22. Cited in Edward Greenspon and Anthony Wilson-Smith, *Double Vision: The Inside Story of the Liberals in Power* (Toronto: Seal Books, 1996), pp. 235–36.

23. Kevin Clinton and Mark Zelmer, "Constraints on the Conduct of Canadian Monetary Policy in the 1990s: Dealing with Uncertainty in the Financial Markets" (Ottawa: Bank of Canada, 1997), p. 26.

24. Edward Greenspon and Anthony Wilson-Smith, *Double Vision: The Inside Story of the Liberals in Power* (Toronto: Seal Books, 1996), p. 235.

25. Ibid, p. 256.

26. Ibid.

27. William Glasgall, Bill Javetski, Rose Brady and Robert Neff, "Hot Money," *Business Week* (20 March 1995), p. 47.

28. Christopher Farrell, "The Dollar Doesn't Deserve This Thumping," *Business Week* (20 March 1995), p. 51.

7/CORPORATE BOARD GAMES

1. Allen Sloan, "The Hit Men," *Newsweek* (26 February 1996).

2. Greg Ip, "Shareholders vs. jobholders," *Globe and Mail* (23 March 1996).

3. Louis Uchitelle and N.R. Kleinfield, "On the battlefields of business, millions of casualties," *New York Times* (3 March 1996).

4. Figures drawn from the *New York Times* (25 February 1996) and Michael Useem, *Investor Capitalism: How Money Managers Are Changing the Face of Corporate America* (New York: Basic Books, 1996), p. 2.

5. Canadian Centre for Policy Alternatives, *Monitor* (Ottawa: October 1997).

6. Louis Uchitelle and N.R. Kleinfield, "On the battlefields of business, millions of casualties," *New York Times* (3 March 1996).

7. Robert J. Eaton, "The New Ownership of Corporate America," Speech to the Economic Club of Detroit (18 March 1996), in *Vital Speeches of the Day* 62, No. 14 (1996), pp. 430–34.

8. Allen Sloan, "The Hit Men," *Newsweek* (26 February 1996).

9. Cited in Robert J. Eaton, "The New Ownership of Corporate America," Speech to the Economic Club of Detroit (18 March, 1996), in *Vital Speeches of the Day* 62, No. 14 (1996), pp. 430–34.

10. Adolf Berle and Gardiner Means, *The Modern Corporation and Private Property* (New York: Commerce Clearing House, 1932).

11. Michael Useem, *Investor Capitalism: How Money Managers Are Changing the Face of Corporate America* (New York: Basic Books, 1996), p. 5.

12. Jeffrey S. Maurer, "Corporate Restructuring in America," Speech to the Albert B. Merrill Fund Lecture, Syracuse University School of Management (16 April 1996), in *Vital Speeches of the Day* 62, No. 14 (1996), pp. 505–8.

13. Bill Tielman, "Labour and the pension fund giant," *National Post* (15 March 1999), p. C5.

14. Michael Useem, *Investor Capitalism: How Money Managers Are Changing the Face of Corporate America* (New York: Basic Books, 1996), p. 6.

15. Cited in David Olive, "So who watches the fund managers?" *Globe and Mail* (10 October 1996).

16. Claude Lamoureux, "Remarks to the Senate Committee on Banking, Trade and Commerce" (7 May 1998).

17. Andrew C. Sigler, Testimony before the Senate Committee on Banking, Housing and Urban Affairs, *The Impact of Institutional Investors on Corporate Governance, Takeovers, and the Capital Markets*, Hearing before the Senate Committee on Banking, Housing, and Urban Affairs, 101st Congress, 1st Session (3 October 1989).

18. Ibid.

19. Champion International, "The Role of Pension Funds in Hostile Takeovers and Leveraged Buyouts and Their Impact on the U.S. Economy," Background Paper Prepared for The Business Roundtable Task Force on Corporate Governance, *The Impact of Institutional Investors on Corporate Governance, Takeovers, and the Capital Markets*, Hearing before the Senate Committee on Banking, Housing, and Urban Affairs, 101st Congress, 1st Session (3 October 1989), pp. 96–97.

20. Ibid, p. 94.

21. Ibid, p. 97.

22. Michael Useem, *Investor Capitalism: How Money Managers Are Changing the Face of Corporate America* (New York: Basic Books, 1996), pp. 25–26.

23. Jonathan Charkham, *Keeping Good Company: A Study of Corporate Governance in Five Countries* (Oxford: Clarendon Press, 1994), p. 215.

24. Champion International, "The Role of Pension Funds in Hostile Takeovers and Leveraged Buyouts and Their Impact on the U.S. Economy," Background Paper Prepared for The Business Roundtable Task Force on Corporate Governance, *The Impact of Institutional Investors on Corporate Governance, Takeovers, and the Capital Markets*, Hearing before the Senate Committee on Banking, Housing, and Urban Affairs, 101st Congress, 1st Session (3 October 1989), p. 100.

25. Ibid.

26. Matthew Barrett, "How Bank of Montreal got a leaner, meaner board of directors," *National Post* (15 May 1999), p. D5.

27. Michael Useem, *Investor Capitalism: How Money Managers Are Changing the Face of Corporate America* (New York: Basic Books, 1996), p. 24.

28. "Getting Rid of the Boss," *The Economist* (6 February 1993), p. 13.

29. Cited in Edward McCarthy, "Pension Funds Flex Shareholder Muscle," *Pension Management* (1 January 1996).

30. "Share Options: Share and Share Unalike," *The Economist* (7 August 1999), p. 18.

31. Ibid.

32. Cited in Greg Ip, "Shareholders vs. jobholders," *Globe and Mail* (23 March 1996).

33. "Share Options: Share and Share Unalike," *The Economist* (7 August 1999), p. 18.

34. George Fenn and Nellie Lang, *Corporate Payout Policy and Managerial Stock Incentives* (Washington, DC: Federal Reserve Board, 1999).

35. Cited in Greg Ip, "Shareholders vs. jobholders," *Globe and Mail* (23 March 1996).

36. Ibid.

37. Deirdre McMurdy, "The Bottom Line: Taking Stock of Options," *Maclean's* (28 April 1997), p. 49.

38. Cited in "Share Options: Share and Share Unalike," *The Economist* (7 August 1999), p. 18.

39. Cited in Greg Ip, "Shareholders vs. jobholders," *Globe and Mail* (23 March 1996).

40. Cited in Murray Dobbin, *The Myth of the Good Corporate Citizen: Democracy under the Rule of Big Business* (Toronto: Stoddart, 1998).

41. Stephen S. Roach, "The Hollow Ring of the Productivity Revival," *Harvard Business Review* (November/December 1996), p. 82.

42. Ibid.

43. Beth Belton, "Despite humming economy, workers sweat job security," *USA Today* (2 March 1999).

44. Cited in ibid.

45. Louis Uchitelle and N.R. Kleinfield, "On the battlefields of business, millions of casualties," *New York Times* (3 March 1996).

46. *Business Week* (20 April 1998).

47. Cited in Aaron Bernstein, "Is America Becoming More of a Class Society?" *Business Week* (26 February 1996), p. 86.

48. Ibid.
49. Ibid.

8/THE POLITICS OF THE NEW INVESTMENT CULTURE

1. Brian Barry, "A Survey of Fund Management: All Capitalists Now," *The Economist* (25 October 1995).
2. James Glassman, "The growing investor class," *Washington Post* (7 April 1998), p. A23.
3. Figures drawn from Paul Ferley, *Rising Net Worth Provides a Better Indication of Household Finances Than Falling Income*, Bank of Montreal Special Report (3 July 1998) and Jim Stanford, *Paper Boom: Why Real Prosperity Requires a New Approach to Canada's Economy* (Toronto: James Lorimer and Co. Ltd., 1999).
4. Bruce Little, "Turning to the stock market with our savings," *Globe and Mail* (27 July 1998), p. A4.
5. Louis Uchitelle and N.R. Kleinfield, "On the battlefields of business, millions of casualties," *New York Times* (3 March 1996).
6. Robert Samuelson, "Hell No, We Won't Save!" *Newsweek* (27 April 1998).
7. Robert Samuelson, "Why We're All Married to the Market," *Newsweek* (27 April 1998).
8. Pam Woodall, "Who's in the Driving Seat? A Survey of the World Economy," *The Economist* (7 October 1995), p. 38.
9. Ibid.
10. George Church, "Mexico's Troubles Are Our Troubles," *Time* (6 March 1995), p. 35.
11. Investment Funds Institute of Canada, "Mutual Funds: A Strategy for Everyone," Advertising Supplement, *Maclean's* (12 January 1998).
12. Cited in Aaron Bernstein, "Sharing Prosperity," *Business Week* (1 September 1997), p. 67.
13. Ibid.
14. Cited in Jonathan Chevreau, "Funds held by 40% of households, survey finds," *Financial Post* (26 September 1996).
15. Robert Ginsberg and Edward Wolff, "Do We Really Live in Wonderland?" *Investor's Business Daily* (11 March 1999), p. 22.
16. Andrew Willis and Andrew Bell, "Mutual fund mania," *Globe and Mail* (1 February 1997).
17. Author's interview with Laura Curtis, manager of Communications and Public Relations, GT Global, Toronto (28 November 1997).

18. Brian Barry, "A Survey of Fund Management: All Capitalists Now," *The Economist* (25 October 1995).

19. Shirley Won, "Investing: how to catch a rising star," *Globe and Mail* (13 September 1997).

20. Ian Cowie, "A risk of two halves for fans of football," *Daily Telegraph* (11 January 1997).

21. Konrad Yakabuski, "Desjardins launches Quebec mutual fund," *Globe and Mail* (20 June 1997), p. B10.

22. Securities and Exchange Commission, *Excerpts from Recent Polls and Studies Highlighting the Need for Financial Education*, Press Release, Washington, DC (24 February 1998).

23. Association of Unit Trusts and Investment Funds, *Annual Report and Accounts 1996* (London: AUTIF, 1996).

24. Author's interview with Laura Curtis, manager of Communications and Public Relations, GT Global, Toronto (28 November 1997).

25. Cited in Paul Slade, "Cash on the curriculum," *Sunday Telegraph* (22 February 1998), p. B21.

26. Investment Company Institute, "The Facts on Saving and Investing Campaign," ICI Web site.

27. Brian Barry, "A Survey of Fund Management: All Capitalists Now," *The Economist* (25 October 1995).

28. John Leland, "Blessed by the Bull," *Newsweek* (27 April 1998), p. 52.

29. Richard Nadler, *The Rise of Worker Capitalism*, Policy Analysis No. 359 (Washington, DC: Cato Institute, 1999).

30. Ibid.

31. James Glassman, "The Growing Investor Class," *Washington Post* (7 April 1998), p. A23.

9/MAKING WHAT'S GOOD FOR FIDELITY GOOD FOR NORTH AMERICA

1. Stephany Griffith-Jones, *Global Capital Flows: Should They Be Regulated?* (London: Macmillan Press, 1998).

2. M. Pacelle et al., "Hedge funds gird for more to come," *Wall Street Journal* (Reprinted in the *Globe and Mail*, 28 September 1998).

3. George Soros, *The Crisis of Global Capitalism: Open Society Endangered* (London: Little, Brown and Company, 1998), p. 192.

4. Ibid.

5. Paul Krugman, "The return of Dr. Mabuse," *New York Times Magazine* (November 1998).

6. Jim Stanford, "The Economics of Debt and the Remaking of Canada," *Studies in Political Economy* 48 (Autumn 1996), p. 131.

7. International Monetary Fund, *World Economic Outlook May 1997* (Washington, DC: IMF, 1997), p. 67.

8. Senate Standing Committee on Banking, Trade and Commerce, *Corporate Governance: A report of the Senate Standing Committee on Banking, Trade and Commerce* (The Kirby Report) (Ottawa: August 1996).

9. Jim Stanford, *Paper Boom: Why Real Prosperity Requires a New Approach to Canada's Economy* (Toronto: James Lorimer and Co. Ltd., 1999).

10. Deirdre McMurdy, "The Bottom Line: Taking Stock of Options," *Maclean's* (28 April 1997), p. 49.

INDEX